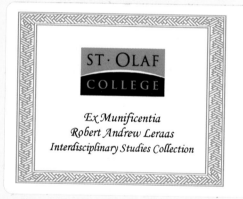

THE DURGA TEMPLE AT AIHOLE

THE DURGA TEMPLE AT AIHOLE

A Historiographical Study

GARY MICHAEL TARTAKOV

DELHI
OXFORD UNIVERSITY PRESS
CALCUTTA CHENNAI MUMBAI
1997

Oxford University Press, Great Clarendon Street, Oxford OX2 6DP

Oxford New York
Athens Auckland Bangkok Calcutta
Cape Town Chennai Dar es Salaam Delhi
Florence Hong Kong Istanbul Karachi
Kuala Lumpur Madrid Melbourne Mexico City
Mumbai Nairobi Paris Singapore
Taipei Tokyo Toronto

and associates in

Berlin Ibadan

ISBN 0 19 563372 5

Typeset by Guru Typograph Technology, New Delhi 110 045
Printed at Pauls Press, New Delhi 110 020
and published by Manzar Khan, Oxford University Press
YMCA Library Building, Jai Singh Road, New Delhi 110 001

For my parents,
Lester Tarr and Dena Roitgering Tarr,
and my wife Carlie,
who have made this work possible.

Preface

The value of this study lies in its double vision, the self-conscious focus upon historical method along with the history of one of India's major monuments. This is thus an essay on the art of history at the same time that it is an essay in the history of art. By the visual power of its of architecture and the beauty of its sculpture, the Durga temple has commanded a central place in histories of India's ancient art. Its unique forms and the sophisticated explanations historians have found for this unique quality, have given it a crucial place in the interpretation of that history. The ultimate goal here is to explain a particular monument and thereby increase our understanding of the total history. The path toward that goal is unusual in the emphasis placed on historiography as a means for better understanding of the meaning of its conclusions. The result is a deeper look than usual into the ways in which we construct the meanings of our great monuments, and so a deeper than usual look into the development of Indian art history over the past century and a half.

Art historians labour in three distinct fields of understanding, each nestling within the other. They consider particular objects, the social contexts that produced those objects, and finally, the all encompassing universal realities that include and link those contexts with their own. Of the three, the most easily controlled is the study of the specific artifacts they intend to interpret. The cultural context can be studied in equal detail, but because of its broader scope, never so thoroughly. Still, this context, too, must be mastered sufficiently to understand the processes by which, and the institutions for which, the objects were created. The global realities which encompass everything, in both the distant world of the objects' creators and that of the historians, throw up the questions of how we are to understand the objects and their histories. The questions we ask emerge from our own world views, as much as from the objects and contexts under consideration.

Each of these three fields is understood differently by different people and, significantly, each is itself in a state of continual change. An object's form may appear differently over time or from different viewpoints. Paint fades, dust and varnish build up. Aspects of the object not visible at one moment may appear at another. Obscuring structures, such as frames, may be removed or added. Some analysts may be more thorough, others may have better access to the object. New techniques of investigation, such as x-ray photography or comparative stylistic analysis, may reveal or explain previously invisible evidence.

Changing techniques of recording may allow one student to compose understandings with greater accuracy than another. Apparently inadequate or false conclusions are weeded out of literature. There may be paradigm shifts in vision as methodology and ideology change and develop. It took until the late eighteenth century for the Europeans who wrote the first histories of India's art to realize that Indian culture could not be interpreted solely on the basis of European information, and figures like Ardhanari Shiva, with a feminine breast on the left side but none on the right, could not be explained as Amazons. Similarly, the eclectic sampling of temples and inscriptions typical of early nineteenth-century antiquarian research was transformed by the archaeological surveys' systematic collection of measurements and records.

There can be no such thing as an objective art history as historians are irremediably subjective. However transparent the historian's vision of an object may seem, it is derived from a different situation and from different interests than those of the object's creators. Historians themselves change. Not only is one replaced by another, but individual historians and their interpretations tend to change and develop. Difficulties in obtaining a satisfactory history also arise because, as historians often tell us, the evidence for the past is frequently sparse and fragmentary. Moreover, the process of interpreting that evidence is far more complex than historians like to admit.

The goal of historical consideration is to understand the past's reality. This involves translating it into language and filtering it through the medium of the written record. Just how limited and imperfect such transcriptions can be is easily illustrated by newspaper descriptions of current events, particularly when we have heard or read alternative accounts. There are differences likely even among accounts offered by relatively disinterested spectators due to their different vantage points or skills. Put the events back a few decades or centuries and the difficulties mount ferociously. We often refer to both the actual happening and its record as 'history', continually forgetting the difference between the two, and that the record is not the reality.

We always need to maintain an awareness of the record's limit as an interpretation. Testimony about evidence is too often referred to as evidence, while what is called proof is often merely agreement among our sources. Sophisticated historians tend to bury this ambiguity in the conclusions they present, while naive ones ignore it. When any historical statement is made there is a tacit implication that the record on which it is based is assumed to be accurate. This often leads the historian to act as if the record is indeed accurate. The only defence we have against these many limits to the construction of a simple or correct interpretation is historiography, the self-conscious study of our historical practice.

The major intent of this volume is to explore the implications of self-conscious historiography for the interpretation of art history. The specific work explored, the Durga temple at Aihole, is one of the touchstones of India's art history and so one of its most commonly discussed monuments. It is possible from this example to gain interesting insights into the field of Indian art history as a whole. A chronological reading of the literature on the temple allows us to identify the methods and attitudes of its historians as well as their conclusions. It is my contention that this will allow us to interpret their conclusions more cogently. Our current record of India's early art is a construction of the nineteenth and twentieth centuries, composed largely in the language and traditions of a conquering caste of Englishmen. As Jan Myrdal points out, writers' explanations reveal as much about their traditions of telling as they do about the traditions they attempt to explain. The effective passing of Indian art history into Indian hands is an important occasion to consider the impact of that viewpoint.

The interpretations that have carried it through the past century and a quarter have identified the Durga temple with the worship of Shiva, Buddha, Vishnu, the Jina, Surya-Narayana, Devi, Brahma and Aditya. The dates for its creation have ranged from 'earlier than the tenth century' to the seventh, the eighth and most commonly, to the fifth and sixth centuries, before returning more recently through the seventh to the eighth. Its style has been called Buddhist, Jaina, Chalukya, Dravidian, Gupta, Mannerist, Vesera, northern, southern and a mixture of northern and southern.

More importantly, its historical significance has been continually reinterpreted as the perspectives applied to it have shifted. What was first presented as a distorted Buddhist monument has more recently become recognized by some as a brilliant Brahmanical one. As we move toward the twenty-first century it is time to recognize not only the difficulty of historical interpretation but also that our interpretations are embedded in the interests of our interpreters. To understand the history we read we must learn to maintain an awareness of our historian's intentions as much as we do of their subject matter. The two essays on the Durga temple here attempt to exemplify the value and use of such an awareness.

A NOTE ON QUOTATION AND TRANSLITERATION

In order to facilitate reading, diacritical marks have been omitted from the Sanskrit terms, except in the cases where precise explanation of a translation or quotation of another text makes them necessary. The most important of these terms are given with their diacritical markings in Appendix XVII. Because nineteenth-century writers used a variety of different systems of orthography and transliteration, some terms will appear in a variety of different forms in the quotations. It has been my rule to be true to the source rather than to introduce an anachronistic uniformity. Where references to this volume's illustrations appear within square brackets in the quotations or appendixes, they indicate illustrations from the original texts.

Acknowledgements

The number of people who have contributed to this book is greater than I can possibly list. They include the teachers and students who have instructed me, the bus conductors and librarians who have led me through the sites of study, and all those who, like the tea-stall proprietors of Pattadakal and Aihole, have sustained me in between. In particular I want to thank those whose material and spiritual support have made this work possible. First and foremost are my wife, Carlie, and my parents, Lester Tarr and Dena Roitgering Tarr, who provided me with the support to write. John Brentlinger and Alan Austin offered suggestions about the writing of early drafts. Dr M. S. Nagaraja Rao, former Director General of the Archaeological Survey of India, has been associated with much of my work in India. Further assistance has come from the Graduate College and the College of Design at Iowa State University, the American Institute of Indian Studies, and the Asian Cultural Council.

Contents

List of Illustrations and Maps

*AIIS: Photo copyright the American Institute of Indian Studies, Centre for Art and Archaeology, Varanasi.

**Letters and numbers indicate location on diagram 6.

All photographs, unless indicated otherwise, are by the author.

MAP

DIAGRAMS

PART ONE

Changing Views of the Durga Temple

Surfacing

THE DURGA TEMPLE emerges into the world of art history through the antiquarian literature of colonial India. It is first noticed as the 'Shivite' temple of 'Iwullee' in a collection of photographs made by a British artillery officer named Biggs.[1] Sometime in the middle of the nineteenth century, Colonel Biggs produced a set of photographs of architectural ruins and inscriptions found in the northern Karnatak villages of Aihole and Pattadakal, in what was then called the Bombay Presidency. Eventually these photographs and their negatives were presented to the Bombay branch of the Royal Asiatic Society. The architectural photographs of this collection were published first, included in a lavish volume entitled *Architecture in Dharwar and Mysore*, printed in London in 1866 under joint British and Indian sponsorship.[2]

Architecture in Dharwar and Mysore was a collection of large sized photographs of monumental remains, by three different photographers, accompanied by a brief 'Historical and Descriptive Memoire' by Colonel Meadows Taylor, and 'Architectural Notes' by James Fergusson. The current state of historical studies is revealed by Meadows Taylor's inability to date the Chalukyas of the sixth to eighth centuries any more specifically than as 'the earliest known Karnatak Dynasty'. The state of art history is seen in Fergusson's inability to link the Durga temple to any of the dynasties on Taylor's list, or to date it more precisely than 'probably anterior to the tenth century'. Four views of the Durga temple are to be found: three photographs showing it from the east and a photograph-based woodcut showing it from the south-west (Figs 1–4). It is clear from his discussion that Fergusson knew the structure only from these pictures. (Significant portions of Fergusson's texts have been reproduced in Appendix I.)

Though Fergusson, an unabashed Orientalist, did not think much of the Durga temple as a work of art, he was interested in it for what he felt it might reveal about other architectural works with which he was already familiar, the Buddhist *caitya* halls of western India. It was the only apsidal construction with an exterior, as well as an interior, that he knew. So, his description centres on the semicircular form of the temple's west end, shown in the woodcut, which he says, 'correctly reproduces what the great cave at Karlee would have been had it been a free standing structural building'.

We can see what he was referring to if we look at views of the Karli excavation that he had previously published. The *caitya* hall is an elongated chamber shaped to enclose the form and the ritual of the Buddhist reliquary mound, the *stupa* or *caitya* (Fig. 28). The hall's form follows and expresses the contours of the *stupa*'s domed-cylinder shape with its barrel-vaulted ceiling and apsidal layout. The colonnade on the interior marks the path of the worshippers' encircling procession. The verticals of the pillars and the arches of the ceiling, repeating down the hall, reinforce the *stupa*'s profile and the worshipper's passage around it (Fig. 29). The arch for the vault is the focal element of the exterior facade (Fig. 30). Despite clear evidence in every element of the rock-cut designs that they are stone sculptures depicting wood and plaster prototypes, none of the free-standing structures of this period have survived. And though a few representations in painting and relief did exist to hint at what the exteriors of these 'structural' halls looked like, their actual form was a mystery.

His interest in the temple's apsidal form led Fergusson directly to his conclusion about its sectarian origin. He supposed the apsidal plan to be a Buddhist form. Colonnaded apses were a salient characteristic of these familiar Buddhist structures, while all but unknown to the antiquarian literature on Brahmanical temples. Most of his note is therefore devoted to demonstrating that the temple's current Saivite identification was the result of a Brahmanical take-over, of what he believed to be a structure more appropriate to Buddhists.

Fergusson thus introduced the structure to its audience by fitting what he could make out of its form into the previously established intellectual framework. European antiquaries of Fergusson's time held a long-standing interest in the spectacular rock-cut architecture of the west Indian *caitya* halls. Several well-published examples were located in close proximity to the European settlements of Bombay and Pune.[3] By contrast, nothing was known to them of the early traditions of the Deccan, to the south, before the publication of *Architecture in Dharwar and Mysore*. As we continue through the literature, we will see how Fergusson's initial interpretation of Biggs' photographs was nurtured and refined by generations of later writers. It is equally significant that Fergusson by and large ignored most of the complex subject of Biggs' pictures, to concentrate almost exclusively on the few details that he could fit into the tradition in which he was writing.

When he inserted the Durga temple into one of his comprehensive histories of Indian architecture a year later, Fergusson revealed more fully how he integrated its new evidence into his existing framework. Fergusson's original vision of the history of Indian architecture was a racial-religious evolution.[4] He divided Indian art history into four stylistic eras. The earliest remains, created before the twelfth century of the Common Era (CE), were considered Buddhist. These were followed by an overlapping era of Jain art, between the eleventh and the thirteenth centuries, and parallel movements of Brahmanical and Muslim art, from the twelfth to the eighteenth century.[5] Though this arrangement seems absurd today, we need to remember that Fergusson's was the first comprehensive history of Indian art ever published. Following this scheme he devoted a separate section of his book to each of his religious styles. In this notice the Durga temple was placed in the section on Buddhist architecture, at the beginning of the chapter on rock-cut temples, as a preface to his consideration of the *caitya* caves.

Fergusson's interest in the Durga temple here again lies in its potential for explaining the exterior of the Buddhist *caitya*. The text is thus illustrated by his woodcut of the temple's apsidal end (Fig. 1). The other two remains to which he referred served the same purpose. Too little remained of Sanchi's temple 18 to be informative, but the 'Mahavellipore rath' (the Sahadeva *ratha*) was another story. It too was a temple with an apsidal exterior Fergusson could cite to illustrate what he surmised to be the outer form of the ancient Buddhist's *caitya* (Fig. 31). And it looked to be a more complete example than the Durga temple. Its form included a barrel-vaulted upper story where the upper part of the Durga temple was in ruins. However, because he believed the *ratha* to be a Brahmanical work of a much later period, he confined his mention here to a note, and discussed it more thoroughly in the later section on Brahmanical structures.

In his previous comprehensive history, a decade earlier, Fergusson put the Sahadeva *ratha* into an ambivalent class of Brahmanical works he thought 'imitated' the forms of earlier Buddhist architecture and placed his views in a special chapter at the end of his Buddhist section, so forming a bridge between that section and his discussion of Jain art.[6] There he described the *ratha* as 'the only representation I know in India of such a temple as those cut in rock at Ajunta and elsewhere',[7] the very words he now used to introduce the Durga temple.[8]

The discovery of the Durga temple thus allowed Fergusson to develop two themes he had proposed previously. The first was his explanation of the form of the *caitya*-hall's exterior. In 1855 he used his drawing of the *ratha* (Fig. 31) to show 'the rounded apsidal end' which was 'nowhere else represented that I am aware of'.[9] However, he lamented, because this monument was itself rock-cut it raised some questions. The outer aisle seemed to be 'open externally', which was 'not the case in the caves hitherto explored, though it probably was so in buildings', and 'it would evidently be impossible to represent this feature in the rock'.[10] The Durga temple's exterior colonnade offered a clear illustration of this (Fig. 1). At the same time its apparently earlier date reinforced his other conviction, that the apsidal form was peculiarly appropriate to the Buddhists. He was now able to reinforce that position with what seemed to be a genuine Buddhist structure, to locate into the place in his argument where he formerly had to make do with a later, Brahmanical 'imitation'.

A few years later, the epigrapher, Bhau Daji, undertook an analysis of the inscriptions Biggs had included in his volume of field notes. Bhau made no direct reference to the specific temples illustrated in *Architecture in Dharwar and Mysore*, but he was able to certify that inscriptions at the site of Iwullee dated to a particular dynasty. In one record, which Biggs had located on a 'Gateway of the Town' but which he associated with the 'wall of a temple', Bhau found the titles, 'Satyāśraya Srī Prithvi Vallabha Mahārājādhirāja', common to several rulers of the early Chalukya dynasty. Another inscription, appearing on what Biggs identified as 'a Shivite Temple', also at 'Iwullee', included a direct mention of the early Chalukya king Pulakesin II, and a date he read as *Saka* 506 (584 CE), indicating it to be the earliest structural temple yet identified by antiquarians in southern India. (Significant portions of Bhau Daji's text will be found in Appendix II.)

Like Fergusson, Bhau Daji had more to say about the bearing of his new evidence on other pending cultural issues than about the structures upon which they stood. But, he was able to suggest a dynasty and even a century within which to date the monuments of Aihole.

And thus, in the 1860s the Durga temple surfaced in the literature of the English writing and reading public of Indian antiquarians, as an inglorious, structural version of a Buddhist *caitya* hall, appropriated by Brahmanical Hindus and buried under rubble at a site of the ancient Chalukya dynasty. The newly 'discovered' work was introduced into the literature by integrating it into pre-existing conceptual schemes. Its form was explained by inserting it into a place in the existing history. It fit the niche in the existing framework formerly occupied by the Sahadeva *ratha*. And fitting better than its predecessor, it partially displaced it.

Pioneering Investigations

THE MOST IMPORTANT individual in effecting the transition from the eclectic, amateur literature of the antiquarians to the systematic art history of the later nineteenth century was James Fergusson. Fergusson went beyond his predecessors, such as the Daniells, Salt and Babington, by combining and refining their various talents at drawing, description and speculation about prominent remains into a comprehensive vision. He also made a first-hand study of a far wider number of monuments, spread over a wider geographic area, than anyone before him. Coming on the scene more or less at the same time as the camera, Fergusson was able to go beyond the limits of his own, rather limited drawing skills to assemble the first comprehensive visual record of Indian architecture.[11] He was the first to study India's architecture comparatively and systematically.[12]

Fergusson was, however, limited in his access to his subject. Coming to India as a youth and eventually succeeding as an indigo planter, he amassed a considerable fortune as well as a remarkable store of racial prejudices. He began his career as a writer on architecture in 1842 only after he left India, never to return. His developed work was thus conducted long distance from Victorian London, through other people's accounts and illustrations, and most prominently through his collection of photographs, which had begun to appear in the 1850s. His writing provided the model for later students. His first and foremost successor in India was James Burgess, one of the earliest professional historians of India's art.

On his appointment as the British colonial government's Archaeological Surveyor of Western India, Burgess took Fergusson's advice in choosing Aihole as one of the sites to be covered in his first tour of exploration. One of the expressed purposes of this tour was to explore the questions Fergusson had raised about the structure and internal arrangements of the Durga temple photographed by Biggs. Fergusson believed it could be the one bearing the Pulakesin II inscription read by Bhau Daji. So, in the spring of 1874, Burgess proceeded to make the first direct art historical examination of the temple itself. (Significant portions of Burgess' texts will be found in Appendix III.)

What is most striking about Burgess' *Report* is how faithful he remained to Fergusson's general interpretation of the temple, despite finding many fundamental errors and misconceptions, which first-hand observation enabled him to correct (Figs 5–9). Confined to what he could see in middle-distance photographs, Fergusson guessed the tower was missing and the sculpture contained 'nothing that might not be found in later Buddhist erections'. Against this, Burgess found the major figure sculptures and decorations all to be Brahmanical deities. Most significantly, there was an image of Garuda over the *mandapa* (hall) doorway, which he took as an unquestionable demonstration of the structure's dedication to Vishnu. He listed the major figures of the hall's exterior niches: 'Nṛsiñha, Maheśāsurī, Varāha, Vishṇu, Arddhanāri, Śiva, &c . . .'. Burgess was thus convinced that the structure was Brahmanical, and yet he organized his detailed description of the architecture around Fergusson's likening of the structure to the Buddhist *caitya* hall.

Besides adding a considerable amount of detailed description to the published record of the temple, Burgess' investigation was able to clear up confusion on several matters. He was able to see that the rubble which Fergusson had supposed to have 'replaced the spire' actually formed 'a ramp round' a spire that was still in place (Fig. 5). Further, he saw that the Vikramaditya inscription, which Biggs had associated with a town gateway and Bhau Daji had associated with a temple wall, was actually located on the wall of the gateway of *this* temple. The sixth-century Jain inscription mentioning Pulakesin II turned out to be elsewhere.[13]

Finally, Burgess was able to compare the temple with several structures he had seen in the nearby sites of Badami and Pattadakal, as well as the much more distant Ajanta, and was the first to consider its place in India's art history. Based upon both inscriptional and stylistic evidence, he was able to provide the first useful estimate for the temple's date. The Chalukya king mentioned in the gateway inscription was now identified through direct investigation and a better copy as Vikramaditya I, who ruled in the middle of the seventh century. The style of the interior appeared to be appropriate to the 'century after' Badami's Cave III, dated by inscription to 578 CE (*Saka* 500), and published for the first time in this same volume (Fig. 32). And so, what the people of the site called the 'Durga' temple, because of its location in the town's fortification-wall, or *durga*, Burgess recognized as a seventh-century Vaishnava temple.

Two years later, in 1876, James Fergusson returned to the lists with his masterpiece, the *History of Indian and Eastern Architecture*. Though confined to architecture, Fergusson's study of Indian temples was the first chronologically and geographically comprehensive history of Indian art. The study, which appeared first in 1855 as a section of one of his universal histories, was doubled in 1867, and brought to full bloom in a lengthy and lavishly illustrated, independent volume. Now Fergusson, who was quite up to date on Burgess' progress in the field, altered his earlier views to accommodate Burgess' findings on the temple's iconographic programme, style and date. He did not, however, change his original conclusion. Rather, he maintained his primary conviction about what he believed to be the temple's most significant characteristic: its preservation of a unique moment in the evolution of the Buddhist *caitya* hall tradition. He did this by means of the somewhat amazing proposition that the religion of the Vaishnavas and that of the Jains were indistinguishable at that time, and that this was also true of their temples, which he saw as derived from Buddhist temples. (See Appendix I.)

Fergusson assigned the temple to *c.* 650, while holding out for a possible non-Brahmanical[14] attribution to the Jain sect, on the basis of his understanding of the only iconic image from the temple yet published in a readable view (Fig. 6), and against the reasoning of Burgess' list of Brahmanical deities (as yet unphotographed or at least unpublished). The figure on the left of Burgess' plate is a totally nude male in a symmetrical pose typical of Jain Tirthankaras. His interest in the temple remains unchanged. He finds it an important example of a stage in an evolution he supposes to connect the circular forms of the Buddhists to the square forms of the Brahmanical Hindus. It was thus still a fulfilment of his original contention: a trivial example of an intermediate step in a significant evolution.

The temple's extensive Brahmanical imagery, described at length by Burgess, is thoroughly ignored. As are all aspects of the architecture that fail to bear witness to the theme of the temple's supposed evolution out of the Buddhist *caitya*. Fergusson is only interested in the structure as it can be conceptualized within the abstract framework of his original evolutionary hypothesis.

These ideas have received serious, if contradictory, support as well as revision in subsequent accounts. The third volume of the *Archaeological Survey of Western India*, appeared two years after Fergusson's book. In it John Faithful Fleet presented a thorough analysis of the inscriptions on the Durga temple, based on the photographs and copies collected and illustrated by Burgess in volume 1 (Fig. 9; significant portions of Fleet's texts will be found in Appendix IV).

The Vikramaditya inscription on the gateway was now edited by an epigraphist with access to a good quality copy. Fleet supported Burgess' assertion that the Chalukya king mentioned was named Vikramaditya, but he disagreed with Burgess as to which Vikramaditya this was. Rather, following his fellow epigraphist Bhau Daji, he referred the palaeographic style to the eighth century, and so attributed it to Vikramaditya II, who ruled from 733/4 to 744/5. In his translation he saw the inscription as a grant of tax revenue to 'Adityabhatta, a priest of the temple'.

Fleet had more to say the following year, in his continuing *Indian Antiquary* series, 'Sanskrit & Old-Canarese Inscriptions'. There he offers a reproduction of a rubbing and a slightly fuller translation of the gateway's revenue inscription, with added support for his attribution of it to Vikramaditya II. The article also includes a repetition of his translations of the two shorter inscriptions, and the first discussion of a fourth, which Burgess only mentioned in passing. This is the short label appearing on a basement moulding of the temple, on the south, above the panel with the flying figures pictured in the *First Report* (Fig. 6). On the grounds of palaeographic style he supposed its letters 'to have been cut by the hand of the very same man who engraved the inscription of Vijayaditya on a pillar in the porch of the temple of Mahakutesvara at Badami'. That is, it belongs to the period of the father of the second Vikramaditya, two generations after Vikramaditya I.[15] His translation of it, as 'the holy temple of Jina', supported Fergusson's attribution of the temple's deity. (See Appendix IV.)

In his first-hand reading of the gateway inscription, with his new impression, Fleet was able to read the fifth line he had had to leave undeciphered in his earlier attempt. Beyond the better reading of the object there is also the possibility of different explanations of its meaning. In his first version of the gateway inscription, Fleet said the tax revenue went to 'Adityabhatta of the temple', who in his comment he called 'a priest of the temple'. In his later edition he says that the revenue went to 'the venerable Aditya of the temple', separating the title *bhatta* (actually *Bhaṭara: priest, lord* or as here *venerable*) from the proper name *Aditya*.

Fergusson's initial contention, that the temple should be Buddhist, was based on his belief that apsidal forms were essentially Buddhist. When Burgess saw the Garuda over the doorway to the temple's hall and the sculpture of its wall, he became convinced that the structure must have been Vaishnava, not Buddhist. He, quite as reasonably, associated Garuda, the vehicle and cognizance of Vishnu, with a temple of that God. In each case the conclusions reached were based on a rationalization of the forms under view. Burgess' description lists the identities of the Brahmanical Gods of the veranda, but omits that of the one he illustrates (Fig. 6). By contrast, Fergusson discusses the identification of that one only, while omitting the others. In each case non-material suppositions entered into the formula to sway the conclusion and in each case we shall see them proven wrong.

At this point another issue comes into view: the *form* of the discussion, and its life in print. While Biggs, Fergusson, Bhau, Burgess and Fleet were measuring their evidence against the temple, each also had to measure it against previous writings. None could merely present their observations or conclusions. Each had to contend with the others' conclusions. Some of these contentions pertained to what the temple was, others pertained to how one or the other thought the temple ought to be interpreted. Although he found flaws in both Fergusson's analysis of the structure's form and in some of his conclusions, Burgess also found it useful to maintain much of the rhetorical shape of Fergusson's argument. On the one hand he offered a modification of Fergusson's essential thesis, rejecting the contention of Buddhist identification for the weaker alternative of Buddhist inspiration. On the other, he continued to describe the temple with reference to its similarity to the more familiar Buddhist structures. As time went on the background understanding of Indian architecture grew progressively more sophisticated and the foreground grasp of the Durga temple's features grew more detailed, but the rhetorical form into which the temple's material relationships had been translated was hardening into factitive logic with a rationality of its own.

In this way real objects and documents are reified into verbal alter egos which regularly replace them in discussions, and although these words ought to carry limited weight, in comparison with the objects described, few people actually have the opportunity to approach the temples, monuments, constitutions or other primary documents themselves. For those unable to work with the object at first-hand, their verbal simulations carry a greater weight than the objects they represent. So strong is the impact of what is published that often even those who gain direct access to the object are so predisposed, by what they have read that they fail to look critically or to make an adequate record of their own analysis. Thus for most, the actual object has a less important presence than its various records.

Fergusson's last living words on the Durga temple come in a surprising but brief reference within an extended discussion of the Sahadeva *ratha* at Mahabalipuram, devoted to his perennial interest in evidence recreating the lost exterior of the Buddhist *caitya*. Following a plan of the *ratha* and one of the Durga temple Fergusson discusses the row of miniature cells surrounding the vault on the exterior of the Sahadeva *ratha* (Fig. 33). He offers the following in his attempt to understand the temple's roof line. 'There is one temple at Aihole dedicated to Siva which does show the external aisle and apsidal termination, and is probably of about the same age as this Ratha. Unfortunately it has been used as a fortification, and its upper storey and room removed, so that it is of little more use to us now than an interior would be for judging of what the effect of the exterior may have been above the first storey.'

There is no explanation given for him calling the temple Shaiva this time. It is possible that Fergusson had forgotten his entire argument and was just quoting Biggs' original notes. At any rate, Fergusson's new woodcut (Fig. 33) showed the sort of vaulted, apsidal superstructure he supposed to have once risen over the Durga temple. As earlier, he continued to believe that the original superstructure had been 'removed', despite Burgess' statement that it was merely covered up.

Thirty-five years after his original visit to Aihole,[16] when he wrote his last interpretation of the Durga temple, Burgess had besides the ten pictures[17] in his possession in 1874 and the eight notices of his own and others' writing, his field notes and what he could interpret from those photographs and notes. Still, though the pictures contained much information as yet undiscussed in the literature, he wrote only about those relationships already lodged in the record. A selective list of abstracted characteristics had virtually replaced the original object for him.

His illustrations of the three slabs leaning up against the side of the temple's basement (Fig. 6) provided Burgess with an opportunity to discuss sculptural style. It provided Fergusson with evidence of Jainism. In fact, Fergusson was wrong about the temple's iconographic programme. There are no Jain temples with Vishnu, Durga, Narasimha, Varaha and Ardhanari as their main wall images. The figure he read as a Jain Tirthankara can be better recognized, from its luxuriant hair, sacred thread and agitated female admirers, as Bhiksatana: Siva as a wandering ascetic.[18] In Fergusson's time, however, the Jina was well established in the English record as India's naked male; Bhiksatana Siva was not so well known there yet. So, in 1876 Fergusson's guess was not so obviously mistaken, to those whose knowledge of Indian deities was from records written in English, just about the only language for nineteenth-century literature on the subject. Indeed, it seemed to gain great support from Fleet's subsequent use of the same picture in reading the inscription on the temple's basement, as indicating that it was a 'temple of Jina'.

Though unable to read it himself, Burgess had the good investigative sense to include the evidence in his report, enabling others to improve on his interpretations later. It is the historian's charge to provide the evidence as well as possible and to explain it on the basis of the understandings available.

He wrote on the temple twice more. In neither case did he significantly alter his previously stated views, although he did attempt to add further evidence to support his arguments. In 1897, he republished two of the photographs of his *First Report*, along with one not printed at that time, in a large collection of famous monuments. The caption accompanying the full view of the temple (Fig. 5) repeats Fergusson's boiler-plate. 'It is unique as a structural building', he says, 'and bears a close analogy in plan to the Buddha cave-temples, illustrating how the latter developed into the later forms of the Jaina and Hindu temples.' The 'new' photograph is a view of the temple doorway whose elaborate decoration included the Garuda that buttressed his contention that the structure was Vaishnava (Fig. 10). It also shows the state of the interior of the structure at the time of his visit, the roof collapsed and the hall filled with debris. (See Appendix III.) Fleet's assignment of the inscription to Vikramaditya II (733/4–744/5) is mentioned, but interpreted as an addition to the structure that Burgess' judgement of style places a century earlier, in the time of Vikramaditya I (654/5–681). The 'Sri Jinalayan' label-inscription is rationalized as the possible result of Jains taking over the temple temporarily, at some date after its original creation.

Burgess' last word on the temple is found under Fergusson's name. It is the 1910 edition of the *History of Indian and Eastern Architecture* where Burgess only takes credit for editing, though the work would be better termed a collaboration. It is better known today than Fergusson's original work. Burgess' rewrite expanded the original by about twenty-five per cent, to accommodate the development of the field during the thirty-five intervening years, and to accommodate Burgess' personal evaluations, which in many cases not only deviate significantly from Fergusson's but thoroughly negate them. Fergusson's essential organization of Indian art into racial-religious styles was recast here with a significantly different emphasis as regional styles, and most of the overt expressions of Fergusson's racial ideology were eliminated. The section on 'Construction' of 'Jaina Architecture', in which Fergusson placed his discussion of the Durga temple, was retitled 'Hindu Construction', and transferred into the book on 'Dravidian Style', in a section on plans. (See Appendix III.)

Most of the text is Fergusson's, but Burgess has made two types of determining alteration. First, he has inserted what was necessary to bring it up to date, such as noting Fleet's interpretations of the structure's inscriptions and the more recent recognition of the existence of other structural, apsidal temples at Ter and Cejerla.[19] Second, he has inserted new elements and transformed existing ones, to bring the interpretation into line with his conviction of the temple's Vaishnava dedication, while dropping Fergusson's contention that it was Jain. The main framework and content, however, remained focused on Fergusson's thesis, interpreting the work's apsidal structure as a formal stage in the Buddhist to Brahmanical evolution.

The argument has softened, however. Where Fergusson wrote of 'how the plans of the Buddhist Chaitya Halls became converted into those of the Jaina and Hindu temple', Burgess rewrote as 'how the plans of such halls were related to those of Hindu and Jaina temples'. Sections describing the Buddhist *caitya* and having nothing to do with the Durga temple remain, as does the orientation of the temple's description around the idea that it was equivalent in form to earlier Buddhist temples and that an appropriate Brahmanical form had not yet been developed. That is, the structure's interest lay in what it revealed about the more important Buddhist *caityas* elsewhere, and the influence of the Buddhists on later, non-Buddhist temple architecture.

The problem of the *caitya*'s exterior form and its lost structural representatives was now solved without reference to the Durga temple. Two new structural survivals in the apsidal mode had appeared in the literature, one at Cejerla in Andhra and another at Ter in Maharashtra (Fig. 34), and seemed to tell all that Fergusson originally desired of the Durga temple, and more. These structures now accompanied Sanchi's temple 18 in the discussion of structural sources of the Buddhist *caitya* hall, where the Durga temple had made its entrance onto the literary stage. In both cases the structures were brick, and their characteristic vaulted superstructures were found intact. So, the rhetorical slot in the evolutionary paradigm allotted to the structural example of a Buddhist *caitya* was finally filled by structures that seemed to be Buddhist, and this time they were ones with vaulted exteriors, not visible at the Durga temple. Neither example had the open veranda that Fergusson wondered about, but both showed effectively what the apsidal vault looked like from the outside. The brick structures of the newly discovered pair seemed to guarantee their early age, and there seemed to be no question but that they were originally Buddhist, though they too had been found under Brahmanical worship.[20]

Henry Cousens, the Durga temple's third major interpreter, was a life-long officer of the Archaeological Survey of India who had visited the Durga temple several times during the course of his service. In contrast to Fergusson, whose dislike of Indians was manifest,[21] Cousens was a man who decided to remain in India when it was time for his retirement. Cousens wrote with the benefit of having read Fergusson and later historians such as Bhau, Burgess, Fleet, Bhandarkar and Fergusson's nemesis, Alexander Cunningham. He based his work on a direct study of the temple and related Chalukya monuments, offering his interpretation along with a new and expanded set of photographs and diagrams. Like Burgess, Cousens reinterpreted his predecessors' conclusions in order to account for an expanded number of closely related monuments. Cousens' field work began under Burgess and extended through the first decade of the twentieth century. His first essay, written for the *Archaeological Survey Reports for 1907–8*, was not published until the year after Burgess' 1910 edition of Fergusson. His two subsequent essays do not seem to have been written much later, though they were not published until 1926, over a decade after his retirement from the Survey.[22] The two later views, in any case, show very little difference from his original interpretation, and no further research. Like the rest of his work on Aihole, they are based on the photographs and diagrams completed before the *Annual Report for 1907–8*.

That Cousens was Burgess' protege, as Burgess was Fergusson's, is evident. Despite first-hand familiarity with its structure his interpretation is in many respects a reinterpretation of theirs. Cousens referred to all the established issues, the Buddhist *caitya* lineage, the sectarian affiliation and the date. But, significantly, he had his own, sometimes quite different, observations and conclusions to offer. His contributions were based on two new factors. The first was his greater familiarity with this temple and with a larger number of early Chalukya monuments than known to his predecessors. The second was his adoption of an evolutionary scheme, modelled partially on Alexander Cunningham's, for explaining the development of Hindu temple architecture as linear progress from cave-like, towerless structures preceding the fifth century, toward the familiar, tower-bearing structures of later times.[23] In particular his interpretation grew out of his analysis of the unusual properties of the Lad Khan, a large temple at Aihole, apparently unknown to Fergusson and Burgess (Fig. 37). In terms of the framework of his discussion, while Cousens continued his predecessor's habit of describing the Durga temple as a Brahmanical take-off on the Buddhist *caitya*, he replaced their Buddhist to Brahmanical *sectarian* evolution, with a flat-roofed to towered *formal* evolution. In terms of the temple, he revealed himself to be the first one familiar enough with its contemporary style to recognize its artistic merits. Thus he began by declaring the Durga temple to be 'without doubt, the finest . . . temple at Aihole'.

Cousens' evolutionary scheme is based on the supposed development of the Brahmanical temple's tower and the location of its shrine in relation to its rear wall. His discussion of the temple fits into his evolutionary sequence after the flat-roofed temples and at the beginning of towered ones. (Significant portions of Cousens' text will be found in Appendix V.)

Cousens' major alteration of the previous interpretations lay in his addition to the discussion of the Lad Khan and other local temples and in his consequent pushing back of the temple's date by more than a century. He did this on the basis of its formal style. His location of the temple into his evolutionary scheme for Aihole places it between the Lad Khan and the Meguti. For Cousens, following Cunningham's logic, the Lad Khan is mid-fifth century because it lacks a tower,[24] and because its shrine is against its rear wall (diagram 2c). Later temples in his sequence have their shrines free from their back walls and support towers. The Meguti is mid-seventh century, inscribed 634/5. It has an isolated (*sandhara*) shrine (diagram 2a) and a superstructure that appeared to be the beginning of a tower (Fig. 86). The Durga temple was *sandhara*, and it had a tower, but its apsidal plan and sloping roofs reminded Cousens of earlier Buddhist rock-cut architecture.[25] Thus we have the Durga temple as mid-sixth.

Responding to Burgess' lead, Cousens also based his evaluation of the temple's date on the relation of its interior pillars to those of nearby Badami's Cave III, dated 578. But, unlike his mentor, Cousens found the Durga temple less, not more, developed than the cave, and went beyond Burgess by giving his reasons. Cousens believed the Durga temple to be later than the Lad Khan because its pillars (Fig. 7) were 'less massive' than the Lad Khan's (Fig. 37). He believed it to be earlier than the cave, because its pillars were less 'elaborate' and less 'varied' in form than those found there (Fig. 32). The photographs already published help us to understand what Cousens meant. This conclusion, repeated in his longer study,[26] that the temple dates from after the Lad Khan of the mid-fifth century and before Cave III of 578, was to be all but universally followed for the next five decades.

Although he did not refer to it specifically, Cousens' photograph of the temple (Fig. 11) had an important place in the developing understanding of the temple. It was taken from about the same location of Burgess' earlier view (Fig. 5) and not too far from Biggs' (Fig. 3). Together they tell the tale of the gradual uncovering of the temple's roof, that allowed Burgess to recognize its tower's survival under the rubble, and later Cousens to discuss both the tower and the roof. Besides this new view of the temple, cleared of debris, Cousens also offered a plate of drawings depicting four of its stone window grills, and a refined plan showing more about the interior (cf. Fig. 12).

Along with the extension of his predecessors' Buddhist subtext, Cousens was the first to develop the analysis of the Durga temple beyond the horizontal plane of the ground plan and layout to a serious consideration of its elevation. He did this through his discussion of the sculptured entablature found above pillars and the varying heights and slopes of the central and flanking ceilings of the interior. The entablature he compared to those found in the *caityas*, citing one at Ajanta. The greater height of the central hall and the lower, and sloping, angles of the side aisle roofs he explained as an attempt to simulate the vaults and half-vaults of the *caitya* within the limits of pillars and lintels.

Cousens' *Chālukyan Architecture of the Kanarese Districts* (1926) is still the best known and most authoritative research interpretation of the Durga temple, and of Chalukya architecture as a whole, more than half a century after its publication. It was, until recently, the most extensive study of Chalukya architecture, containing a comprehensive study of a large number of temples at their major sites in Karnataka outside of Aihole: Badami, Pattadakal and Mahakuta. Its treatment of the temples at Aihole is a rewrite of his 1907–8 report, expanded to include a detailed description of the temple's forms. Its conclusions stem directly from the earlier note, with a few minor nodes of development and one major new blossom. In this version of his interpretation, Cousens discusses the Nagara (north Indian) *sikhara* atop the temple (Fig. 14), which was revealed by a photograph though not discussed in the report (Fig. 11). Also in this version he comments, without explanation, that the temple's dedication might have been to a particular form of Vishnu: 'Surya-Narayana'. And, he adds some new illustrations, including a site plan of Aihole (Fig. 13), locating the temple's position there.

This second version differs from Cousens' earlier report largely in the extension of description and detail and in the polished arguments and illustrations. A sketch of a *caitya* hall plan was added to the plate with the Durga temple's plan (Fig. 12) as it was printed in the earlier article, to further demonstrate the *caitya* lineage theme. While illustrations of the temple before his time had ambiguously suggested that the temple was topped by a vaulted superstructure, the clearing of Cousens' time revealed that no such vault existed (Fig. 11). Rather, there was a Nagara style tower, with angular contours. Thus new effort had to be expended if the *caitya* hall lineage was to be maintained.

In his detailed description Cousens reveals the control, we have grown to expect, of previous writing over independent observation. For example, he repeats Burgess' list of the six Brahmanical deities found in niches of the hall wall. Burgess (1874) listed these images randomly, without an interest in their sequence on the structure, and he mistakenly identified the Harihara as Ardhanari. Cousens, who should have known better, repeats Burgess' unsequenced list verbatim, modernizing the spelling but failing to correct the misidentification.

He does add significantly to our understanding with his explanation of the tower and a little to our knowledge of the pillar sculpture. But he fails at the same time to take any advantage of the new evidence of the basement mouldings or other information available in the two somewhat different views he adds to the visual record. Cousens does not explain his change from Burgess' designation of the temple's deity as Vishnu to the syncretic, if still Vaishnava, Surya-Narayana.

The closeness of the interpretation in *Chālukyan Architecture* to that of the 1907–8 *Report* suggests that they were written about the same time. That Cousens retired from the Archaeological Survey shortly after the publication of the report, and that the latest bibliographic citation is to the 1910 Burgess-edition of Fergusson's history, seem to confirm this supposition.

Cousens' third notice of the Durga temple was published in the same year as the *Chālukyan Architecture*, in his more modest *Architectural Antiquities of Western India*. The interpretation there is a close variation of the others,[27] though in this case the tower is cited as a difference between Brahmanical temples and Buddhist temples. Adding to the ambiguity he produced earlier, the dedication is first said to be 'Vaishnava' and then (in contradiction or extension?) to be 'quite possib[ly] . . . to the Sun-god, Surya'. The difference between this version and the other two lies in the emphasis. Now issues already prominent in the literature are stressed, while contradictory details are screened. The writer's focus upon Buddhism dominates the field-worker's familiarity with the Brahmanical building.

During the sixty years between its first art historical notice and Cousens' authoritative summation, there appeared an increasingly more accurate and detailed record of the temple's form in photographs, diagrams and descriptions, as the structure emerged by successive stages from beneath the weeds and rubble that dominate Biggs' first views. As this occurred there was a progressive reevaluation of the structure's sectarian attribution, likely date, aesthetic value and historical significance. And yet, it was still being discussed in terms of the issues that first attracted Fergusson.

Over time, in the process of repeated approaches, written descriptions and analyses of the Durga temple accumulated. Each succeeding analyst was therefore required to study two separate versions of the temple: the stone structure being slowly cleared of its obscuring layer of rubbish and vegetation at Aihole, and the verbal representation growing ever more detailed and elaborate in the literature. No interpretation could be simply a study of the actual building, or a record of reality; each had to be something more complex and less empirical: a painstaking correlation of the author's understanding of the monument with his understanding of the literature, as focused by the particular writing project at hand.

Synthesis from a Distance

About the time of World War I we enter a new phase in the Durga temple's histories, and find more abstracted discussions by writers whose knowledge is based almost exclusively on earlier reports. These studies are global surveys, seeking either to situate the Durga temple into the evolution of Indian art, or oblique analyses that address select aspects of the temple's design in attempts to answer more limited questions. The result, on the one hand, was an expansion of understanding through attempts to connect the temple with the wider range of India's architecture, while on the other it lead to a shrunken stereotype of the temple, which replaced more detailed and nuanced observations of the structure.

Havell's *Ancient and Mediaeval Architecture of India* resuscitates Fergusson's project of explaining the lost Ashokan *caitya* hall, in order to put forward his own racial theory. (Significant portions of Havell's text will be found in Appendix VI.) Unlike Fergusson, who disparaged traditional temple art for being tainted by Dravidian or Hindu origin, Havell wanted to show that the Brahmanical temple was essentially Aryan and so as worthy of western respect as India's already admired idealist philosophy.

The prolific and uncritical Havell adapted Fergusson's 1876 explanation of the temple, with a bit of Burgess' report mixed in, to reject Fergusson's anti-Brahmanical attitude. His illustrations were mostly drawn from Burgess' fieldwork. He makes an interesting attempt to analyse the temple's form on the basis of the ritual and social interests, but he subverts his own purposes with his characteristic sloppiness. In order to bolster his desired conclusion he ignores consistent explanations of the temple's name and attributes its dedication to the goddess. He creates a unique and ill-starred conception of northern style towers as appropriate to Vishnu and southern (or Dravidian) towers as appropriate to Shiva, in the belief that the temple has a domed, southern tower, when Cousens' report of four years earlier had already shown unobstructed views of an unambiguously northern one (Figs 11 and 14).

In his illustration Havell offers alternative views of the *gandharva-apsaras* ceiling panels, found in Burgess' *Report* (Fig. 6) and the opinion that these panels had been destroyed.[28] His mistaken guess that the panels were destroyed after Burgess' visit, was not without foundation in a world of imperial British archaeologists, where Brahmanical art was regularly denigrated and often treated both carelessly and contemptuously. Comparison of the two plates shows that the photographs published by Havell were actually taken earlier than those published by Burgess,[29] and that in the interim the figures had sustained some damage. The *apsarā* accompanying the *gandharva* with the wine cup seems to have lost her left hand. The *gandharva* with the tufted *cakra* has lost part of his right foot plus a good deal of his left arm and hand, the *apsarā* with him has lost a bit of her trailing foot. Her left foot and most of his left leg were lost later.[30] Thus discovery by the antiquarian community was potentially as dangerous for the record as beneficial. The possibility of recognizing some new element of design was accompanied by the possibility that the object might lose part of its material form as well.

In 1922 Gurudas Sarkar referred to particular aspects of the Durga temple without attempting a comprehensive analysis. His aim was to show, contrary to European interpretations from Fergusson to Havell, that the northern-style temple tower does not trace to foreign or Buddhist sources. His reference to the Durga temple appears in his consideration of the views of W. Simpson, who referred to the temple towers of Aihole and Pattadakal as 'evidence of the fact that Brahmins constructed temples more or less in imitation of *chaitya* halls . . . the *shikharas* constructed over the cellas . . . ''*Dravidian* in style'' and quite distinct from the character of the northern *shikhara*'.[31] Sarkar cites the Durga temple both as proof of Simpson's error and as evidence of the northern style's early date. The authority he cites is Cousens' report, though his photograph is more recent than the one Cousens used.[32]

Sarkar refers to the contrast between the northern (*Nagara*) and southern (*Dravida*) styles which can be seen in Fergusson's early woodcut of both types at Pattadakal (Fig. 35).[33] Like Cousens, Sarkar compares the Durga temple with the Parasurameswara of Bhuvaneswar.[34] The southern style is characterized by its domed *stupika* crown, comparatively squat, pyramidal proportions and clearly defined horizontal story structure, as seen on the left in the woodcut. The northern style is more vertical in its emphasis, composed of many narrow horizontal layers within a gently curving outline, accented by prominent vertical *ratha paga* strips. Its crowning member is a cogged wheel or melon shape called an *amalaka*. Both are normally topped-off by a *purna kalasa*, water pot finial. The Durga temple's tower fits into the northern style without question, despite its damaged peak.

Ananda Coomaraswamy's *History of Indian and Indonesian Art*, 1927, offers a comprehensive synthesis of the Durga temple into the history of Indian art. It is the classic survey complement to Cousens' analysis. Coomaraswamy follows Cousens' suggestions, adapting to Cunningham's theory of an evolutionary development of the Hindu temple, from a flat-roofed stage in the fifth century to a tower-bearing stage in the sixth.

Writing on an India-wide scale, Coomaraswamy separates his discussion of the Durga temple from his 'Early Cāḷukya' chapter, placing it into an earlier section on the Gupta period, where architecture is discussed under a series of formally related categories which he offers as an evolutionary sequence: '(1) *stupas*; (2) excavated *caitya*-halls and *viharas*; (3) structural *caitya*-halls and apsidal Hindu temples; (4) flat-roofed temples; (5) *sikhara* shrines, and . . . (6) Palaces and domestic architecture.'[35] He gives the Durga temple two separate places in this scheme. First he uses it as an apsidal temple with a flat roof, to bridge between apsidal Hindu temples (3) and flat-roofed temples (4). The apparent contradiction between having a flat roof and a *sikhara* is explained in his second gloss. This time the Durga temple is brought up between the section on flat-roofed temples (4) and the section on *sikhara* shrines (5), as a temple whose tower seems inappropriate and may, therefore, 'just possibl[y]' be added. (Coomaraswamy's text will be found in Appendix VII.)

Only a year later than Cousens' authoritative Archaeological Survey volume, Coomaraswamy's photographs of the Chalukya monuments (by Johnston and Hoffmann of Calcutta)[36] are significantly more recent. The layer of sod, still visible at the time of Cousens' Survey photographs (Figs 11 and 14), has been removed (Fig. 15). In this they match Sarkar's illustration, as they do in the presence of the scaffolding used for repairing the roof on the south-east.

In O. C. Gangoly's popular little book, *Indian Architecture* (Calcutta, 1928), of the following year there is the now obligatory reference to the Durga temple's plan, linking the discussion of the Buddhist *caityas* to that of the Brahmanical temples. In this Gangoly has settled for the most convenient fit in a conventionalized survey outline, as framed by Fergusson and dated by Cousens. The picture used is the same as Coomaraswamy's, and typical of Gangoly's work the temple's name is mistaken for its dedication.

George Moreas' *Kadamba Kula* (Bombay, 1931) was a pioneering attempt to reconstruct the history of the Karnatak royal house that preceded the Chalukyas. Moreas uses the Durga temple there in his attempt to give the Kadambas their own dynastic architectural style, an honour the literature had already accorded to the Chalukyas and the Hoysalas. He based his speculations on the reasonable logic that the Chalukyas were likely to have built upon the traditions that preceded them, and on his opinion that the very plain, horizontally layered *śikhara* common in the South Kanara region (e.g., Fig. 38) was the indigenous ancient style.[37]

Despite its apparent logic, Moreas' vision is a hodgepodge of little critical value. It combines Fergusson's idea of a square Brahmanical architecture based upon round Buddhist forms with Gravely and Ramachandran's speculation about the layered *sikhara* forms of Karnataka, the northern style of the Durga temple's tower and the southern style of other towers in the Chalukya region and beyond (which he refers to as 'Pallava').[38] His conclusion is that the Durga temple, and so the early Chalukya style, is a combination of derived elements, soon to be replaced by yet other derivations. He selects elements of Cousens' writings that support his logic, such as his Buddhist interpretation of the temple's layout. But he ignores, without comment, elements that conflict with his vision, such as the Lad Khan temple type, which Cousens considers earlier than the Durga temple.

Moreas illustrated the Kadamba style temple tower of 'horizontal stages' by the much later temple at Halsi. No one else has accepted his likening of the Durga temple's tower to such layered structures.[39]

Percy Brown's vision of the Durga temple, a decade later, is an elaborated version of Coomaraswamy's in which the major themes are rationalized, a good deal of Greek terminology added and the conclusions coarsened. What Coomaraswamy achieves in paragraphs Brown does in chapters. Where Coomaraswamy is prudently tentative, Brown is heavy-handedly definite. The temple that for Coomaraswamy 'follows the plan of the apsidal *caitya*-halls' and has a *sikhara* that 'it is just possible' to consider added, becomes for Brown, 'a Brahmanical version of the Buddhist caitya hall' to which 'a *shikara* has subsequently been added'. In captions he dates the temple to the year 500. Following the logic found in Coomaraswamy exactly, he considers the temple twice. The first description of the body of the temple is given in the chapter on early Chalukya temples without towers, that Brown places (following Cousens) between 450 and 650. Then, in the chapter on early Chalukya temples with towers, attributed to the period between 600 and 750, we are given the temple's superstructure. (Significant portions of Brown's text will be found in Appendix VIII.)

It is typical of Brown's encyclopaedic work that while his text adds little new information to the record, his insights and illustrations do squeeze new and developed understandings out of the information previously available. He produces an isometric reconstruction, sketching the temple as if seen from above, with the tower simplistically restored (Fig. 16), a photograph of the southern side of the porch after the clearing (Fig. 18), and the first published view of the interior of the surrounding porch (Fig. 17). He examines the tower and points out the survival of its *amalaka* crown, visible on the ground below in Coomaraswamy's photograph (Fig. 15). He also points to the unusually straight profile of its surviving section, which he explains as evidence of its early or 'primitive' nature. Most significantly he provides a hard-edged reduction of Coomaraswamy's impressionistic sketch, declaring the tower to be an addition to what was originally a flat-roofed temple copied from the Buddhists, thereby reinvigorating the two Victorian evolution theories for another generation.

Though Stella Kramrisch has no focused discussion of the Durga temple in the text of her *Hindu Temple* (Calcutta, 1946), she mentions it several times, indicating that she has followed Percy Brown's discussion of its tower and accepted his conclusions. She sees the structure as a flat-roofed temple with sloping side roofs,[40] to which a tower was experimentally added 'as an afterthought'.[41] In a manner, now becoming conventional, she mentions the temple twice: once for its plan and once for its tower. Her reference to the temple's layout is contrastingly agnostic. It comes in relation to the rock-cut temples. Following recognition that the earliest surviving apsidal halls are heterodox—Ajivaka, Jain and Buddhist—she points out for the first time that such apsidal ground plans are legitimate Brahmanical forms according to the *smrti* literature. The particular term she quotes from the *Samaranganasutradhara* is 'hastijatiya' or 'elephant shaped'.[42] As significantly, and unlike her predecessors, she seems careful to avoid references to Buddhism or to suggest that Buddhist art is its source.

By contrast A. V. Naik's 1947 treatment of the Durga temple, which he dates to *c.* 557–600 in his 'Structural Architecture of the Deccan', is a cut-up and repaste of Cousens' summation in the *Chalukyan Architecture of the Kanarese Districts* and Percy Brown.

With the work of Benjamin Rowland in the early 1950s we come to the flowering of a genre we might characterize as the 'literary' or 'second-hand survey'. Early survey writers, from Fergusson to Percy Brown, attempted to synthesize a coherent picture of the history of India's art from first-hand accounts and illustrations. Now there seems to be a decided shift toward the syntheses of previous survey writers. Coomaraswamy and Brown, the master integrators of field reports, now seem to replace those reports as the source of information.

Benjamin Rowland's treatment of the Durga temple, in his *Art and Architecture of India* (Middlesex, 1953), is, along with many portions of his book, largely a variation on Coomarswamy's synthesis of previous writers. He discusses the Durga temple along with Buddhist apsidal structures in a chapter on the Gupta period. His opinions of the site, 'an overgrown wasteland', and his description of the temple echo Cousens, from whom many of his illustrations are taken. His combination of Greek temple and Christian church terminology parallels Percy Brown. And, it is interesting to note, he explicitly rejects elements of Fergusson's religious evolution. (Significant portions of Rowland's text will be found in Appendix IX.)

S. K. Saraswati's history of Indian architecture, spread through the various volumes of the *History and Culture of the Indian People*, discusses the Durga temple in volume III, in a chapter devoted essentially to the Gupta period. It takes a form we might call the Cousens' summation of the Fergusson thesis.[43] Coming just after a mention of the temples at Ter and Cejeṙla, it defines all three as structural versions of the Buddhist *caitya* hall.

Herman Goetz' summary of the monuments at Aihole seems to reflect his reading of the literature more than what he saw on his visit to the site.[44] His several treatments of the Durga temple, published in 1959, echo Percy Brown: the culmination of the first or '6th century' phase at the site, where temples were 'mere adaptations of the later Buddhist monastery type', of flat-roofed structures witnessed in the Lad Khan and Konti-gudi. However, he adds, 'The temple was completed much later, in the 7th century, so that its sculptures cover all the transitions from homely figures in the manner of the Lad Khan to great masterpieces of the later Gupta style.'[45]

Goetz illustrates one of the temple's magnificent pillar figures (cf. Fig. 66), but mistakenly he attributes it to the eighth-century Virupaksa temple at Pattadakal,[46] and judges the style to 'retain the elegant dignity of the Gupta tradition of Pulakesin's time, though more mannered and far less monumental'.[47]

The same year, Goetz was responsible for a series of notes on Indian art in the *Encyclopaedia of World Art.* He referred to the Durga temple on six different occasions but confined his comments to architecture, repeating the same basic themes of Buddhist and Gupta derivation from several points of view. He does, however, make the interesting point: that *pradaksina* 'is a rite constituting a corporeal participation in prayer; in some cases it was translated into architecture and an ambulatory, the *pradaksinapatha*, was provided. It is this element which gives the Durga temple at Aihole the basilical plan—exceptional among Hindu temples—of the Buddhist chaityas.'[48] Though neither circumambulation nor the plan of a shrine surrounded by outer aisles are uncommon for Brahmanical temples,

Goetz' focus upon the ritual functions explaining the temple's structure is insightful for its time.

It is in his rhetoric of derivation, tracing every element possible to a source somewhere outside the Chalukya tradition that Goetz makes his personal mark: 'Buddhist chaitya model', 'basilical plan', platform of the 'Gupta type', 'pillars like Ajanta', and the whole 'based on the rock-cut sanctuary type' with a 'north-Indian shikara' and sculpture derived from north India. Otherwise Goetz' vision is merely a crude reprise of Percy Brown. His dependence on surveys rather than the research literature is revealed by his misunderstanding of the temple's dedication, and his refusal to consider any issues beyond the tower and the plan.

Goetz' interest in discovering even more remote sources can be seen in his tracing of one of the temple's images beyond India. In another article of 1959 he traced the source of the famous flying figures of the ceiling to Rome (Fig. 46). India's 'flying Gandharva (Vidyadhara) couples', he says are, 'the Nayads and Tritons of Hellenistic typology dressed up in Indian costumes, whereas the single Gandharvas were inspired by the flying Victories. The similarity goes so far that the Gandharva women on the ceiling of the Durga Temple at Aihole hold a flying scarf exactly as on Roman sarcophagus reliefs.'[49]

The second-hand survey continued through the nineteen sixties, based largely on the research completed before the first world war. In Charles Fabri's popularizing *Introduction to Indian Architecture*, the development of the temple is fitted into a rigid formal evolution from a single, towerless cell to an elaborate combination of cells and towers. As Cousens suggested, Fabri places the Durga temple into this sequence at the point where they imagined the tower was invented as a primordial, pseudo-tower. Ambiguously he refers to its 'little turret, a veritable little spire, an obvious ancestor of the *sikhara* of the next century'.[50] He concludes that 'This style, following the strictly classic period of AD 320 to 500, is called the "mannerist".'[51] Interestingly, Fabri makes no reference to Buddhist derivation.

In his widely read *History of Far Eastern Art*, published in 1964, Sherman Lee includes the Durga temple in his chapter 'Early Hindu Art in India'. There the architecture of Aihole is described as a 'development beyond the single cell and *chaitya* type, previously seen in Buddhist architecture of the Gupta and earlier periods'.[52] (The significant portions of Lee's text are found in Appendix X.) In a popular survey covering most of Asia, Lee has even less interest than an Indian generalist in offering new information. Rather he chooses to present the temple as part of a synoptic evolution. His writing is much more concerned with heuristic concepts, such as the difference he draws between sculptural and architectural form. His distance from the actual structure is revealed by his confusing suggestions that the temple's roof has 'a single stone covering the main area', and that the 'rudimentary tower is carved with numerous representations including figures and Buddhist *chaitya* facades'. These are the mistaken guesses of someone dependent upon survey opinions and photographs, who has not bothered to seriously consult the research literature, much less the structure.[53]

P. K. Agrawala's inclusion of the Durga temple in his *Gupta Temple Architecture* came a full century after Fergusson's first notice. It is a brief rewrite of Coomaraswamy's gloss on Cousens, following similar treatments of Cejerla and Ter, all of which have now been reduced to formulae.[54]

The 1950s also saw the development of two quite different approaches to temple art. On the one hand was the commercial success of publications focused on aesthetic enjoyment of visual imagery: popular picture books or 'art books'. These added both illustrations and a new appreciation of the structure to the record, as well as an awareness of the temple's figurative sculpture. On the other hand, interpreters of religion and culture began to provide alternative interpretations of the structure's meaning. Both of these approaches were to have important effects on art historians.

The photographer Louis-Frederic and the team of Pierre Rambach and Vitold de Golish, writing in French but quickly translated into English, produced two of the best known art books. Typical of the genre, Rambach and de Golish confused some of the facts while they enhanced the visual record. Emphasis was placed on the rhythmic sensuosity of the sculptors' art and their sensitivity to nuances of human feeling projected by the portrayal of the human form in stone. Rambach and de Golish provided evocative views of one of the *mithuna* couples of the porch interior, and a miniature couple from one of the hall's door jambs (Fig. 19). They also offered vivid close-ups and a detail of the flying *vidyadhara* couples of the fallen ceiling panels, glimpsed previously in Burgess' archaeological record plate (Fig. 6) and reproduced with little comment by Havell and an earlier picture book by Odette Monod-Bruhl.[55] And finally, we get views of some of the splendid images of the *mandapa* niches, listed by Burgess: the Siva (Fig. 20) and the Varaha (Fig. 21). These were the first photographs of the temple's sculpture to be published since the single plate in Burgess' first report, eighty years before, on which basis alone the impact of this little picture book was important. It opened up a major dimension of the temple's art barely considered before this time: its magnificent figure sculpture. It is perhaps fortunate that they did not bother to discuss the individual pictures they reproduced considering their entertaining lack of interest in the printed record.

Louis-Frederic's work also adds to our visual impression of the temple. Its text is confined to explanations of three plates, and is in no way inferior to those of the second-hand survey historians.[56] His pictures include a standard view of the east facade, a view comparable to Percy Brown's of the porch interior, and the *nagaraja* ceiling. He noted curved brackets on the facade (cf. Fig. 61), but failed to realize that they were modern restorations by the Archaeological Survey, which do not appear earlier.[57] His discussion of the elegant *nagaraja* image of the porch ceiling (cf. Fig. 74) confuses the *naga*'s fringe of secondary snake-heads with another being, and calls the two visible *nagini* a couple, when they are the two survivors of what was originally a quartet. Still, it offers a long awaited view of the quite impressive panel referred to by Burgess.[58]

Joseph Campbell's mid-fifties edition of Heinrich Zimmer's 1941 essay on the transformations of symbols in Indian art brings up the Durga temple in a chapter titled 'Indian Ideals of Feminine Beauty'. It focuses on figurative imagery of the goddess in sculpture, beginning at Bharhut and continuing on to the vision of later Brahmanical culture. The amount of space given to architectural description (in this figurative context) is explained by Zimmer's apparent misunderstanding of the temple's title, as indicating it to be a goddess temple. (Significant portions of Zimmer's text will be found in Appendix XI.) It is notable in that it is the earliest published discussion to treat it as a Brahmanical temple, created to function in Brahmanical worship. The photographs here add a third of the hall niches' *avaranadevata*, the Mahisasuramardini (Fig. 22) and another pillar couple (cf. Fig. 59).

Zimmer explained the symbolic nature of the temple as a stone worship structure representing the form of the deity's heavenly palace and the figurative imagery as the population of that abode. Though the illustrations chosen for the volume included the magnificent Durga Mahisasuramardini of the veranda wall, it was not discussed in the text. This lack was repaired by Jitendra Nath Banerjea a year later in the second, expanded edition of his seminal *Development of Hindu Iconography*, significant portions of which are to be found in Appendix XII. Banerjea moved the study of the temple into serious consideration of its iconography with discussion of the Durga plus the Shiva, published by Rambach and de Golish. Following a discussion of the Kailasa, Ellora's relief of the goddess attacking the demon Mahisa, in the form of 'a full-scale man of her stature with buffalo horns',[59] Banerjea goes on to discuss previous forms of the demon used in depicting this confrontation. In the description of the goddess, Banerjea relates the temple's sculptural style to its assumed architectural date. His description of Shiva illustrates the trend, coming into prominence at mid-century, of reference to ancient ritual lore.

The two figures on fallen ceiling panels came into constant illustration in the fifties, when they were transferred from Aihole to the galleries of the National Museum in New Delhi. The first in this renewed consideration was C. Sivaramamurti, who as head of the museum travelled to the site to select them. Since he discussed them as sculpture, Sivaramamurti referred little to the temple or its literary *alter ego*.[60] His interest was in interpreting the images for the significance they illustrate. Thus his consideration extends to another set of records, those of the traditional Sanskrit literature, which come from roughly the same period in Indian culture and offer a wealth of appropriate Sanskrit terminology with which to explain the activity of these figures and define their accoutrements. Though first-hand analysis of the temple is not an explicit element of the note, it is apparent that the author has been to the temple, since no previous writer had noticed the *Ramayana* panels of the porch interior (cf. Fig. 68). In his explanation Sivaramamurti compared the imagery of the *vidyadharas* to similar expressions of the same seminal, Indian vision seen in the *Ramayana*.

In 1961 when he discusses the temple again, in his *Indian Sculpture*, his list of deities omits Burgess' oft repeated and mistaken reference to an Ardhanari among the *avaranadevata*. A decade and a half later, however, in his sumptuous *Art of India*, the benefit of his first-hand familiarity is lost, and we get a mechanical gloss based on photos and a return to Cousens, which includes Burgess' mistaken list of deities—demonstration enough of how even fine scholars may be trapped by the literature when they apply its conclusions, rather than search its store of evidence critically. By the time this was written photographs showing all the deities of *mandapa* wall had been published.[61]

The goal of Nelson I. Wu's impressionistic comparison of Chinese and Indian architecture, subtitled *The City of Man, the Mountain of God, and the Realm of the Immortals*, of 1963, is not a record of the Durga temple *vis-à-vis* Indian art, but a more speculative 'search for the essential meaning behind the true achievements of the . . . two glorious traditions', of Indian and Chinese architecture. His is consequently a more personal and poetic approach than a specialist's. However, his view still reflects the written record of conventional histories, and his own photographs,[62] used to illustrate his text, show how much his view of the monument has been influenced by his predecessors.

Renewed Analysis

THE DECADE FOLLOWING 1947 saw India's colleges, archaeological surveys, museums and publishing houses taken into Indian hands. As a result there was a shift among Indian specialists, and some others, toward a reappraisal of the record, away from the literature and back towards analysing the monuments. Across India, known monuments were re-examined and the set of monuments under consideration was vastly expanded. At the same time there began a critical examination of past approaches and a search for more indigenously oriented explanations. Interpretations of the Chalukya monuments reveal this trend in their developed scope, refinement and understanding. The first signs of this shift in the literary image of the Durga temple took the form of a more critical review of the published record, and the application of traditional Indian, Agamic, approaches to descriptions of the temple's structure and imagery.

The mid-century saw textual scholars of history and religion reconsidering the Vikramaditya inscription on the gateway. In alternative readings, Fleet's understanding about gifts made to a priest named Aditya was reconstrued as gifts to the god Aditya. This may not be the case with H. D. Bhattacharyya, who mentions the temple in his discussion of solar cults in the fifth volume of the *History and Culture of the Indian People*.[63] But when K. A. Nilakanta Sastri offered this conclusion in his carefully constructed history of the early Chalukyas there is no question as to the reasoning or source involved. Nilakanta Sastri was rereading and retranslating the temple's inscription itself. The significant change is found in his recognition of the line 'for the benefit of the shrine of Āditya', as signifying not a priest but the deity of the temple. The spirit of the new translation is independent and critical, going back to the original inscription and reinterpreting its evidence. It is quite a different performance to his art historical treatment of the temple in his earlier *History of South India*, which—he testifies in his preface—is based upon the 'excellent guidance furnished by Percy Brown's monumental survey'.

We can pick up the art historical trend toward an increasingly critical grasp of the structure with K. V. Soundara Rajan's article on temple layouts. Soundara Rajan combines a variation on the Buddhist derivation thesis with a reconsideration of the evidence. After following Cousens and others in deriving the plan of the Lad Khan temple from the Buddhist *vihara* (dormitory), he goes on to derive the plan of the Durga temple from the *caitya* hall in an embroidered rendition of the Percy Brown synopsis, to which he has added an interesting twist of his own. After accepting Cousens' extreme assertion of the *caitya* hall imitation thesis, Soundara Rajan has gone on to suppose that an apsidal vault, of the sort found at Ter, Cejerla and Mahabalipuram, once actually stood above the roof of the Durga temple.[64] His basis for this was a look at Biggs' photographs, published by Meadows Taylor (Figs 1–4).[65] It is the remains of such an elephant-backed tower that Soundara Rajan sees surviving in the rubble of the early pictures. The Nagara *sikhara* visible today he takes to be a replacement, placed there after Biggs's photographs. But, as both photographs and the literature attest, he was mistaken on several counts. Observation of the early photographs show that the *sikhara* visible in Cousens' publication of 1911 (Fig. 11) can be seen within the stone piling of Burgess' picture of 1874 (Fig. 5) and peaking through even the thicker encrustation of rubble found in Meadows Taylor's time (Figs 2 and 3).[66] What we see today was there when the first photographs were taken. (Significant portions of Soundara Rajan's text will be found in Appendix XIII.)

His assertion that the temple's form was a 'Buddhist formula' and so for Brahmanical worshippers 'a blind alley', and 'totally unsuitable to their aspirations and requirements', had already been contradicted by testimony found by Kramrisch and others in the texts. The very term Soundara Rajan uses for the apsidal vault he supposed *gajapṛishṭha*, or elephant-backed, is drawn from those Brahmanical texts.

In an interesting footnote Soundara Rajan mentions the development of apsidal shrines. In fact, there were by this time a dozen apsidal Brahmanical temples recorded in the literature, dating from the tenth century and after, and it was growing apparent that this was a standard, if infrequent, Brahmanical form. As K. R. Srinivasan, another officer of the Archaeological Survey, said the same year while speaking of the Brahmanical remains excavated at Nagarjunakonda, 'The main shrines are apsidal, except in one or two cases where they are square, there being no difference between them and the contemporary apsidal Buddhist *chaityas* attached to the larger *stupas* or monasteries at Nagarjunakonda and other places in the Andhra area, thus indicating that the forms of temples were common to all the creeds.'[67]

Though we may reject Soundara Rajan's contention that the tower visible in Meadows Taylor's time is different from the one in place today, we cannot miss the evidence here of the two characteristics shared with Nilakanta Sastri and lacking in the secondary surveys. There is a renewed interest in the monument's structure, and a more scientifically critical attitude toward the literature. This is the first time since Coomaraswamy's tentative proposal that the tower may 'just possibly' have been added that anyone attempted to offer evidence to support that contention, based on observation of the temple's form.

The idea that the Durga temple's tower was tampered with by restorers was repeated and developed a year later, in an official report by Srinivasan, the Superintendent of the Temple Survey for southern India. However, given the slowness of publication and the likelihood of sharing information within the Archaeological Survey, it is impossible to know whether it was Soundara Rajan or Srinivasan who came up with the restoration theory. It is clear, however, that the theory had begun to circulate that the supposedly incompatible northern-style tower's existence at its current location could be traced to conservators shifting it from another temple.

The idea was not preposterous. The same review of *Architecture in Dharwar and Mysore* that produced the faulty reading of the rubble-obscured superstructure, could easily have noted that the *amalaka* shown on top of the 'Bengalee' temple (the Kasivisvanatha) in Fergusson's engraved view of the site (Fig. 35) did not exist in the photographs of the temple (Fig. 36). The *amalaka* in the engraving was, in fact, transferred via the engraver's hand from the nearby Galaganatha (Fig. 103). Site conservators at Aihole could have done in stone what Fergusson seemed to have arranged in ink. However, it seems clear from all evidence that they did not.

Two years later M. Rama Rao showed the potential for a revolutionary reappraisal of the temple in a consideration remarkable not only for its interest in direct analysis of the structure, but also for its ideological reconceptualization of the discussion. Rama Rao describes the temple's forms in detail according to the traditional Agamic terminology found in the Indian priests' and architects' texts devoted to temple construction, rather than the English, church-Latin or Greek favoured previously. Since this was likely to be closer to the terminology of its creators, the potential significance of this development for achieving a more precise and deeper understanding of temple architecture was immense. His discussion is constructed around a list of temple types, according to the numbers and placement of architectural spaces, to which he has been led by his consideration of ancient Brahmanical lore as well as the contemporary art history. He describes the temple by listing the elements he can identify in the following manner. 'It has five distinct parts—an entrance porch, an apsidal outer *pradakṣiṇa*, a porch, and a closed *pradakṣiṇa* beyond containing the *garbha gṛha* with a porch before it. The temple stands on a high *adhistāna* containing *upana*, moulded *paṭṭa*, fluted *tripaṭṭa*, narrow *gaḷa*, *kapōta* adorned with gables containing heads inside and a row of *yāḷis* above . . .' And so on.[68]

Rama Rao's analysis is notable for its independence as well as its eccentricity. However difficult we may find this detailed transcription of the temple into elements designated by traditional Sanskrit terminology, it is based on important textual lore, long ignored. Awareness of the traditional *Agama* and *Sastra* literature was brought to the antiquarians by Ram Raz in the early nineteenth century.[69] But little interest was shown in it by art historians, and after Rajendra Lal Mitra's controversy with Fergusson few efforts in that direction were made.[70] It was not until the twentieth century that the works of Coomaraswamy, P. K. Acharya, N. V. Mallaya, Stella Kramrisch and others offered art historians a traditional Indian terminology, more appropriate to the conceptualizations of the original builders.[71]

Later writers may dispute some of his specific identifications or terms,[72] but Rama Rao has overcome the art historical literature's fixation on itself and returned to primary sources for understanding the temple: the structure itself and its creators' language. In doing so he also maintained a strong focus on what was there, as opposed to what was not, and noticed details that others had not previously reported. He focuses on elements with which the builders themselves were concerned, such as the particular mouldings and pillar details, for which they had technical designations. He adds to the literature notice of the leonine-*yali* leaping across the pillar-corbels, the presence of Narasimha slaying Hiranyakasipu and Ardhanari on the pillars of the porch, the elaborate, inhabited architecture of the temple's inner architraves, and the fact that paint had been used in at least some of the decorations. These had not been mentioned previously.

And finally, almost a century after the temple's emergence in the literature, we are given the identities of the major images on the hall wall in their correct number and order—though one of these is misidentified and another inappropriately included.[73] It is notable that in the midst of this welter of terms and painfully unillustrated descriptions there is no reference to supposed Buddhist sources.

In the same article Rama Rao also refers to a second Chalukya apsidal temple, he first published and illustrated three years earlier (Fig. 39).[74] The temple is a single apsidal cell, topped by an apsidal vault of the sort found at Ter, Cejerla and wrongly-supposed by Fergusson and Soundara Rajan to have once stood over the Durga temple. His discussion is interesting partly as a complement to what we know about the Durga temple, and partly because his categorization makes it clear that he does not follow the view proposed by Soundara Rajan, that such structures are inappropriate for Brahmanical worship.

K. R. Srinivasan's full interpretation of the temple the following year, though more refined and accessible than Rama Rao's, is marked by precisely the same characteristics of first-hand observation and intrinsically traditional viewpoint. It was an official Archaeological Survey of India presentation, on the occasion of the Twenty-sixth International Congress of Orientalists, held in New Delhi, and included in a survey of the southern style of India's 'structural' architecture. Like Rama Rao's note, Srinivasan's is without the benefit of illustrations, but unlike it there is recognition of the literature of the field that has come before. He begins by making the significant point, unrecognized before him, that the Durga temple is, despite its striking northern style tower, largely a work of the southern style. (Significant portions of Srinivasan's text will be found in Appendix XIV.)

Srinivasan mentions five new issues: the southern style of the architecture as a whole, contrasted with the northern style of the tower; the (parallel) mixture of both styles in the niche-fronts of the veranda; the existence of the *upapitha*, second (or sub-) basement; the morphologically 'late' form of the corbels and the presence of a *pranala* (run-off from the sanctum). His unusual eighth-century date is supported concretely with this information, in contrast to the arbitrary sixth-century date that has ebbed and flowed in the wake of Cousens' evolutionary logic. He softens with a 'perhaps' his earlier contention that there was once an elephant-backed tower, fit to the plan of the sanctum, and then goes on to elaborate it with fuller detail.

When he later expanded this treatment of the southern style architecture to book length, Srinivasan offered greater refinement, specificity and detail, but only two relatively minor changes. The first of these changes was a further backing-off from the transferred-tower thesis, to a more scientifically tentative 'odd clumsily-fitted northern-type square *śikhara* which would be aberrant if of original design or incongruous and inapt if a later addition.' The second was a growing confidence in the eighth-century date, which he refined to the first quarter of the eighth century. He remained unsure of the dedication.[75]

Srinivasan's analysis has been taken by many as authoritative, though it has not put an end to controversy about the date or much else. In the same volume as Srinivasan's first article appeared a complementary chapter on temples of the northern style that also included the Durga temple. Krishna Deva's note is similar to Srinivasan's in its empirical spirit, though different in dating the temple as 'sixth to seventh century'.[76] This one too formed the basis for a somewhat longer treatment of its topic. There, after characterizing the tower as an 'early experimental variety, representing a prototype of the characteristic north Indian tower' and 'lately placed' upon the structure, the tower is explained as 'a heavy *shikhara* . . . of 3 rathas and more than 2 storeys indicated by *bhumi-amalakas*'.[77]

The chronological order of the literature does not exactly follow the order in which understandings were formed or even that in which they were written. Publication is irregular and on occasion one writer will know of another's work and be able to respond to it before it reaches print. The inscriptions published in the fifteenth volume of the Archaeological Survey's *South Indian Inscriptions* were collected in the years 1928 and 1929 in what the British called the Bombay-Karnatak (B.K.).[78] A variety of individuals within the Survey may have been aware of them after that time; a few epigraphists may have been aware of them from observation at the site, but they were not published until 1964. The inscriptions from the Durga temple recorded there were given in Old-Kannada characters, but translations could have been acquired by scholars who were interested. One of these repeated the name of Komarasinga, the temple's *yajamana* (patron), previously noted in the gateway inscription, on the body of the temple. The other five were names of artisans who worked on the structure. Four of these began with the honorific 'Sri' thereby suggesting that the 'Sri Jinalaya(n)' inscription noticed by Fleet was not a description of the temple as he had surmised, but the name of one of its builders.[79]

The next notice of the Durga temple comes in relation to a major piece of new evidence: the first recognition by art historians of yet another apsidal early Chalukya temple. This time it is one nearby and closely related. The article, by R. S. Gupte, describes a small stone temple, found only a day's walk west of Aihole, at Chikka Mahakuta (cf. Fig. 40).[80] Its architecture, he says in a close paraphrasing of Percy Brown on the Durga temple, 'adapted the Buddhist caitya hall to the needs of the Brahmanical creed'. He concludes that it is a temple of the northern style, from between 475 and 525, which he, unaccountably, considers part of the early Chalukya era, which others consider began in 542/3.

Gupte considers the temple to originally have been Vaishnava, but converted in early Chalukya times into Shaiva, on the basis of the Garuda of its doorway and the linga on its altar. He reads the remains of its missing tower as square and so 'Indo-Aryan', or northern. His photographs show northern style *udgama* niche crowns. His dating of it, explained by a history of the apsidal type, is, to say the least, confusing and filled with logic and assumptions that range from the controversial to the absurd. What is important, for those interested in the Durga temple, is that the academic world now had an early Chalukya temple with an apsidal layout and a northern style *sikhara*, at a nearby site. The crucial combination of features was no longer unique.

Gupte followed this article with *The Art and Architecture of Aihole*, the most ambitious study yet attempted of the site of Aihole, a photographically rich volume covering more temples than Cousens did, and discussing them in greater detail, if not with greater understanding. The main theme of the volume was a simplistic evolutionary scheme, derived from Cousens and Coomaraswamy, in which every temple that happened to catch his attention at the site, is lined up in single file, ending at the Meguti of 634/5, according to an evolution from flat to towered roofs and from rear-walled to isolated sanctums. There is a good deal of ambiguity about the date of many of these temples, but no question that Gupte counted many tenth-century temples, such as the north-eastern temple in the Konti-gudi group and the Ambiger-gudi, on his early Chalukya list. The Durga temple appears late in this scheme, although it is dated, as was then usual, to the mid-sixth century. Though highly limited in its understanding of both the temple and the site, Gupte's discussion was important for its empirical observations.

His discussion of the temple comes in two sections, first the architecture and then the figurative imagery. His method is to describe the object in great detail, citing Sanskritic terms where he can, while fitting it into his simplistic interpretation of the site's development. His description of the temple's architecture is full, detailed and to some extent original because it is based on direct observation. The quality of the observation is uneven, however, and the conclusions are limited to the long established, conventional understanding to which he adheres. Once again the temple is seen as an adaptation of a Buddhist design, though Gupte adds consideration of the intermediary step of the Chikka Mahakuta temple, which he believes preceded it.

Where Gupte refers to the apsidal plan as an 'imitation of Buddhist *chaitya* architecture' he is unlike most Indian writers from the mid-fifties on, who had rejected this theme to consider the building as a Brahmanical structure. He does not base his discussion of the temple on that analogy, however; he only refers to it in passing. The new elements he notices in the architectural design are details in the *mandapa* doorway decoration. He points out the unusual presence of multiple *naga*s running from Garuda, the presence of *purnakalasa* (brimming pots), and the river-goddesses, Ganga and Jamuna, in the miniature architectural frame supporting miniature towers. He mistakenly cites a Garuda on the sanctum doorway.[81]

As he continues, Gupte becomes the first to discuss and illustrate the temple's sculpture, including all its large *avaranadevata* images, in almost full range and detail. The sixteen pillars of the temple's eastern end have large images on either one or two sides. Most of these are *mithuna* (couples), but some are particular deities or scenes. He lists mos of these and illustrates many, describing their attributes, gestures and dress.[82]

Although much of the description in this section is an enumeration of details, taken with the illustrations it adds a great deal to available knowledge of the tem presence of the large pillar figures had been illustrated since Biggs' first photo this is the first time they are considered seriously as sculpture or illustrated ef *mithuna* (couples) and deities include some of the most magnificent sculpture of the early Chalukya era. Only three had been illustrated before this time: one drawn on Burgess' plan plate, one in Zimmer and the one (mistakenly attributed to the Virupaksa at Pattadakal) by Goetz. Gupte describes thirty-two and illustrates fourteen. The sculpture of the Durga temple now begins to come into its own, recognized as the splendid art that it is.

From pillars he moves to ceilings and the major deities of the niches of the *mandapa* wall, visible from the open porch. Gupte is the first to give a full discussion of these figures, including the Harihara mistaken as Ardhanari by Burgess, and Vishnu by Rama Rao. With the exception of the last two, which he reverses, he presents them in sequence, moving from the south-east clockwise around the temple, the usual direction of ritual circumambulation. What this reveals about the difficulty of fieldwork and the confusion that still existed after a century is worth noting.

Gupte's survey of the temple's figurative decoration is, like his survey of the architectural imagery, a listing of its elements from the point of view of empirical perception and Agamic terminology, to which he has added a highly positive aesthetic appreciation. He finds the sculpture here the peak of early Chalukya figurative art. It is indeed the high point of the site, and indeed one of the great treasures of Indian art. A particularly interesting, but unexplained, assertion is the idea that one of the sculptures, the previously misidentified Harihara, is 'reminiscent' of the later, Rastrakuta period.[83]

The scope of this analysis is important. With Gupte's work the literature has now attained a relatively full description and illustration of the temple's significant imagery. It is a century and a year since Fergusson's original publication of Biggs' photographs. The structure has finally been recognized as a major work of art in its own right.

The Second Century

R. S. GUPTE'S *Art and Architecture of Aihole* concluded a century of conservation, research and exposition that brought a rather complete image of the Durga temple into the discourse of Indian art history. There was now a commercial market for superficial picture books with an abundance of repetitive glosses.[84] On the other hand, scholars were also testing the temple's structure for new and interesting elements.

In the second half of the twentieth century, a combination of the growing highway and bus systems along with the arrival of 35 mm photography and high speed films significantly expanded the accessibility of India's monuments while opening up their inner forms to recording and consideration. A growing number of students were able to acquire an increasingly intimate and thorough knowledge of a vastly enlarged number of temples. With increased time at the sites, easier communication between them and more flexible photography to record observations, the study of temple art moved from middle distance views of their outlines and towers up onto their platforms to analyse concrete elements of their figurative imagery and decorative details, formerly out of sight. As they were able to take these views away with them in the form of photographs, specific details from one site could be studied and compared with details from others in a way not possible earlier. The effect was revolutionary. What had been a broad study of temple exteriors, now became close up consideration of entire structures, from their contexts to their finest details.

Among the set of investigators to come on the scene in the second century of the Durga temple's interpretation were specialists in comparative analysis of figurative imagery. They considered the temple's forms from the point of Indian imagery as a whole. Aschwin Lippe, the first of these men, looked at the Durga temple in a series of articles on early Chalukya sculpture, published in the late sixties and early seventies. In the German tradition typified by Goetz, Lippe developed the supposition that Chalukya sculpture could be explained by tracing its inspiration to far-away sources. In concert with some suggestions by K. V. Soundara Rajan, Lippe was particularly interested in the idea that a good deal of Chalu art was based on the art of their dynastic rivals, the Tamil-speaking Pallavas to the either inspired in the wake of the Chalukya invasions of the Pallava region or cr Tamil artists. Lippe's approach, to reveal what he saw as stylistic 'diffusions' mental 'alterations', was the comparative analysis of isolated stylistic and motifs. He compared details of large numbers of Chalukya sculptures with each other and then with other images throughout India.

In an article on the ceiling panels, door-guardians and doorways Lippe compared the sculpture of the Durga temple with that of other early Chalukya temples.[85] He pointed out the similarity between the Garuda of the Durga temple and that of Aihole's temple 7. In another reference he goes beyond the Chalukya region to compare the cross-legged pose of several Chalukya door-guardian figures, including one of the Durga temple's beautiful pillar figures (Fig. 66), with a variety of images, concluding that the *dvarapala* wears a 'flower-pot' crown like the doorkeeper of Badami Cave I, which convinces him that they are all Pallava imports from the south.

Lippe's fullest and most comprehensive treatment of the temple and of the alteration theme is offered in an article concerned with what he sees as 'additions and replacements' to the sculpture of early Chalukya temples. There he gives a chronology of early Chalukya art designed around a hypothetical Pallava period in Chalukya art, during which Tamil artists are supposed to have recut a series of Chalukya monuments and significantly 'influenced' Chalukya artists, following the Pallava army's crushing victory at Badami in 642.

Like Gupte, Lippe's method involved a close description of individual images, but where Gupte's system involved attaching Sanskritic terms to whatever he described, Lippe's way was to offer a more western art historical analysis, focused on the progressive development of formal style through a comparison of images. He pays particular attention to the technical handling of particular motifs, and their presence or absence. Typical of this are his references to the crossed legs of the door-guardian or the 'spoke-haloes' of the Durga and the Vishnu contrasted with the 'lotus-petal' halo of the Siva. On occasion the number and variety of these comparisons can be bewildering.

Noteworthy is his emphasis on the closeness of the Durga temple's sculpture to that of the Malegitti of Badami, as for instance in the likeness of the Durga temple's Harihara (Fig. 73) and the Malegitti's Vishnu (Fig. 42). Notable also is his emphasis on the chronological development of the elements he follows, and their contribution to his solution of the still controversial issue of the temple's date. A particular contribution to this discussion is the citing of the presence of the leaping *yali* beneath the temple's pillar brackets (Fig. 76) as a common feature of the temples of Vikramaditya II's time at
...agrees with Srinivasan. His belief that the Harihara is one
...ver, stands in distinct contrast to Gupte's opinion that it
... one that has been added later.[86]

... his contention that not only the tower but a number of
...vere later additions to the temple's original form. In
...asimha, and possibly the Vishnu, the Siva and the Durga,
...its' for images done in what he sees as the original style,
...ara. His comparison of the Narasimha here (Fig. 70) with
...s 32 and 43) may be instructive. 'The Kevala-Narasimha
...een inspired by the Pallava addition to Badami Cave III.'

When examined, however, the two images are not so peculiarly similar as to prove either was specifically copied from the other. But beyond this, the degree of generalized naturalism they do share distinguishes both from the significantly more stylized lion face characteristic of Pallava art, to which he wants to trace them (e.g., Fig. 44).[87]

More important, however, is the act of bringing the temple's gateway into focus. After others had ignored this major element of the temple's design for over a century, referring to it only as 'a rubbish shoot' or the bearer of the Vikramaditya inscription, Lippe points out the similarity of the gateway's doorframe to that of the temple, and the presence of an image of Surya (or Aditya, the Sun) above it. The dedication of the temple to Aditya finally has figurative confirmation.

In his supplementary thoughts on 'additions and replacements' Lippe extends his former consideration to account for the Chikka Mahakuta apsidal temple and the Jambunatha temple at Badami, of which he has apparently only now become aware.[88] In the earlier article Lippe followed the usual convention. He saw an 'apsidal plan derived from the Buddhist *chaitya* hall. On top of the flat roof, over the sanctuary, sits what remains of "northern" type *sikhara*. Structurally and esthetically, the superstructure has no relation to the temple and certainly is a later addition. . . .' Now he says, 'We stand by the remarks concerning the Durga temple superstructure. However, the small apsidal Chikka-Mahakuta (near Mahakut) has remains of a superstructure which does not seem to be apsidal either (cf. Fig. 40).'[89]

The last of Lippe's articles is devoted to the large iconic sculpture. Here he goes over the Varaha and Harihara comparisons again and adds to his consideration of the Mahisasuramardini and the Ardhanari of the porch. He continues to emphasize the late position of the Durga temple's sculpture in the Chalukya tradition and the idea that elements are derived from a variety of distant sources.

Lippe finds some interesting likenesses among various traditions but does not know how to explain them, except by means of a crude influence theory which traces everything to somewhere else. 'On both the Aihole cave and Durga temple reliefs we note the presence, as a spectator, of Durga's lion, who at Mamallapuram enters the fight, carrying the goddess to victory . . . We may conclude that the lion in this context is a southern element that migrated with the Chalukyas.'[90] Though the early Chalukyas shared some types of Mahisasuramardini imagery with the Pallavas, the type found on the Durga temple was a distinctly northern variety, *not* found south of the Chalukya region. And so, it cannot be considered a 'Pallava influence' as he suggests. There is certainly no element here that can be traced to Mahabalipuram or that can meaningfully be traced to anything that might be called a 'Mamallapuram formula' as Lippe suggests.[91] Lippe's descriptions take us close
to the images in the examination of particular forms of drapery or techniques of modelli
but because his discussion is impressionistic rather than systematic we are directed
existence of visual similarities without exactly understanding their relationships.

In 1972 James Harle analysed early Chalukya sculpture against the same b
of traditions considered by Lippe. He too found much of the sculptural style i
in contrast to Lippe, he traced the art to the north rather than the south. Ha
to divide early Chalukya sculpture into two distinct style traditions: a high

north Indian style of Gupta and post-Gupta (Gurjara Pratihara) elements, and a local, indigenous, 'crude' or even 'brutish' style. He sees both these traditions on the Durga temple. Most of the temple's sculpture he finds crude, but the niche images and a few pillar *mithuna* fit his imported style in its later stage. Again the discussion is widely and eclectically comparative. Among the images in the veranda's niches Harle sees the style he calls 'imported' in the Vishnu (Fig. 71) which, he says, 'resembles to a marked degree' the Vishnu of the Malegitti temple at Badami (Fig. 42). 'It is inconceivable', he says, 'that this change could have taken place by AD 700.'[92]

He sees both imported and local styles in the *mithuna* pillar figures. The more solid, round-bodied figures, 'mannered poses and elaborate crowns and head dresses' he calls post-Gupta (Fig. 65). He sees the 'simpler' style in the *asvamukhi* (Fig. 23). He relates both styles to certain figures on the porch of the Lad Khan, and feels the pieces in the simpler style could be by the same hand on both the Lad Khan and the Durga temple (Figs 23 and 45). Harle never explains how his supposed foreign style reached northern Karnataka. One of the more interesting conventions of Indian art history through most of the twentieth century is that almost any regional tradition can be called upon to explain work in another by the ubiquitous *deus ex machina* of 'influence'.

Harle's decision not to insist on the usual chronological interpretation of Chalukya architecture allows him to arrive at the rather interesting conclusion that the Durga temple and the Lad Khan are nearly contemporary. What is more, he agrees with Lippe, the other specialist in sculptural style, that the Durga temple's figurative imagery is eighth century. So both agree with the general date that K. R. Srinivasan had arrived at for the architecture.

When K. V. Soundara Rajan included a description of the Durga temple in his *Indian Temple Styles*, he confused first-hand observation with recent book-lore. His account reinforced the importance of the gateway to understanding the temple and pointed out for the first time the fact that the temple's circular altar is prepared to take an image with a rectangular base. The circular shape of the altar was first noted in Cousens' plan of 1911 (Fig. 12). The rectangular socket is visible on that diagram, but until now no one had drawn attention to it. Soundara Rajan takes the temple to be early seventh century, Vaishnava. And ... still believes that it carried a *gajaprstha* tower, or none at all, before the arrival of the ... He places the Chikka Mahakuta temple after it, in contrast to Gupte, ... dhism. Nor does he make any mention of his earlier ... ed to the Vesera style. His handling of the inscriptional ... efers to the Bombay-Karnatak collection but mentions ... re. Not only does he fail to mention the gateway ins... the temple's founder, but he specifically denies there

... *Calukyan Temples* is the most extensive and thorough ... t of Karnataka, and the first thorough re-evaluation of ... detailed descriptions along with carefully measured ... Chalukya structures at Badami, Mahakuta, Pattadakal ... an, plus an elevation and a section of the Durga temple.

In his text Michell outlines what has previously been published and then offers his own empirical analysis, from an architect's point of view, but no new judgements as to dedication or date. He mentions the Buddhist-origin hypothesis only in a footnote, and neither derives the temple from it nor arranges his analysis around it. (Significant portions of Michell's text will be found in Appendix XV.)

In his discussion Michell distinguishes between the 'inner temple' and the wider structure supported by the plinth. More important, he discusses the added-tower hypothesis in terms of its material attributes. Unlike previous authors, who had little more than distant photographs and theoretical generalities to offer, Michell's analysis is based upon careful empirical study. His drawings (Fig. 25) are based upon direct measurement of the structure. He climbed up to see what was there, and his conclusion is that the tower *is* 'supported on the *garbhagrha* walls'. Though it is an 'awkward' fit into the ceiling slabs, which required a 'cutting back of the slabs roofing the *mandapa*', which 'suggest[s] that the superstructure may be a later addition.' Still, 'if this is so, then it must have been added within the Early Western Calukyan period.' Be that as it may, he goes on to specify those elements of its form that show the tower to be a structure of the early Chalukya period. He sees the Cikka Mahakuta temple as of a later date.

When considered with the information on elevation and sections, Michell's discussion is extremely rich in new information. He combines Sastric terminology with a strongly empirical vision, biased toward issues of construction. He points out the difference between the elevation at the eastern (porch) end of the structure and that collateral with the *mandapa*. He describes the rich articulation of the porch balustrade. He describes the fit of the tower to the temple's body. His photographs give us our first look at the *kostha* niche architecture (Fig. 68), the elaborate miniature architecture of the interior architraves (Fig. 24), doorways, entablature and the *Ramayana* frieze of the inner porch, mentioned by Sivaramamurti. But most significantly, he gives the literature its first comprehensible appreciation of the way the architectural decoration delineates every element of the structure, inside and out, and the hierarchical nature of the whole organization, inner *above* outer—the sanctum within the hall, the hall within the colonnaded platform. He supposes that marks on the roof suggest the former existence of a parapet.[94]

Michell then proceeds to give attention to the gateway, which he illustrates in a plan, an elevation and a section. Since this is a structure larger than many early Chalukya temples, and mentioned regularly since Burgess, it is truly amazing that it took a century to enter the discussion of the temple, through Lippe's references to its doorway and Surya image. Michell is the first to consider its architecture and the first to illustrate it (Fig. 26). Though, by doing so in a separate section, he severs much of its relationship to the temple.

Michell rejects Soundara Rajan's impression that the rubble wall (standing at the site up to the mid-1970s) may have been the temple's intended *prakara* (wall).[95] He notes the *hamsa* under the lintel and the location of the inscriptions. He refers to a trefoil over the doorway which he believes to be 'almost certainly misplaced'. This is the one bearing the Surya cited by Lippe. Besides the inscriptions, he notes no important relationships between the gateway and the temple in terms of either design or placement. Of greatest significance are his measured plan, section and elevation (Fig. 26), that allow us to compare it to the temple. If separate, we can see that their structures are cognate.

Michell's new site plan for Aihole (Fig. 27) goes beyond Cousens' (Fig. 13) by including the gateway and three other structures in their vicinity. It shows the relationship of the structures roughly, while omitting the rubble wall.

As a doctoral dissertation, *Early Western Calukyan Temples* offers an extended look at the Durga temple that attempts a full consideration of its significance in relation to the full corpus of published studies and in line with current approaches to the Chalukya tradition as a whole. It is a model work of academic thoroughness and sophistication, aimed at the most advanced scholars in the field. The contrast to Michell's subsequent treatments of the temple in brief survey notes, intended for non-specialists, is interesting. The first of these came only two years later in his *Hindu Temple*, where the Durga temple appears in a section on the Chalukya's northern style temples. The description there is a brief synopsis of his earlier detailed treatment, omitting all reference to the gateway. A noticeable shift of key, however, occurs in the caption of the drawing plate, where the Buddhist derivation thesis is returned to prominence: 'Durga temple, Aihole, eighth century: the semi-circular-ended plan is rare in structural architecture, deriving from rock-cut Buddhist sanctuaries.'

A year later, in a 1978 issue of *Marg* magazine, also published as a book, the paragraph describing the temple is led by a reference to the supposed Buddhist derivation. Here the emphasis is, to some extent, on the temple's 'celebration' in the literature, where its Buddhist connection is unarguably prominent. It is also interesting that now the tower is simply accepted as original. The caption, accompanying the photograph and elevation of the temple's exterior, goes even further with the Buddhist derivation theme: 'The Buddhist apsidal plan of Ter and Cezerla and the rock-cut chaitya hall were sought to be integrated with a northern sikhara above the three layers of the roof.'[96] It would seem that the more popular the audience addressed, and the briefer the notice, the more the understanding slips backward to the temple's stereotype in survey literature and further from the sophisticated approach of more recent specialized scholarship. The Brahmanical temple is once again portrayed as an atrophied remnant of Buddhism.

The first suggestion that the Durga temple may have been dedicated to the Sun god came from Henry Cousens, who first called it 'Vaishnava' and added ambiguously 'possibly Sūrya Nārāyaṇa' (apparently a form of Vishnu as the Sun). Cousens later said it was 'quite possible' that the temple 'was dedicated to the Sun-god Surya', following which this thesis received no support for many decades. Art historians continued to refer to the temple as most likely Vaishnava. Iconographers, epigraphers and other historians eventually investigated the solar possibility, however, as noted in Bhattacharyya's reference and Nilakanta Sastri's explanation in a *re*translation of the Vikramaditya inscription on the temple's gateway. Aschwin Lippe was the first art historian to add weight to the point, in his 1970 citation of the Surya image over the gateway's entrance. Though he denied its place on the gateway was original, George Michell, who agreed, did include this little finial in his elevation (Fig. 26).

Although it had been suggested as early as Cousens that the Durga temple might have been dedicated to the Sun, it was left until 1976 for K. V. Ramesh, an epigrapher and historian of the early Chalukyas, to offer a clear reconsideration of the inscription. Going beyond Nilakanta Sastri's simple statement of an alternative translation, Ramesh bases his own interpretation on a carefully-explained rereading of the orthography found in impressions of the inscription (and later verified by study at the site). To make the change clear he refers in detail to Fleet's analysis. Fleet transcribed: 'Rēvaḍibaddar-Āṭada-Āḷekomara-Siṅgana dēgulada Āditya-bhaṭārage koṭṭudu', which he translated as 'the gift of Rēvaḍibadda . . . to the venerable Āditya of the temple of Āṭada-Āḷekomara-Siṅga', taking the builder of the temple to be 'Āḷekomara-Siṅga of the games'. But, according to Ramesh the relevant portion of the inscriptional text actually reads: 'Rēvadi baḍḍa-rāūḷa āḷe Komarasingana dēgulada Āditya-bhaṭārange koṭṭudu' which Ramesh translates as 'the gift made to the god Āditya of the temple of Komarasiṅga by Rēvaḍi who was administering the *baḍḍa-rāūḷa* tax.' His conclusion is that the gift was made to 'the god Āditya' and that the temple was built by the patron Komarasinga.[97]

Ramesh's new reading was followed up almost immediately by Srinivas Padigar in a thorough art historical and epigraphical analysis that leaves little doubt that the temple was indeed dedicated to some form of Aditya, not only at the time of Vikramaditya's inscription, but from its original construction, if that was at all earlier. (Significant portions of Padigar's text will be found in Appendix XVI.)

Padigar sums up all pending information on the temple's dedication in the literature and adds important new observations of his own. In terms of the epigraphical evidence, he supports Ramesh's improved reading of the gateway inscription with references to parallel usages in other contemporary inscriptions and additional evidence of his own. *Bhatara* in the singular, as in the Durga temple inscription, refers to deity, he explains, where in reference to kings or venerable individuals the term is rendered in plural as *bhatarar*. Then, shifting to the temple's visual imagery, he shows a greater knowledge of its iconographic programme than any previous author. The Garuda over the doorways is recognized as a device without sectarian significance in early Chalukya temple architecture. In a note elsewhere Padigar cites Cousens' *Chālukyan Architecture* and Soundara Rajan on this.[98] More to the point, several images of Aditya are found in crucial locations on the structure and around it. One of them is over the entrance to the *mandapa*, recorded, but too small to be read, in either Burgess' photograph of 1897 (Fig. 10) or Michell's of 1975, but finally recognized in print here. Another, looking in towards the sanctum from the entablature of the inner porch, was now noticed for the first time, here and in another article published in the same volume by S. Rajasekhara (cf. Fig. 75).[99] The image over the gateway (mentioned by Lippe) is cited, as are two loose images in the vicinity of the gateway, unnoticed by earlier writers. The suggestion that the pillar couple of a male struggling with a horse-bodied female (Fig. 64) represents the chastisement of Chaya (one of Aditya's wives and so a Saura subject) is original and most likely correct.

Padigar's remaining doubt, stemming from the presence of the 'Sri Jinalayan' inscription, may worry others less than it does him. He gives the main reason for discounting its significance, syntactically: it may be read as a man's name, rather than a reference to the temple. More significantly, he has noticed a fragmentary inscription on the temple itself referring to Komarasinga, who was cited as the temple's patron on the gateway.

If Padigar lays to rest one of the temple's longest standing controversies, Philip Rawson approaches another. Rawson, a prolific writer on many Asian art topics who made perfunctory references to the Durga temple in a number of popular publications during the nineteen-seventies,[100] contributes a new attitude to an old issue in one of these. In a book on Indian culture published in 1977, Rawson dates the Durga temple to the sixth century. But his comment about the sculpture being 'worked on well into the 7th' indicates the growing view, repeated in his other notices, that the figurative imagery cannot be so early. The most interesting elements of his discussion are no less contradictory. On the one hand he abandons the long-held contention that the apsidal form has a peculiar relation to Buddhist culture, maintaining quite reasonably that there is no particular need to consider the apsidal temples of Cejerla and Ter to have been originally Buddhist. On the other hand, he follows this independent judgement with a description of the Durga temple that is yet another variation on the *caitya* theme, though significantly his 'inversion' of the theme is based upon the idea of variation, not derivation.

The last treatment of interest to be published before 1980 comes from A. Sundara, who approached the temple in the course of an article once again considering the possibility of alterations to early Chalukya temples. As so many before him, Sundara considers the temple's tower to be 'added' to its originally 'flat-roofed' form.[101] A more unusual element of his analysis comes in a note where he offers the proposition, already argued against convincingly by his own student Srinivas Padigar, that the temple was dedicated to Brahma.

As with Padigar's article, it is unfortunate that readers were not able to see the visual evidence upon which the claims of Aditya and Brahma are based. But also like it, first-hand observation of the temple and the site are the basis of the analysis. Considering the weight of Padigar's argument, Sundara's contention is hard to accept without evidence such as a photograph of the supposed Brahma. The image is an ambiguous one that may be read as easily as Brahma or as Surya, or as another deity altogether (Fig. 79). Brahma temples are, in fact, quite rare; I know of none in southern India.

Summing Up

ON THE DURGA TEMPLE

SURVEYING MORE THAN a century of writing on the Durga temple we can see where the development of our analytical and theoretical techniques have brought our historical understanding of this fascinating structure. By far the greatest amount of what has been written about the temple has been unexamined repetition of conventionalized understandings that did not withstand the careful scrutiny of later students. And yet, there have always been critical students who have continued both to cull out the worst misunderstandings and to add new and useful insights to our collective vision. Though little benefit has come from uncritical writers such as Havell or Goetz, other students such as Cousens and Srinivasan, willing to measure the verbal claims against the material record, have refined the record and led us to an increasingly meaningful grasp of the temple's reality. It has in fact been true that there has never been a time when critical, creative study did not produce new understandings and a refinement of old understandings.

As the field has expressed itself in its literature, our collective vision of the Durga temple has undergone amazing fluctuations and developments. The temple's dedication has been attributed to eight different Gods, from Biggs' original Siva, to Fergusson's Buddha and Jina, Burgess' Vishnu and Cousens' Surya-Narayana, with momentary lapses into the semantic error of the goddess Durga, before arriving at what seems to be a solid determination among specialists of Aditya, although, this too has been questioned by the unlikely, further suggestion of Brahma.

The dates to which the temple has been assigned have ranged as widely. Beginning with the crude original surmise of 'earlier-than-the-tenth century', they stabilized quickly to early Chalukya possibilities, with art historians preferring the sixth to seventh century or the fifth to sixth century, and epigraphers holding out for the early eighth. The fifth to sixth century date, with an earliest point of 478 and regular estimations of *c.* 500 or 550, was a staple of the literature from the nineteen-twenties to the nineteen-sixties. Then specialists in both architecture and sculpture settled upon the early eighth-century period, assigned to its inscriptions.

As the field developed from Fergusson's racial-religious categories to more modern regional, dynastic and Agamic ones, the temple's style has been termed Buddhist, Jain,

Chalukya, early Chalukya, Dravidian, Gupta, Vesera, Mannerist, southern (Dravida), northern (Nagara) and a mixture of southern and northern. And yet for all this variety and range of assertions there has been a progressive development of the literature's grasp of the monument and a refinement of the concepts by which it has been defined. There is now rather general agreement among specialists that it is a superb example of an eighth century early Chalukya temple to the god Aditya.

After a century as a star issue in the survey literature, the puzzle of the Durga temple's tower was largely resolved. For most of its literary career the temple's tower has been dismissed as destroyed, removed, buried, restored, added, replaced or transferred from another structure nearby. When it was accepted as part of the temple it was called primitive, inappropriate, or aberrant, more often than 'northern' or 'Nagara'. The trail begun in Soundara Rajan's re-investigation of old photographs eventually led to further investigations of the temple itself, culminating in many new photographs and Michell's measured diagrams of the structure. After a half-century of ambiguity about its existence and another half-century of confident assertions that it was an afterthought or a late addition, we can at least conclude, along with Michell, that however awkwardly joined and unusual it may seem, the Durga temple's tower is definitely early Chalukya and probably original.

This conclusion, unlike the other that so long dominated discussion of the temple, rests on a concrete examination of the original stones of this and associated structures as well as a development of our theoretical understanding of Hindu temple history. The added-tower hypothesis rested on theory alone. It was drawn from Fergusson's conviction of a Buddhist origin for the apsidal plan seen in the first photographs, combined with Cunningham and Cousens' hypothesis of an evolution of the towered-temple out of caves and cave-like, flat-roofed temples. The combination of these two suppositions seemed plausible because of the unusualness of a Nagara tower on an apsidal plan, and its simplistic logic continued to carry weight for those caught in the survey literature with its eminently photogenic selection of Buddhist *caityas* and lack of apsidal Brahmanical halls. But it failed the understanding of those taking a closer look at the Durga temple and its tradition, where other apsidal Brahmanical temples were known.

The added-tower hypothesis was based on a concept of a period of towerless temples in the fifth century followed by the emergence of towered temples in the sixth. An eighth-century date removed the Durga temple from that discourse.

Thus by the time George Michell explored and measured the structure's stones in detail and came to the conclusion that the tower's fit was not only directly over the shrine, but as reasonably neat as any at the site, most of the earlier theoretical support for the old hypothesis had been removed as well. The point of Coomaraswamy's added-tower hypothesis was to explain the Durga temple as one of the oldest, most rudimentary and unusual of Brahmanical temples in South India. But the Durga temple was now recognized as a highly sophisticated structure of the eighth century, in a form that, however unique in the survey literature, fitted comfortably with the Chalukya tradition that gave it birth.

By 1980 most of the temple seems to have been discussed and illustrated. Its architecture has been described in detail in both traditional Agamic and modern English architectural terms. Its decorative and iconic figure sculpture has been illustrated extensively and with some sensitivity. Its fit with a number of structures locally and throughout India has been considered. Its initial patron, Komarasinga, is known, as is the nature of the *vadda-ravula* tax that supported its ongoing rituals.

I shall offer my own interpretation of the temple in the following essay, but it should be clear that the massive presence of this temple, its rich decoration and its fit into traditional Indian culture is well established. If some of the more popular and less critical discussions continue to resurrect discredited cliches of the past, most careful students have learned to avoid them. Caricatural and anachronistic survey glosses may still be produced calling it a primitive Hindu take-off of a Buddhist *caitya*, but the specialist literature has long passed the point of discussing the Durga temple as the pseudo-Buddhist cave it is not, and moved on to considering it as the magnificent Brahmanical temple that it is.

ON HISTORIOGRAPHY

I want to end this consideration of the career of the Durga temple in the history of Indian art with a few words on the value of historiography. The writing of history requires that we not only record evidence but that we form it into a coherent vision. No matter how objective we may endeavour to make our record, essential suppositions will remain a basis for what we see when we look and say when we write. A Hindu will see the Durga temple differently than a Jew, a stone mason differently than a historian. What brings us together is our ability to decentre ourselves and see it from more than our peculiar personal or technical viewpoints. We are self-conscious about the very fact that we as specific individuals are viewing a particular set of events and objects from historically and socially bound locations. While reading or writing history, we need to remain conscious of the fact that we are not only following evidence but also constructing explanations.

One means of achieving this self-consciousness, particularly explored here, has been the rereading of the Durga temple's histories in their chronological order. Every history study begins by a rereading of essential texts, but the approach I have taken here has been to organize this rereading into a sequential order to recapitulate its evolution. The first purpose of this order was to allow us to follow the steps by which the construction of our understanding of the temple took place. It allowed us to observe how one author benefited from another and how one sort of understanding did or did not lead to another. But it had another benefit as well. Besides allowing us to see the history of the Durga temple's uncovering and the evolution of its explanation, it has a allowed us a reflexive view, into the theories and attitudes that underlay that evolution and those explanations.

Reading the histories in sequence allowed us to see some of the structure of our own tradition's historiographic underpinning. Sequential reading allowed a revelation of the analysts' methodological concerns. It raised to prominence the themes that interested the analysts and the changes that took place among those themes. We could see the importance to nineteenth-century British historians of tracing Hindu art to supposedly Buddhist antecedents, and the later interest in tracing a technical and formal evolution of the *sikhara* temple out of flat-roofed temples and rock-cut, cave temples. Still later we saw the method of comparative analysis emerge, and then the tracing of stylistic sources to other regions, and the vein of explaining elements of the design as mistakes or changes in the original conception. We could also see the contrast between a British tendency to describe temples in terms of European paradigms and a later preference, led by Indian historians, for descriptions based upon the terminology of traditional Indian temple lore. We saw the perspective of the literature shift from analysis of the temple's most general outlines to ever more detailed analyses of individual elements, and from its architectural to its figurative imagery.

In important ways these shifts in the methodological focus of the discourse mark shifts in the interests of Indian art history and its historians. If these shifts are followed the tradition in which we read and write is revealed. Significantly, this tradition has not been a neutral discourse on the temple so much as a discourse filled with agendas. The conventional need of writers to include familiar and fascinating designs they have little opportunity or interest to investigate themselves has led to a narrative that dominates its objects. Most of what we have read has been a simple repetition of conventionalized views, not concrete analysis. And where the record has dominated the objects, ideology has tended to dominate the record. The British desire to make the structure understandable to western Christians, trained in the traditions of the classical antique, explains to an extent the use of Greco-Roman and church terminology; the Indian desire to explain it to Indians explains in part the shift to Brahmanical terminology. To see these themes and interests is to see ourselves and the socially embedded nature of our art historical practice more clearly. It also gives us some idea of which issues have proved informative and worth following up and which have lost value over the years.

Indeed the single issue that reveals itself most tenaciously and contradictorily throughout our survey has been Fergusson's original contention that the temple is a Brahmanical derivation of an essentially Buddhist form. Despite Burgess' rejection of every one of his original premises for this suggestion, Fergusson clung to his belief. And despite the subsequent rejection of every new support this primordial vision of the temple has received, later writers have consistently returned to it, to resuscitate it with new evidence or merely repeat it as if its premises had not been stripped away. Somehow the ideological desire to derive this Brahmanical structure from earlier Buddhist ones has been indestructible for many. Thus we are left with the interesting dilemma of a literature carrying on in two distinct recensions. For the specialist there is a discourse devoted to the study of a highly refined Brahmanical temple, while beside it we find the continuing popular and generalist discussions of primitive, Buddhist derivation.

The explanation of this dilemma leads us beyond our subject to the issue of Orientalism and the British imperial and subsequent western need to define India as a defective civilization, where decadence, devolution, disorder and foreign derivation are said to have dominated the arts since the early Buddhist period. I have discussed elsewhere the ways in which Orientalism has perversely influenced the image of the Durga temple in the literature.[102] Here I will only add that the Orientalist drive to depict Indian culture through even its most successful aesthetic creations as flawed has led to some of the more absurd views of the temple in the survey literature, long after they have been dismissed by those with closer contact or sympathy for Indian culture. This is the best explanation I have for the obsessive attempt to explain the temple's most unique features as somehow wrong. It is the peculiar value of a historiographic reading of the literature that it points to the implicit ideological assumptions that lie behind the explicit statements of the discourse and so encourage recognition of such issues.

Every historical study begins with a search of the literature to reveal the subject and identify the issues of historical interest. If they are seldom as thorough or detailed as the one conducted here, they will at least cover a selection of the best known previous notices. The detailed chronological reading of the literature modelled here offers a particular advantage over more eclectic readings, of providing the most acute view possible of the ideological themes that underlay the discourse. Reading all or most of what has been written, chronologically, is the best way to render explicit what is implicit in the individual pieces. It allows one to recognize the patterns of argument in which the concrete details of the various views are set and thus provides a better recognition of our predecessors' deeper interests and a better grasp of our own.

NOTES TO PART ONE

1. 'Iwullee', or 'Aihole' as it later came to be recognized, was first noted as 'Eivolle' in a letter to the Cave Temple Society from Colonel Elliot excerpted in the *Journal of the Bombay Branch of the Royal Asiatic Society*, vol. IV, 1853, p. 460.
2. Meadows Taylor and James Fergusson, *Architecture in Dharwar and Mysore*, London, 1866, preface.
3. A selection of the best-known examples, including some reproductions, will be found in Partha Mitter, *Much Maligned Monsters*, Oxford, 1977. The example at Kanheri was within picnicking distance of Bombay; those at Kondane, Karli, Bhaja, and Bedsa lay along the main trunk road connecting Bombay with Pune and were within a day's journey of Pune.
4. The most detailed adumbration of this system is found in James Fergusson, 'Ethnology from an Architectural Point of View', in his *History of the Modern Schools of Architecture*, London, 1862, pp. 493–528.
5. This system went through many incarnations, but it is stated simply in James Fergusson, *The History of Architecture in All Countries*, London, 1867, vol. II, pp. 445–53.
6. James Fergusson, *The Illustrated Handbook of Architecture*, London, 1855, Part I, Book I, 'Buddhist and Jaina Architecture', ch. VII, 'Transitional Styles and Concluding Remarks on Buddhist Architecture', pp. 65–7. Here too he introduced the temple in the section on *caitya* hall excavations, in the same note just quoted: pp. 21–2, note 4.
7. Fergusson (1855), p. 65.
8. Where in 1855 he refers to the *ratha* as the only *temple* known to him in this shape, in 1866 he refers to the Durga temple as the only *structural* building, and then in 1867, rewriting his note on the *ratha*, he distinguishes it as the only *free-standing monolithic* representation.
9. Fergusson (1855), p. 65.

10. Fergusson (1855), p. 65.
11. A version of his drawing style, tidied up by a wood-engraver, can be seen in Fig. 31.
12. See Pramod Chandra, 'The Study of Indian Temple Architecture', in Pramod Chandra, ed., *Studies in Indian Temple Architecture*, New Delhi, 1975, pp. 1–12.
13. This is the Meguti inscription ultimately attributed to 633/4 CE. See F. Kielhorn, 'Aihole Inscription of Pulikesin II; Saka Samvat 556', *Epigraphia Indica*, vol. VI (1900–1), 1–12.
14. Fergusson, his contemporaries and most writers since have used 'Hindu' as a religious designation, synonymous with 'Brahmanical' as distinguished from Buddhist, Jain, or Sikh. This was the usage before the arrival of the British, who were interested in creating as great a distinction as possible between India's Muslims and all other Indians. Thus the usage today insinuates the incorrect Orientalist contention that Indian Muslims are somehow 'less Indian' than followers of India's other faiths. I, like many others today, would prefer to see it as an appropriate synonym for Indian, and include Jain and Buddhist within that term.
15. John F. Fleet, 'Sanskrit and Old Canarese Inscriptions No. 94: Mahakutesvara temple at Mahakuta', *Indian Antiquary*, vol. X (1881): pp. 102–4.
16. Though it is not known whether he ever returned himself, he was certainly in direct contact with assistants who did.
17. There were eight published pictures at this time (Figs 1–8), and he lists two others he had made. James Burgess, *Report on the First Season's Operations in Belgām and Kaladgi Districts*, Archaeological Survey of Western India, New Imperial Series, vol. I, 1874, p. 45.
18. See Stella Kramrisch, *Manifestations of Siva*, Philadelphia, 1981, p. 40.
19. The Trivikrama temple at Ter (Thair) was first published in 1904, in the *Archaeological Survey of India, Annual Report* for 1902–3, p. 195fn., by Henry Cousens, Burgess' successor as the Surveyor of Western India. Cejerla (or Cezerla) was first recorded in April 1889, in Burgess' bimonthly *Reports of the Southern Circle*, p. 13, after Alexander Rea visited and made sketches.
20. Fergusson (1910). However, both have been subsequently reconsidered as Brahmanical.
21. Pramod Chandra (1983), p. 12fn.
22. Pramod Chandra (1975), p. 17, note 41.
23. See Alexander Cunningham, *Archaeological Survey of India*, vol. IX (1873–76), pp. 41–7; and vol. X (1874–77), pp. 60–1.
24. The structure on the Lad Khan's roof is an upper temple, not a *sikhara* tower over its sanctum. The sanctum is in the rear and has no remaining tower.
25. Several later authors have mistakenly suggested that Cousens questioned the originality of the tower, but such questioning took place only with the theoretician Coomaraswamy.
26. Henry Cousens, *Chālukyan Architecture of the Kanarese Districts*, Archaeological Survey of India, New Imperial Series, XLII, 1926, p. 5, and implied throughout the discussion of Aihole.
27. The latest reference in this work is to a 1916 publication. The accompanying photograph is more or less equivalent to the full view in the *Report* (Fig. 11), and was apparently taken at the same time from a step to the left (south) and later, after several stones had been moved.
28. E. B. Havell, *The Ancient and Mediaeval Architecture of India: A Study of Indo-Aryan Civilization*, 1915, Plate XVI.
29. Like Burgess, Havell seems to credit his photographs to the Indian Office. His source reads 'I. O. List of Photographs'.

30. Compare Fig. 5 of 1874, with Figs 10–11 of Pierre Rambach and Vitold de Golish, *The Golden Age of Indian Art, Vth–XIIIth Century*, London, 1955, p. 9, taken in 1951.
31. W. Simpson, 'Origin and Mutation in Indian and Eastern Architecture', *Transactions of the Royal Institute of British Architects*, vol. VII (N.S.) as quoted by Gurudas Sarkar, 'Notes on the History of Shikhara Temples', *Rūpam*, no. 10 (1922), p. 45.
32. Sarkar, Fig. 4.
33. Originally made for Fergusson and Taylor, 1866, as Fig. 4 on page 43.
34. Henry Cousens, 'Ancient Temples of Aihole', Archaeological Survey of India, *Annual Report*, 1907–8, (1911), p. 197; and Cousens (1926, 1), p. 39.
35. Ananda K. Coomaraswamy, *History of Indian and Indonesian Art*, New York, 1927, p. 75.
36. Ibid., p. 1.
37. Moreas, Fig. 32.
38. F. H. Graveley and T. N. Ramachandran, 'The Three Main Styles of Temple Architecture. Recognized by the Silpa Sastras', *Bulletin of the Madras Government Museum*, vol. III, no. 1 (1934), pp. 1–26.
39. Moreas, however, repeated it almost verbatim half a century later in his Presidential Address in the Proceedings of the Karnataka History Congress, 'Constituent Elements of Karnataka Culture', pp. 1–10, *Studies in Karnataka History and Culture*, vol. II (1987), pp. 8–9. There is an even simpler version of the layered style that is a local variation on the northern style in early Chāḷukya times. It can be seen in Aihole's Mallikarjuna temple [diagram 3b] and temple 10, discussed below. Later this form occurs in both southern and northern forms.
40. Stella Kramrisch, *The Hindu Temple*, Calcutta, 1946, p. 150, note 54.
41. Ibid., p. 285, note 88.
42. Ibid., p. 170, note 100.
43. S. K. Saraswati, 'Architecture', pp. 471–521 in R. C. Majumdar et al., *The Classical Age*, Bombay, 1954, p. 503.
44. Herman Goetz, 'A New Brahmanical Mural of the Sixth Century at Aihole', *Marg*, vol. V, no. 1 (1952), p. 63.
45. Herman Goetz, *India; Five Thousand Years of Indian Art*, London, 1959, p. 124.
46. Ibid., p. 128.
47. Ibid., p. 129.
48. Herman Goetz, 'Hinduism', *Encyclopaedia of World Art*, vol. VII, vol. 433, 1959.
49. Herman Goetz, 'Imperial Rome and the Genesis of Classic Indian Art', *East and West*, vol. X, no. 3–4, (Sept.–Dec. 1959), p. 177.
50. Charles Fabri, *An Introduction to Indian Architecture*, Bombay, 1963, pp. 18–19.
51. Ibid., pp. 18–19.
52. Sherman E. Lee, *A History of Far Eastern Art*, New York, 1964, p. 178.
53. This was altered significantly in the editions after 1980.
54. P. K. Agrawala, *Gupta Temple Architecture*, Varanasi, 1968, pp. 60–61.
55. Odette Monod-Bruhl, *Indian Temples*, Oxford, 1937, Pl. 22 and accompanying note, p. 3, originally *Aux Indes Sanctuaires*, Paris, 1935. Both editions include an introduction by Sylvain Levi.
56. Louis-Frederic is the pseudonym used by the prolific French author-photographer, Louis Frederic Nussbaum.

57. Burgess mentions the location as bare but probably intended for figure brackets, such as those of the cave temples in his report of 1874.
58. Ibid.
59. Jitendra Nath Banerjea, *The Development of Hindu Iconography*, second ed., Calcutta, 1956, p. 499.
60. C. Sivaramamurti, 'Some Recent Sculptural Acquisitions in the National Museum', *Lalit Kalā*, vol. I, 1956, pp. 113–15.
61. R. S. Gupte, *Art and Architecture of Aihole*, Bombay, 1967.
62. Nelson I. Wu, *Chinese and Indian Architecture*, New York, 1963, p. 2.
63. When Bhattacharyya says, 'Possibly, the Durga temple at Aihole and the Papanatha temple at Pattadakal were associated with Sun worship' (R. C. Majumdar and A. D. Pusalkar, eds., *History and Culture of the Indian People*, vol. 4, *The Age of Imperial Kanauj*, Bombay, 1955, p. 334), he is probably paraphrasing Henry Cousens. Cousens ambiguously linked the two in his *Chālukyan Architecture*, saying in similar terms: 'The [Papanatha] was, originally Vaishnava, like the Durga temple at Aihole, and possibly dedicated to Surya [the Sun]' (*Chālukyan Architecture*, p. 69).
64. It is reasonable to wonder to what degree Fergusson had his favourite view doctored when he had it rendered as a woodcut (Fig. 1), in his own attempt to show the possibility. No print from the original negative has been preserved, as far as I know.
65. The only photographs associated with Meadows Taylor are those taken by Major Biggs and published in Meadows Taylor and Fergusson, *Architecture in Dharwar and Mysore*, London, 1866.
66. Three of the stones have been moved, and I will discuss these in Part Two.
67. K. R. Srinivasan, in A. Ghosh, ed., *Indian Archaeology 1959–60—A review*, 1960, p. 84.
68. M. Rama Rao, 'Early Caḷukyan Architecture—A Review', *Journal of Indian History*, vol. XLI (1963), pp. 446–7.
69. Ram Raz, *Essay on the Architecture of the Hindus*, London, 1834.
70. The prime document in this controversy is Fergusson's last work, *Archaeology in India; with Especial Reference to the Works of Babu Rajendralala Mitra*, London, 1885. Mitra argued for an approach to Indian culture that blended western approaches with traditional Indian ones. Also, much to Fergusson's chagrin, Mitra questioned certain European assumptions such as that some of India's art was dependent on western sources. Fergusson rejected Mitra, Indians in general, and Brahmanical Hindus in particular, as racially incapable of the rational and moral understanding found among 'Aryaṇ' (European) races.
71. This Sanskrit of the ritual and artistic texts is as close as we can currently come to the language of those who built the temples. However, local specialists undoubtedly used the local language of Kannada, and because we have no Kannada texts surviving from this era, and few Sanskrit ones from the south of India, we still cannot be sure of their actual language.
72. Particularly his identification of temples with curvilinear towers as Vesera, when all others now seem to agree on Nagara.
73. Rama Rao's list runs counter clockwise: 'Visnu, Mahisaamardani, Varaha, Cakra, Visnu on Garuda, Narasimha, Vrsavahanamurti'. The first image is actually a Harihara; the Cakra is not a sculpture but a window grille.
74. M. Rama Rao, 'Caḷukyan Temples of Satyavolu', *Transactions of the Archaeological Society of South India, 1959–60*, (1960), p. 77 and Figs 7 and 8.
75. K. R. Srinivasan, *Temples of South India*, New Delhi, 1971, pp. 133–5.

76. Krishna Deva, 'Northern Temples', in A. Ghosh, ed., *Archaeological Remains, Monuments & Museums*, New Delhi, 1964, p. 162.
77. Krishna Deva, *Temples of North India*, New Delhi, 1969, p. 17.
78. P. B. Desai, ed., *Archaeological Survey of India: South Indian Inscriptions*, vol XV, (*Bombay-Karnatak Inscriptions*, vol II), Delhi, 1964, p. 342.
79. Transliterations were supplied to me by Government Epigraphist, Dr K. V. Ramesh. 464: Śrī Basavarayyan Kusuvoḷalā Bhaṭṭan; 465: Śrī Surēndrepāḍa (in *Nāgarī* script); 466: Mūṭṭasila Peṇḍirānangan; 467: Śrī Jinālaya[n?]; 468: 1 Śrī Savitaran, 2 Pirireyya puttran; 469: 1 . . . mēre ā vurge, 2 . . ., 3 . . . v. agrahāra . . ., 4 Komārasinga charnadi. The first five are names, it seems, most likely of artisans who worked on the structure; 464, 'Basavarayya of Kusuvoḷalā' refers to an artist from Pattadakal. The last mentions Komarasinga, who is otherwise mentioned in the larger gateway inscription as the patron of the temple. Number 467 is the often mentioned basement inscription.
80. R. S. Gupte, 'An Apsidal Temple at Chikka Mahākuṭa (Dist. Bijapur)', *Journal of Marathawada University*, vol. IV, no. 2 (February 1964), pp. 58–63.
81. R. S. Gupte, *The Art and Architecture of Aihole*, Bombay, 1967, pp. 38–41.
82. Ibid., pp. 92–105.
83. Ibid., p. 104.
84. A record of the less significant notices which I have consulted is in the bibliography.
85. Aschwin Lippe, 'Some Sculptural Motifs on Early Cāḷukya Temples', *Artibus Asiae*, vol. XXIX, no. 1, 1967, pp. 11–12.
86. Aschwin Lippe, 'Additions and Replacements in Early Chālukya Temples', *Archives of Asian Art*, vol. XXIII, 1969–70, pp. 14–17.
87. See Gary Tarr, 'Chronology and Development of the Chāḷukya Cave Temples', *Ars Orientalis*, VIII (1970), pp. 176–8 for a critique of the recutting concept.
88. Odile Divakaran, 'Le Temple de Jambuliṅga (daté de 699 ap. J. C.) à Bādāmi', *Arts Asiatique*, XXI (1970), pp. 15–39.
89. Aschwin Lippe, 'Supplement, Additions and Replacements in Early Chāḷukya Temples', *Archives of Asian Art*, vol. XXIV, 1970–71, p. 82.
90. Aschwin Lippe, 'Early Chāḷukya Icons', *Artibus Asiae*, vol. XXXIV, no. 4, 1972, pp. 285–6.
91. The figure at Mahabalipuram regularly referred to in relation to the lion-riding Durga of the Kailasa is the Mahisasura sainyavadha (or Mahisasuramardini) of the Mahisasuramardini mandapam. For a detailed explanation of this image and the northern connections of the previous image see Gary Michael Tartakov and Vidya Dehejia, 'Sharing, Intrusion, and Influence: The Mahiṣāsuramardinī Imagery of the Calukyas and the Pallavas', *Artibus Asiae*, XLV (1984), pp. 287–346.
92. James Harle, 'Some Remarks on Early Western Cāḷukya Sculpture', in P. Pal, ed., *Aspects of Indian Art*, Leiden, 1972, pp. 68–9.
93. K. V. Soundara Rajan, *Indian Temple Styles*, New Delhi, 1972, pp. 142–3.
94. Michell addresses various details of the temple in later chapters of his book dealing with plans, elevations and so on. There are no major conclusions left uncovered in his initial analysis.
95. Despite its vernacular rudeness, the structure was well-constructed and thoughtfully laid out. It may have been the original rubble core for a fine wall that has either lost its outer surfaces or never received an intended stone finish.
96. 'Temples of the Early Chalukyas', *Mārg*, December 1978, p. 36.
97. K. V. Ramesh, *Presidential Address to the Epigraphy Section of the 37th Session of the Indian*

History Congress, 1976, pp. 15–16; and 'On Some Inscriptions edited by Fleet', *Journal of Epigraphical Studies*, IV (1977), p. 87.

98. Henry Cousens, *Chāḷukyan Architecture*, p. 67; K. V. Soundara Rajan, 'Temples of Aihole and Pattadakal', p. 263, in M. S. Nagaraja Rao, ed., *The Chalukyas of Badami (Seminar Papers)*, Bangalore, 1978, pp. 258–71.
99. S. Rajasekhara, 'Surya Sculpture at Aihole', *Archaeological Studies*, vol. II, 1977, pp. 35–8.
100. Philip Rawson, *Indian Art*, London, 1972, pp. 54–5 (where the Vrsavahana Siva is dated from the ninth century); and pp. 59–60; *Indian Sculpture*, London, 1968, Fig. 129.
101. A. Sundara, 'Some Early Calukyan Temples: Notes on Further Traces and Additions', *Quarterly Journal of the Mythic Society*, LXX/2, p. 110.
102. Gary M. Tartakov, 'Changing Views of Orientalism', pp. 509–22, in Lokesh Chandra, ed., *Dimensions of Indian Art*, New Delhi, 1986; and 'Changing Views of India's Art History', pp. 15–36, in Catherine B. Asher and Thomas R. Metcalf, eds., *Perceptions of South Asia's Visual Past*, New Delhi, 1994.

1. 'Apse of Temple at Iwullee', Woodcut 11, *Architecture in Dharwar and Mysore*, 1866.

2. 'Iwullee. Ruined Temple. From the South-east'. Pl. LXX, *Architecture in Dharwar and Mysore*, 1866.

3. 'Iwullee. Ruined Temple. From the North-east'. Pl. LXXI, *Architecture in Dharwar and Mysore*, 1866.

4. 'Iwullee. East Front of the Temple'. Pl. LXXII, *Architecture in Dharwar and Mysore*, 1866.

5. 'Aiwalli—The Durga Temple'. Pl. LI, *Report on the First Season's Operations in Belgām and Kaladgi Districts*, Archaeological Survey of Western India, vol. I, 1874.

6. 'Aiwalli-Slabs Outside the Durga Temple'. Pl. LIV, *Report on the First Season's Operations in Belgām and Kaladgi Districts*, Archaeological Survey of Western India, vol. I, 1874.

7. 'Aiwalli-Pillar in the Durga Temple'. Pl. LIII, *Report on the First Season's Operations in Belgām and Kaladgi Districts*, Archaeological Survey of Western India, vol. I, 1874.

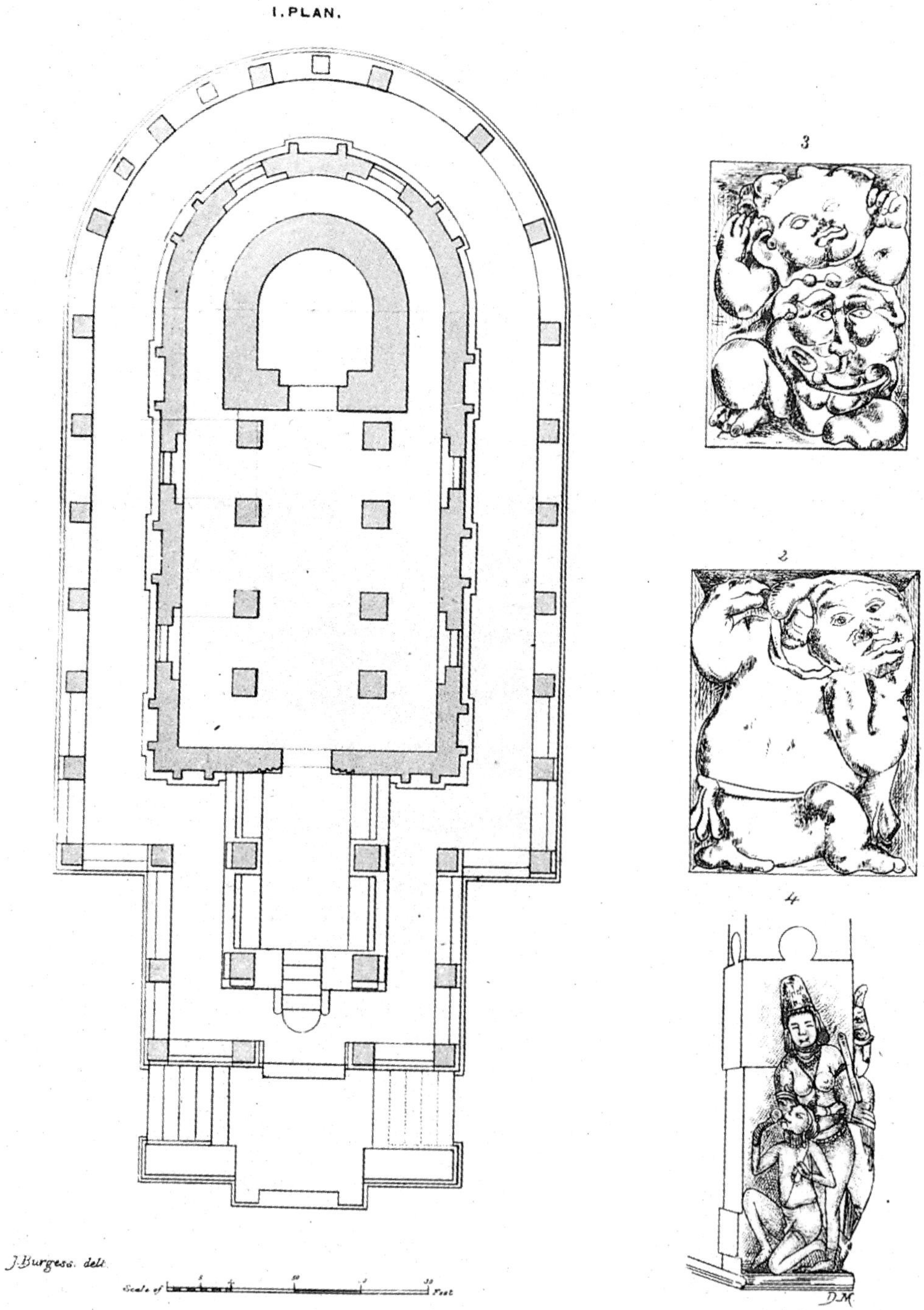

8. ‘Aiwalli—The Durga Temple’. Pl. LII, *Report on the First Season’s Operations in Belgām and Kaladgi Districts*, Archaeological Survey of Western India, vol. I, 1874.

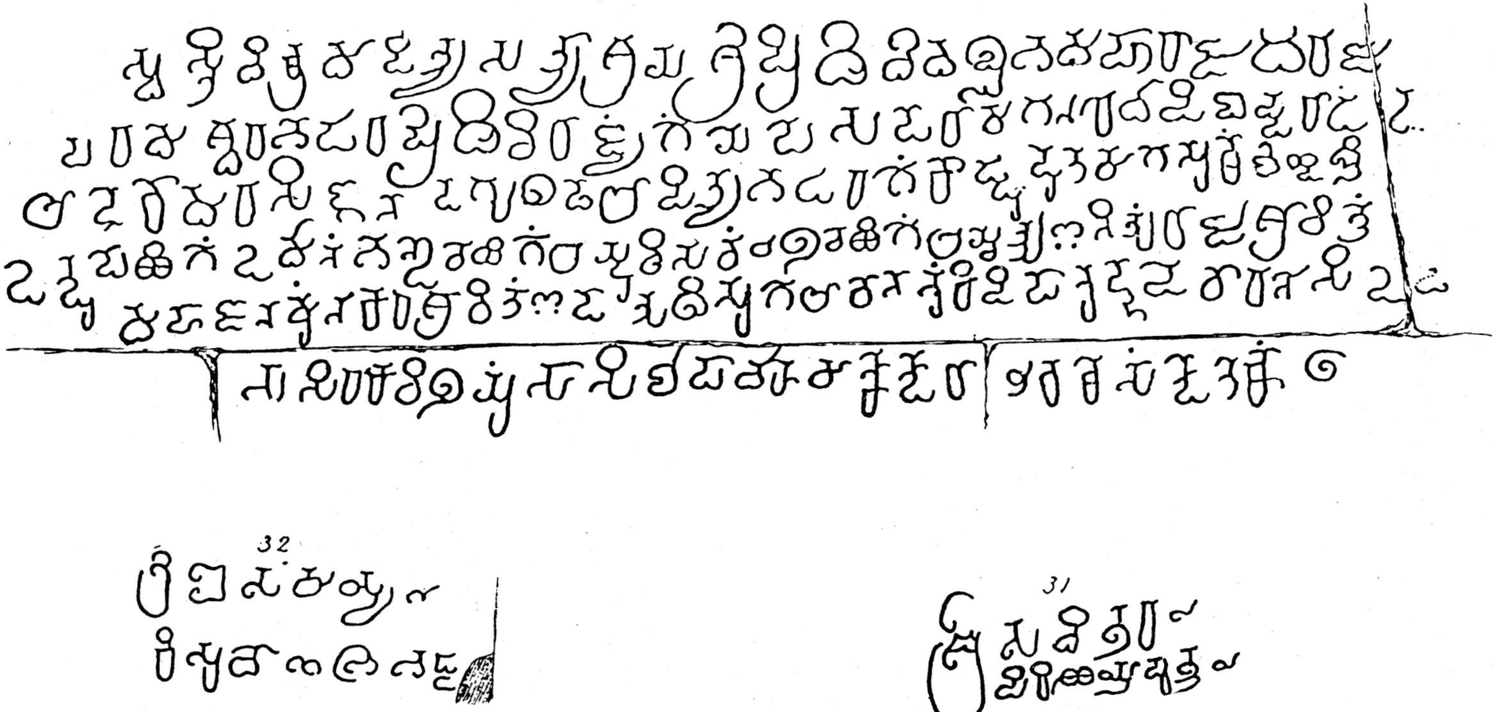

9. 'Aiwalli—Inscriptions'. Pl. LV, Figs 30–2, *Report on the First Season's Operations in Belgām and Kaladgi Districts*, Archaeological Survey of Western India, vol. I, 1874.

10. 'Aihole: Shrine Doorway of the Old Chalukya Temple'. Pl. 268 [right], *Ancient Monuments, Temples and Sculpture of India*, 1897.

11. 'The Durga Temple'. Pl. LXXIIIa, 'The Ancient Temples of Aiholẹ', *Archaeological Survey of India, Annual Reports, 1907–8*, 1911.

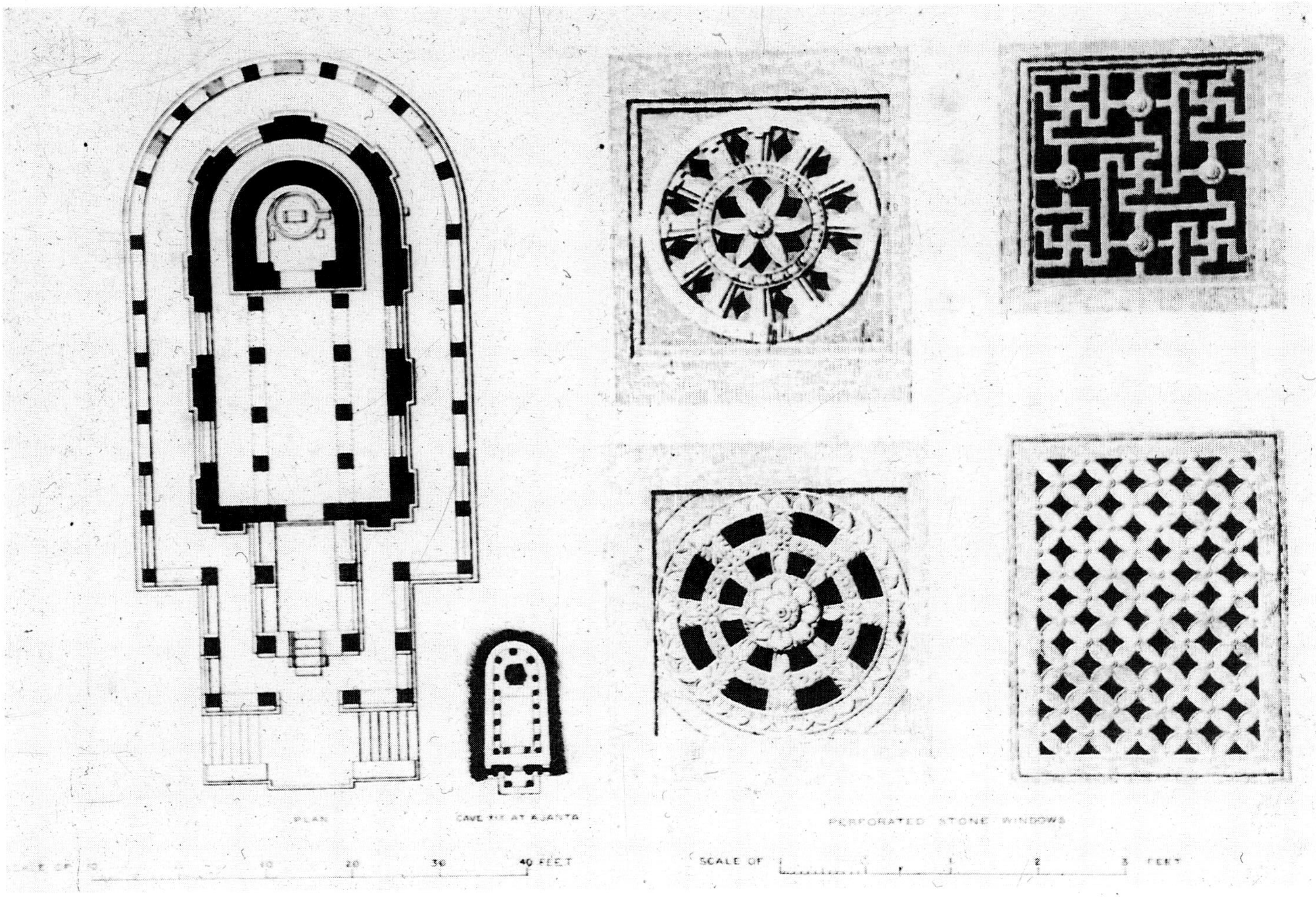

12. ‘Aihole: The Durga Temple’. Pl. XI, *Chālukyan Architecture of the Kanarese Districts*, Archaeological Survey of India, New Imperial Series, vol. XLII, 1926.

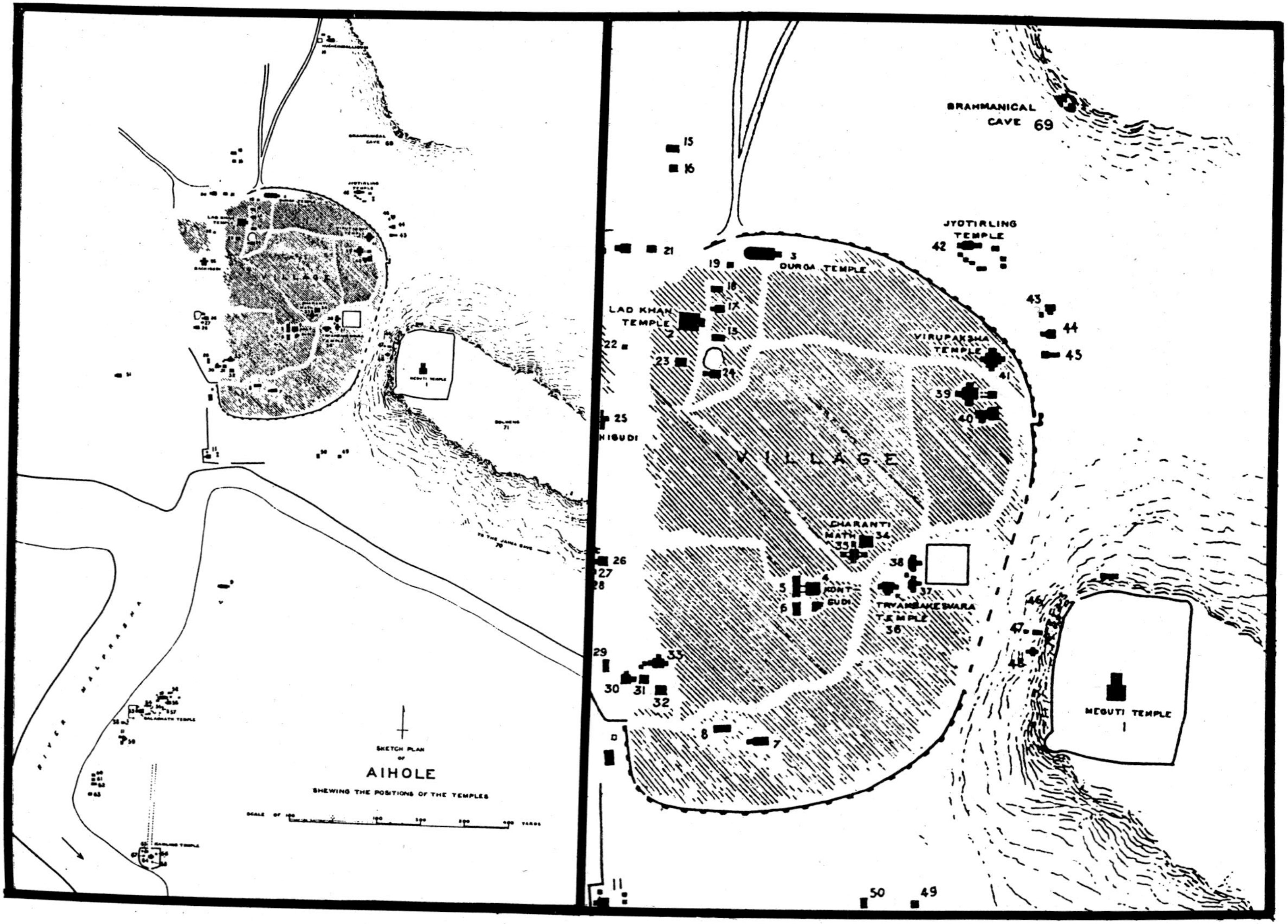

13. ‘Sketch Plan of Aihole’. Pl. II, *Chālukyan Architecture of the Kanarese Districts*, Archaeological Survey of India, New Imperial Series, vol. XLII, 1926. [Inset of the Durga temple is not in the original.]

AIHOLE: THE FRONT PORCH OF THE DURGA TEMPLE.

14. 'The Front Porch of the Durga Temple' and 'The Durga Temple from the North-west'. Pl. X, *Chālukyan Architecture of the Kanarese Districts*, Archaeological Survey of India, New Imperial Series, vol. XLII, 1926.

15. 'Durga Temple, Aihole; sixth century'. Pl. XXXVII, Fig. 152, *History of Indian and Indonesian Art*, 1927.

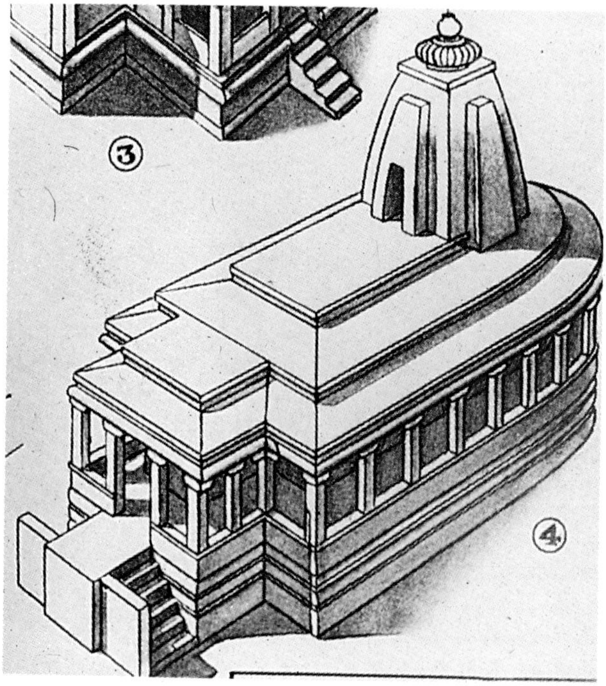

16. 'Durga Temple Aihole. *C.* AD 500', Pl. XXXIII, Fig. 4, *Indian Architecture* [1942].

17. 'Passage (pteroma) round exterior Aihole, Dharwar: Durga Temple, AD 500', Pl. XXXVIII, Fig. 2, *Indian Architecture* [1942].

18. 'Aihole, Dharwar: Durga Temple, portico; *c.* AD 500'. Pl. XXXIX, Fig. 1, *Indian Architecture* [1942].

19. 'Couples. The Temple of Durga, Vth century'. Pls 5–6, *Golden Age of Indian Art*, 1955.

20. 'The god Shiva'. Pls 7–8, *The Golden Age of Indian Art*, 1955.

21. 'Vishnu in his boar incarnation'. Pl. 9, *Golden Age of Indian Art*, 1955.

22. 'Veranda niche, Durga, Slayer of the Titan Buffalo'. Pl. 117, *Art of Indian Asia*, 1960.

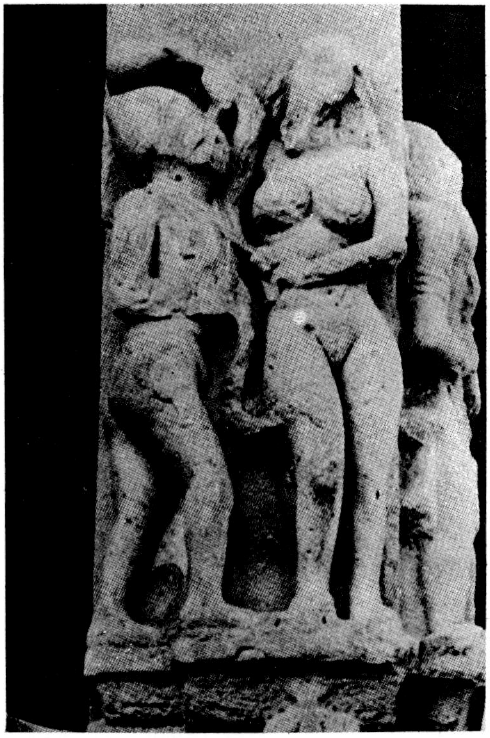

23. 'Asvamukhi group, Durga, Aihole'. Pl. XXXIII [right], Some Remarks on Early Western Cāḷukya Sculpture', 1972.

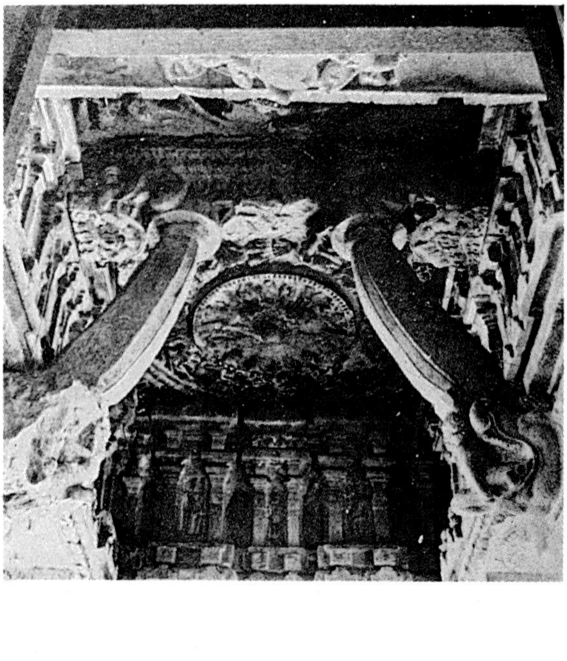

24. 'Aihole Durga, porch'. Pls XIVf, *Early Western Chalukyan Temples*, 1975.

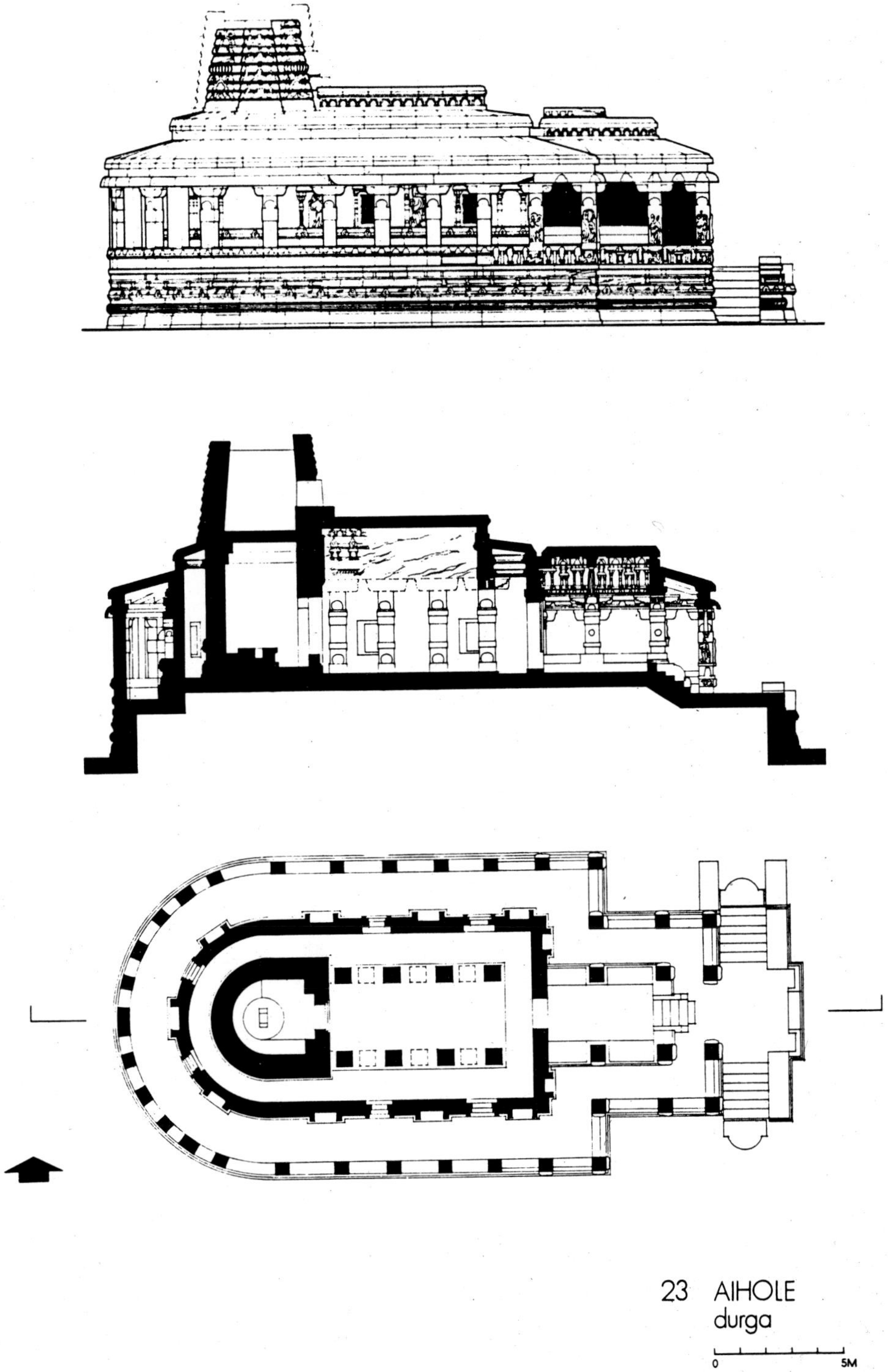

25. 'Aihole Durga'. Drawing 23, *Early Western Chalukyan Temples*, 1975.

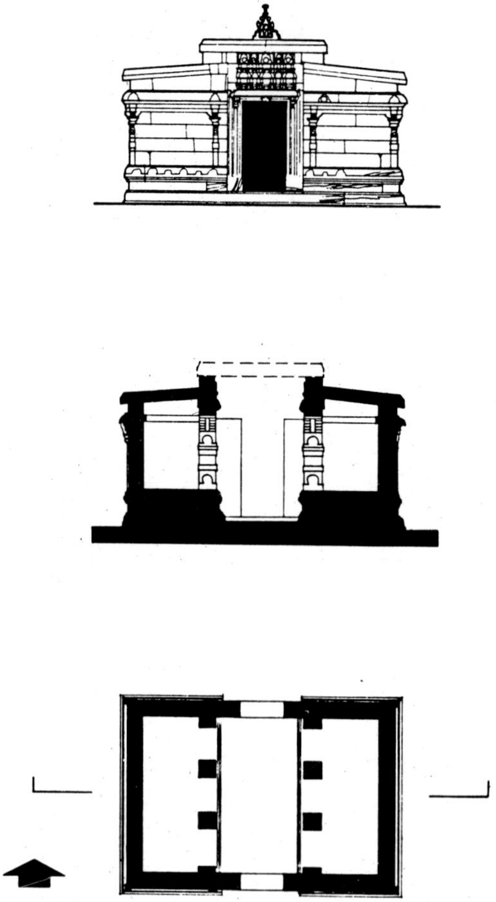

26. 'Aihole Durga gateway'. Drawing 24, *Early Western Chalukyan Temples*, 1975.

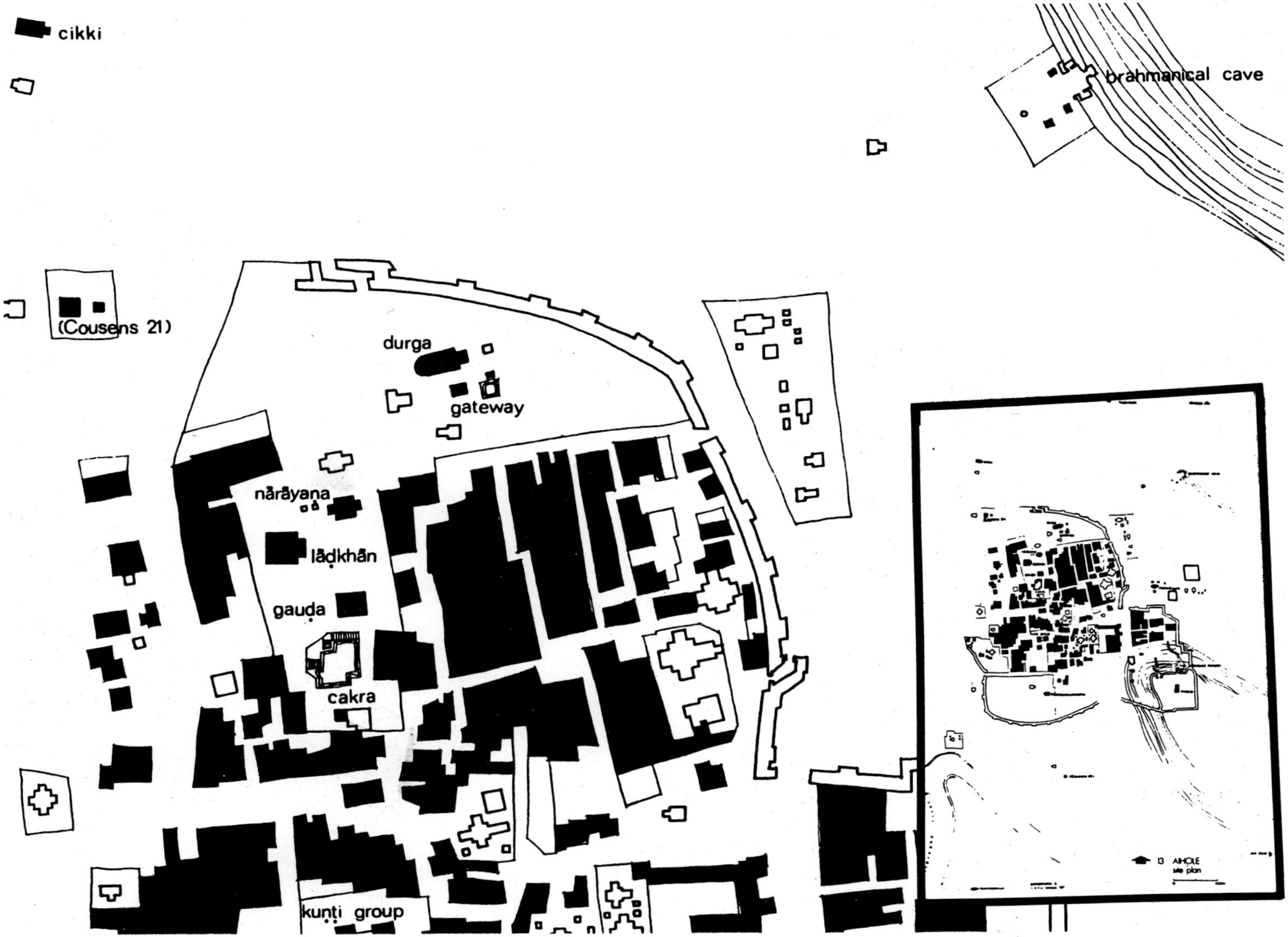

27. 'Aihole site plan'. Drawing 13, *Early Western Chalukyan Temples*, 1975.
[Inset of the Durga temple is not in the original.]

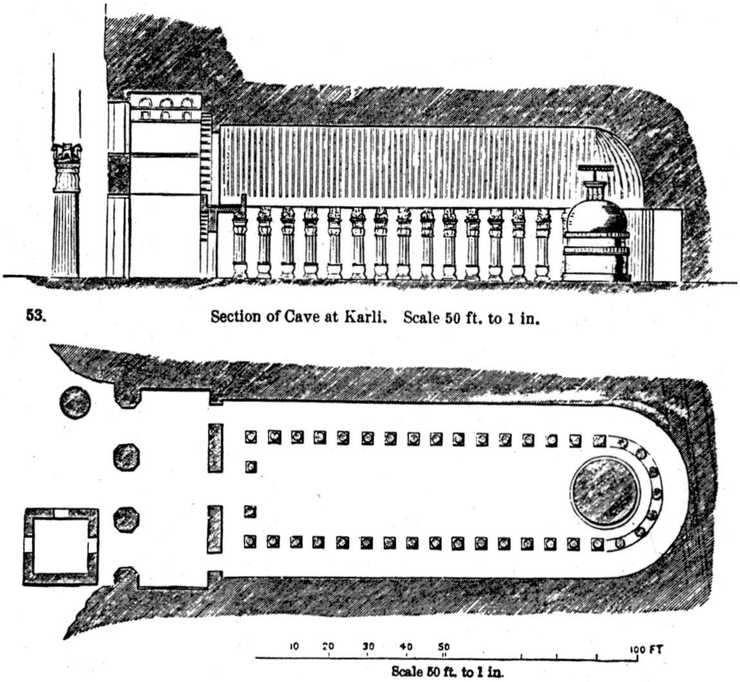

28. 'Section of Cave at Karli', and 'Plan of Cave at Karli'. Figs 16 and 17, *Illustrated Handbook of Architecture*, 1855.

29. 'View of Interior of Cave at Karli. From a Photograph'. Fig. 992, *A History of Architecture in All Countries*, 1867.

30. 'View of Cave at Karli. From a drawing by Mr Salt, corrected by the Author'. Fig. 18, *Illustrated Handbook of Architecture*, 1855.

31. 'Raths, Mahavellipore. From a sketch by the Author'. Fig. 42, *Illustrated Handbook of Architecture*, 1855.

32. 'Badami—Veranda of Cave III from the E. end'. Pl. XXIX, *Report on the First Season's Operations*, 1874.

33. 'View of Sahadeva's Ratha, from a Photograph'. Fig. 38, *Cave Temples of India*, 1880.

34. 'Ancient Buddhist Chaitya at Ter.' (From a photograph by H. Cousens.) Fig. 48, *History of Indian and Eastern Architecture*, 1910.

35. ‘Temples at Purudkul. Dravidian. Bengallee.’ Fig. 4, *Architecture in Dharwar and Mysore*, 1866, p. 43.

36. Detail of Pl. LIX, 'Purudkul. Group of Temples, with Idol Car'. *Architecture in Dharwar and Mysore*, 1866.

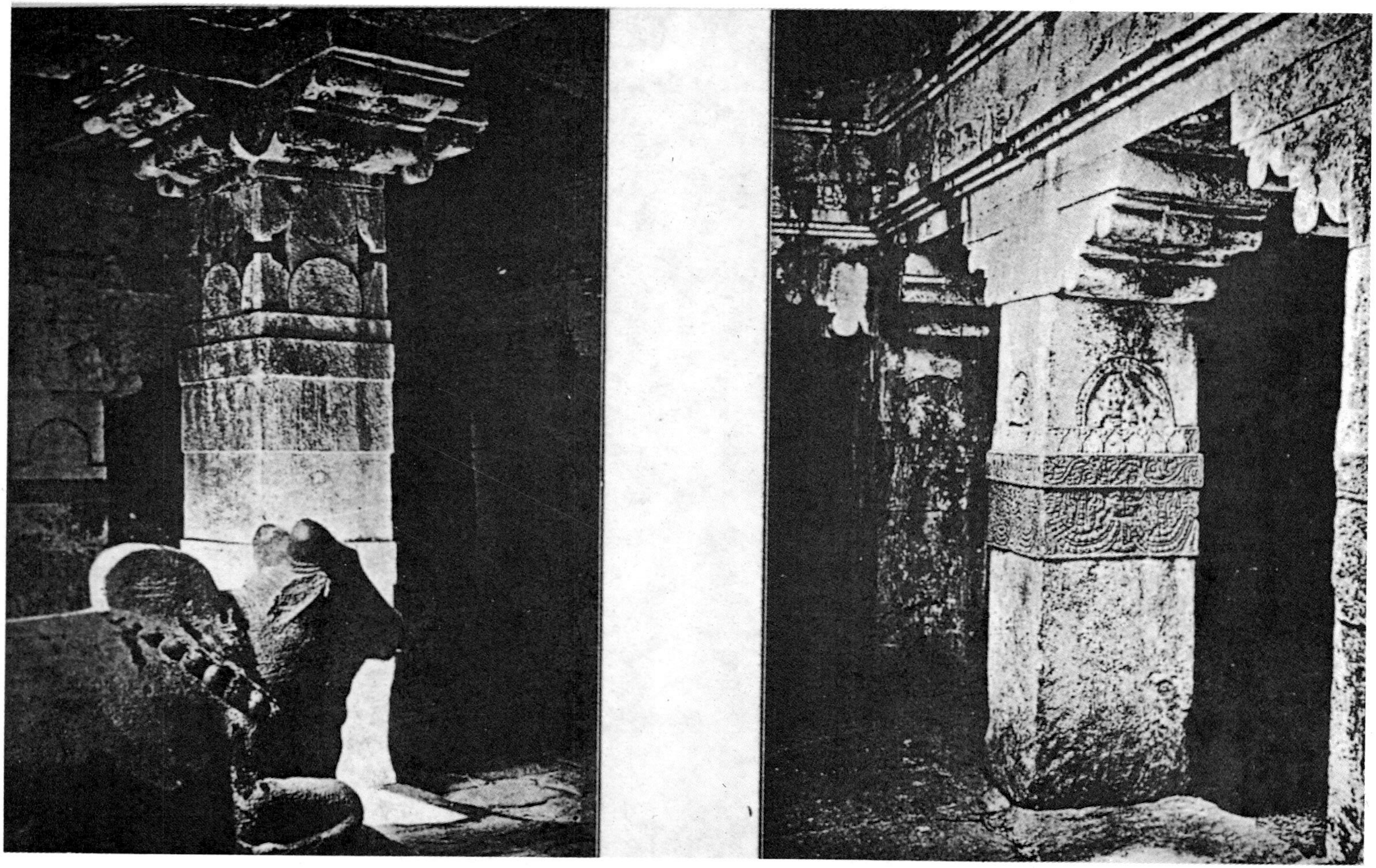

37. ‘Pillars in Lad Khan’s Temple’. Pl. LXXII, ‘Ancient Temples of Aihole’, 1911.

38. 'Halsi, Varaha-Narasimha Temple, Vimana'. Fig. 32. *Kadamba Kula*, 1931.

39. 'Apsidal Shrine—Front View' Fig. 7, and 'Back View' Fig. 8, 'Çalukyan Temples of Satyavolu', 1960.

40. Pl. III, 'An Apsidal Temple at Chikka Mahākuṭa', 1964.

41. 'Badami, Malegitti-Sivalaya, god or guardian slaying a kinnari'. Fig. 11, 'Additions and Replacements in Early Chālukya Temples', 1970.

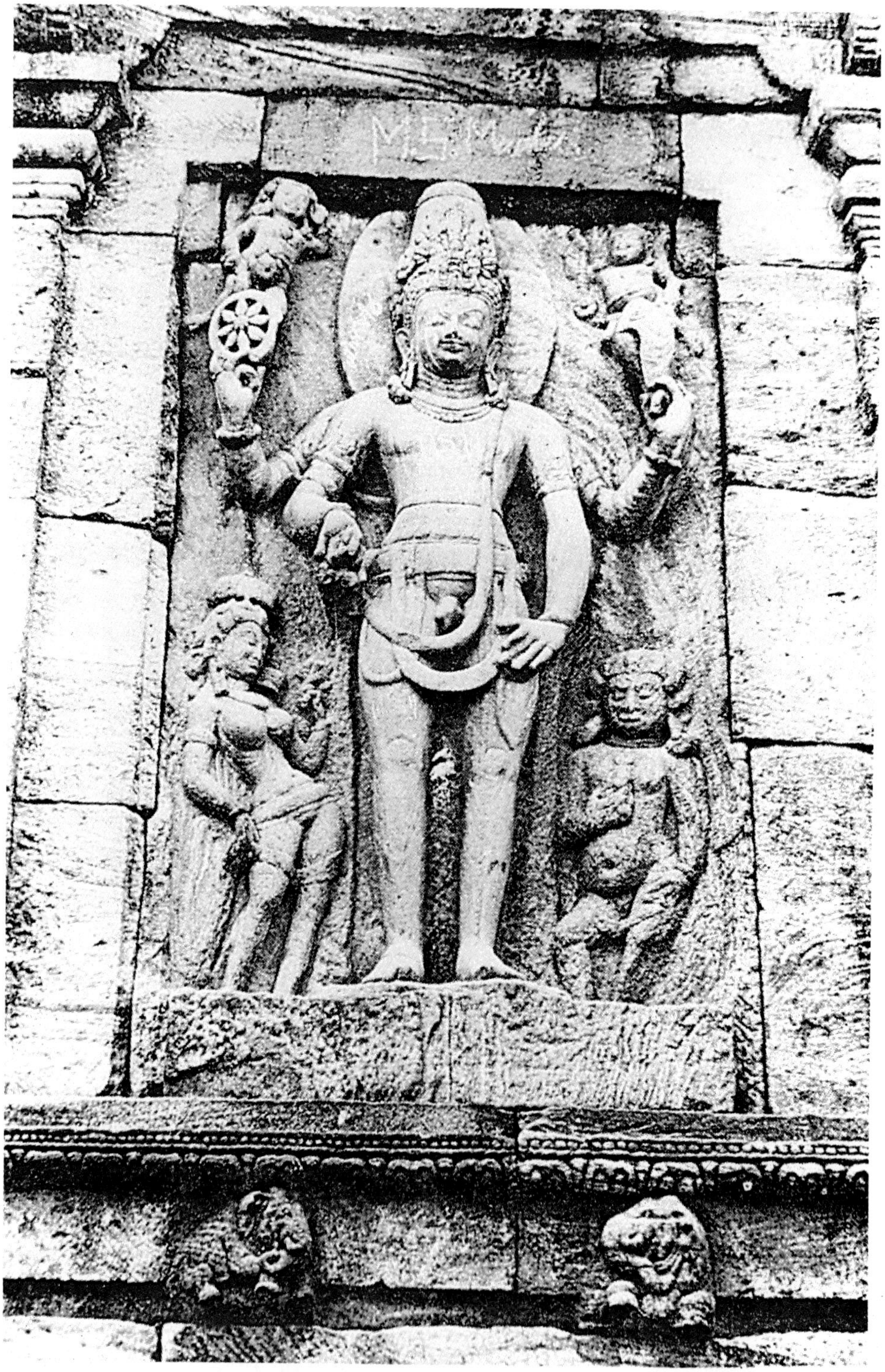

42. 'Badami, Malegitti-Sivalaya, Vishnu and ayudha-purushas'. Fig. 16, 'Additions and Replacements in Early Chālukya Temples', 1970.

43. Badami Cave III, Narasimha (detail).

44. Mahisasuramardini Durga, Kailasanatha temple, Kanci.

PART TWO

The Durga Temple in its Cultural Context

The Durga Temple in its Cultural Context

GETTING THERE

MY FIRST ENCOUNTER WITH the Durga temple took place in 1961 in the 'squalid . . . wasteland' of Benjamin Rowland's Aihole, where it was introduced as 'a late Gupta shrine of the chaitya type . . . a modified structural chaitya-hall with [a] familiar basilican plan . . . a flat roof over the nave replac[ing] the barrel vaults . . . [and] massive bracket capitals . . . severe or rustic version[s] of those in Cave XIX at Ajanta.'[1] The accompanying illustrations were Henry Cousens' 1908 view of the temple from the east (Fig. 11) and a plan. The chapter was entitled 'The Golden Age: The Gupta Period' and it led from Ajanta's Cave XIX through Cejerla to Sanchi's temple 17. I saw as I was directed, that the round end of the temple nicely matched those of the *caitya* caves—its positive their negative. It seemed to fit well into the classic formal development Rowland offered: the rock-cut cave forms had been *translated* into free-standing structural ones.

Two years later, when I had the opportunity of a brief two-hour visit to the site, I managed about five minutes to views and take three or four pictures of the outside of the temple. My main goal was to get a picture of the famous round apse and its contrasting tower, to fit it into the survey I expected to eventually teach. Seeing the Mahisasuramardini Durga in the ambulatory (Fig. 22), I presumed it to be the temple's presiding deity. By then I had been able to read little more than Percy Brown.

Before I returned to study the temples, in the winter of 1966, reading had helped me locate the Durga temple into the tradition of the early western Chalukyas, who ruled the Deccan from the middle of the sixth century to the middle of the eighth.[2] By that time the dynasty's dates were firmly set, beginning with Pulakesin I's fortification of the nearby site of Badami in 542 and continuing through eight reigns to Kirtivarman II's defeat by the Rastrakutas between 754 and 757.[3] A detailed study of the Chalukya's rock-cut temples, based upon the pictures taken on that first visit allowed me my first taste of the technical literature and problems of the region's history.[4] As I understood it at that point, the art of the Chalukyas had been charted by Henry Cousens and detailed by several others, with a certain amount of consistency.

The literature of the time discussed an early Chalukya art that consisted of the six rock-cut temples studied by Burgess and R. D. Banerji,[5] the two dozen nearby structural temples considered by Cousens, and another set of six temples at Alampur in Andhra, noticed by Gulam Yazdani and tied to the Chalukyas by Percy Brown.[6] Henry Cousens worked out his understanding of early Chalukya temples before the discovery of Pulakesin's foundation inscription had led historians to the firm conclusion that the dynasty could not be traced before 542. In his variation on Cunningham's hypothesis of the evolution of 'towered' from 'flat-roofed' temples, Cousens distributed what he considered the early Chalukya temples from the middle of the fifth to the middle of the eighth century. He put the towerless Lad Khan into the fifth century and the Huccimalli-gudi and Durga, with their apparently rudimentary towers, into the sixth. He then placed the more developed-looking Badami and Mahakuta temples into the seventh century and the larger (and more complex) Pattadakal temples into the eighth. In the 1960s most art historians continued to follow Cousens, though anyone aware of the inscriptions could ponder the contradiction involved in placing some structures a century before the dynasty's beginning. On a visit to the Lad Khan, S. R. Balasubrahmanyam dealt with this by noting the Chalukya insignia on one of its porch pillars and, after a consideration of its formal style, moved it up a century to the time of Cave III, around 578.[7] This did not clarify whether or not there were pre-Chalukya temples in the region, but it opened up the question.

The conclusion of my study of the cave temples was that they had all been cut in the third quarter of the sixth century, in the two decades immediately leading up to the consecration of the series climax, the colossal Cave III at Badami, inscribed in 578.[8] This was at the beginning of the dynasty's political activity and the region's aesthetic development in stone, and it gave me a basis for approaching their earliest structural temples, since they would be the ones most closely related to the caves.

My study of the caves had also shown me there was a good deal more evidence in the field than anyone had yet incorporated into the literature. I found nine rock-cut monuments where Burgess and his successors had confined themselves to six. Conventional statements on the caves merely repeated Burgess' or Banerji's conclusions about them without considering all the evidence available in their plans, drawings and photographs.

Around 1960, more Chalukya structural temples began to surface in print. They were the first since the twenties and so far they had appeared only in publications with limited circulation and with little analysis of their place in the tradition. Herman Goetz and others mentioned a temple located by the Archaeological Survey at Nagaral a few miles east of Badami.[9] M. Rama Rao had found a half-dozen more early Chalukya temples in Andhra.[10] There had been, on the other hand, no comprehensive re-evaluation of the tradition that would account for all that had been learned since Cousens. No one had yet compared the Chalukya temples of the Telingana region with their better known Karnatak series. Nor was there yet any analysis of how the structural temples were connected with the rock-cut ones. On a broader plane there was the question of how the Chalukya temples related to the Indian scene as a whole, and particularly the regionally adjacent monuments of Ajanta and Ellora in the north and those of the Pallavas of Kanchi to the east and south.

In their inscriptions the Chalukyas claimed control of the Deccan as far north as the Narmada (see map), and the usual interpretation of the memoirs of the Chinese Buddhist pilgrim Xuan-Zang (Hsuan-tsang) has been that he met the Chalukya emperor Pulakesin II at a capital in Nasik. So they could surely have sponsored art or found artists at these sites. There are painted ceiling panels at Ajanta showing figures in near-eastern dress that were regularly interpreted as representing an embassy of the Persian, Khusrau II, to this same Pulakesin.[11] I expected to find some clues to early Chalukya art among the myriad rock-cut temples there.

There were important organizational features shared by the layouts of the last Ajanta temples and the earliest at Aihole, but there were also distinct differences, suggesting a leap in time. Their doorframe decoration, of miniature architectural elements bordered with foliate and figural mouldings, was generally similar. But very few of the particular moulding courses found at Ajanta could be seen at Badami or Aihole.[12] I had found one striking sculptural parallel between the door guardians of Badami's Cave II and the guardians flanking Siva and Parvati in Ellora Cave 29's Ravana panel (Figs 82–4). But my further research produced an even more striking absence of other similarly close imagery.

Besides my research in the library, the course of my progress toward Aihole led through encounters with a number of scholars. Walter Spink, an American whose outlandish chronology of Ajanta and Elephanta had been one of my early introductions to the field, was then in Pune.[13] In the course of my work on the caves I had made an effort to refute his 'early' chronology which held Ajanta to the fifth century, a good century and a half before the supposed visit of Khusrau's ambassadors, but I ended up agreeing with him. Since the Chalukya caves were discretely independent of the art at Ajanta and there seemed a significant chronological break between them, Ajanta's work could not reasonably have lasted up to the time of the earliest Chalukya work, which would have been under way by the mid-sixth. Spink was equally alone in his dating of the great cave at Elephanta to the early sixth century. Most others then thought it to be eighth or ninth century.[14] Thirty years later, limiting Ajanta to the fifth century is gaining acceptance, and few would date Elephanta later than the sixth.[15]

In the autumn of 1966, I also met and discussed the chronology of the earliest Chalukya temples with M. A. Dhaky in the photo collection of the Archaeological Survey in New Delhi. To both of us, at that moment, this meant the Huccimalli-gudi, the Durga temple and a few others. The outstanding issue was clearly the connection between these temples, with their rudimentary towers, and the earlier 'flat-roofed' temples that Cousens and Percy Brown related to the fifth-century art of the Guptas in north India.[16] The most famous of these, of course, was famous, 'enigmatic' Lad Khan. One temple my new friend was surprised to find on my sixth-century list was Badami's well-known Malegitti.[17] He believed on stylistic grounds that it was late seventh century or even eighth, but he was interested in my comparison of it with the Mahakutesvara temple, which was associated with an inscribed pillar of 601/2.[18]

Map of India: The locations of the Chalukya temple sites are marked **o**.

At Pune I also met B. Rajendra Prasad, who was finishing a doctoral thesis at the Deccan College on the Chalukya temples at Alampur.[19] He pointed out the necessity of direct personal contact with the monuments, climbing right up on them when possible, to get the most accurate understanding. Among other things about the Chalukyas, Prasad assured me that there was a close connection between the Alampur temples and some of those at Pattadakal. Though from Andhra, Prasad had then been to Alampur only a few times, and to the other major Chalukya sites but once. His work was based on a detailed familiarity with the languages and libraries of his region and an intimate first-hand knowledge of the site, but very few pictures. He knew Alampur very well, but relatively little beyond it.

THEORY OF COMPARISON

The first step in doing the art history of the Durga temple is to locate it on the map of a particular tradition. This was a difficult task in the 1960s, because of the inadequacy of the maps available. Cousens' periplus provided a comfortable guide to anyone whose voyage was confined to the literature based upon him, but it failed those hardy enough to venture into the field. Cousens and his successors offered a selection of landmarks, which they related in a variety of ways to each other and to other structures across the subcontinent, but it was necessary now to construct a more comprehensive and systematic map establishing the tradition's regional borders, gazetting its major forms and tracing the paths that linked them.

All understandings of the Durga temple's form were based on its apparent placement within the development of temple traditions. To generalists such as Fergusson or Goetz this meant within the full expanse of Indian temple art. To specialists such as K. R. Srinivasan or R. S. Gupte it meant a development largely confined to a particular regional or local tradition. For others such as Henry Cousens or Percy Brown focus was upon dynastic as well as regional development. At the time of my research I found B. Rajendra Prasad doing a study of the early Chalukya dynasty at the site of Alampur in Andhra Pradesh, and K. V. Soundara Rajan studying all the early Chalukya monuments of Karnataka.

Putting my interest in the sixth-century temporarily aside, I determined to work out the development of the early Chalukya dynasty's art as a whole. To be comprehensive I decided to study all its recognized sites in Karnataka and Andhra, and even north into Maharashtra, where inscriptions showed they had been active. To be thorough I decided to include everything that could be identified with the dynasty: religious or secular, figure sculpture, jewellery, coins, painting or architecture, rock-cut or structural.

The early Chalukya temples were identified as a set by Burgess and their number expanded by Cousens and his successors on the basis of style, the style they shared and the styles of the neighbouring temples with which they contrasted. The common visual characteristics that united them as a set were relatively clear. Nearly all the region's temples were built of locally quarried, buff and gold or plum-coloured sandstone, but those identified as early Chalukya were constructed of significantly larger blocks than the other, apparently, later temples. Their decoration, even among the most developed examples, was consistently more massive and less linear than the others. They were less ornate. Their plans and profiles were simpler. They carried more figure sculpture, and their figures were larger in size.

The identification of this simpler style with the early Chalukya dynasty was based upon the presence of inscriptions in a few of them. Seven of the three dozen accepted examples bore statements specifically linking their construction to the dynasty. A handful of others carried inscriptions associating their use with it. The rest were attributed on the basis of style and location alone.

The current gazetteer was the list of these related structures. Its ordering principle, their relative chronology, was also conjectured largely on the basis of the formal patterns we call style. Without further inscriptional information, and lacking a test comparable to carbon-14 dating, patterns of style were all there were to go on. The seven temples with a year or reign inscribed on them could stand as landmarks by which to plot formal developments from the later sixth century to the mid-eighth. Cave III at Badami was consecrated in 578,[20] the Meguṭi at Aihole in 634, the Sangameswar at Pattadakal was constructed during the reign of Vijayaditya (695–733), and the Virupaksa and Mallikarjuna of Pattadakal were done during the reign of Vikramaditya II (733–45). The Huccimalli-gudi was built before 708, and the Makutesvaranatha of Mahakuta and the Durga temple were built by 745.[21] The rest of the temples, lacking inscriptions, had to be assigned their positions on the basis of their apparent relationships with the formal progression plotted among the dated ones. As with a good deal of India's art, the majority of analysis thus far devoted to early Chalukya architecture took the form of either description or hypothetical explanation of these formal patterns.

A comparative stylistic analysis was thus more or less what everyone writing on the art of the Chalukyas had done, so what could I expect to get out of doing yet another? On the one hand I intended to take the dynasty as my cultural unit and include consideration of a more complete set of its monuments than had been done before. On the other hand, I intended to consider all the monuments from a consistent and highly detailed point of view. Earlier studies had taken various selections of monuments and approached them from a variety of viewpoints. Moreover, previous approaches varied considerably in the quality of their comparisons.

The lateral entrance staircases of the Durga temple (Figs 25 and 57) resemble those found on another well known early Chalukya temple at Aihole, the Meguṭi, on the hill above the town (Fig. 86 and diagram 2a on p. 68). But, how much alike are they? And what does this have to tell us about the Durga temple? It is easy enough to place the two staircases into the same tradition. Both are attached to fabrics bearing early Chalukya inscriptions. Since the Meguṭi is one of those rare artifacts in the early Chalukya tradition that has a firmly established date, its significance for our understanding of the Durga temple can be particularly useful. On the eastern wall of its *mandapa* the Meguṭi carries an inscription quite unequivocally dating the structure's inauguration to *Saka* 556, 634/5. The simple fact of their staircases looking alike is not, by itself, enough to date the Durga temple to *circa* 634.

The crucial elements of a comparison are establishing a specific aspect of comparability, a measure of that comparability, and conclusions about the nature of the relationships involved—most significantly chronological priority and cultural connection. These are three quite different things and, therefore, three distinct tasks.

Most if not all well-formed (*samskrta*) stone temples are raised over basements climbed by staircases running directly toward their halls (e.g., Fig. 47). In a significant if relatively small number of such temples, the stairs are lateral ones, approaching the structures from the side, across the temple's longitudinal axis, as those of the Durga temple. Examples may be found in structures as varied as the Gondesvara temple at Sinnar, the Mahaprasasta Pancaratha prasada described in the *Silpasarini*, the Orukal *mandapam* at Tirukkalukkunram and the Malegitti of Badami (p. 68, diagram 2d).[22] Within this category of temples with lateral stairways, only some have pairs.

Not only are the steps of the Meguṭi and the Durga temple paired-lateral sets approaching a common landing, they are each attached to the longitudinal facade of a forward, pillared *mandapa*. They are both of sandstone, with the risers in each screened by a facing wall articulated in response to the decoration of the temple basements they climb.

However, the stairs of the Durga temple are considerably more refined. They are placed on the temple's facade quite elegantly, blending in a nicely considered and carefully wrought manner with the mouldings of the temple's basement (Fig. 57). Precisely as wide as the porch, their facing wall carries the basement courses around the façade, making the stairs appear to be cut neatly through a continuous set of mouldings.[23] On the front they are articulated by a projecting bay that establishes the temple's longitudinal emphasis with a forward accent. The eight steps to each side begin with an undecorated moonstone.[24] The staircases of the Meguṭi are plainer in nature, and though some of the difference visible today is the result of their physical deterioration, it seems clear that they were neither as elaborately designed nor as finely executed. There are five steps to each side, fitted against the mouldings of the basement and fronted by a screen wall articulated at the centre. Neither their fit to the mouldings of the basement nor their coordination with the plan reveal much care or preparation. So, we can say that the two are distinct as well as similar, but how do we measure the degree of similarity? How close can we tie the Durga temple to the Meguṭi's authors and its date of 634?

Once a field of formal comparability has been established, we need to establish a range within which we can measure the closeness of the relationship. In the case of the early Chalukyas we have about 150 temples of which only six have twin lateral entrance stairs. So, we can say they are relatively unusual within their tradition, though neither their relative rarity, nor the fact that four of them are at Aihole, tells us just how closely connected they may be. Bringing the others into the discussion can give us a scale by which to measure their similarity. The remaining four are found on the Sarangi-math and the Bhagavati temple at Aihole, the Jambulinga temple at Badami and the Papanatha at Pattadakal. Of these four only one bears much relation to the pair we are considering.

The twin lateral stairways of the Papanatha are crude makeshift, completing or replacing more finished work that the temple's refined architecture required (p. 68, diagram 2f). A view of the basement shows that twin lateral stairs were intended, but that those there today are irregularly finished. The form of these stairs was uniquely free in space. They extended in a 'T' shape with arms reaching out on either side of their single-bay (*catuski*) porch. They did not hug the porch wall like those at Aihole.[25] Fragments in front of the Jambulinga suggest that it may once have been intended to have twin lateral staircases, but there is only enough remaining to suggest their form: a shallow landing and an irregular combination of relatively narrow steps (diagram 2b). These steps hug the face of a three-bay porch in the more modest version of the Aihole fashion, but hemmed in as they are by later courtyard additions it is impossible to guess how—or even if—they might have been finished. What remains is too rough and irregular to have been more than temporary.

Returning to Aihole, there are interesting remains on two temples. First there are what seem to be the vestiges of lateral stairs on the seemingly more conventional staircase of the Bhagavati temple (Fig. 87).[26] Like the Durga temple, the Bhagavati is composed of an inner shrine surrounded by an open veranda. The entrance to the veranda today has the usual longitudinal stairs entering directly toward the shrine. On either side of this staircase, however, there are vestiges of three short flanking steps. These seem cramped; they are only about 60 centimetres wide or a third the width the Durga temple's risers. But, they are well cut, nicely fitted to the basement and possess a finished facing, articulated in a projected panel at its centre. A broken slab at the level of the second step marks the point where the current longitudinal stairs were superimposed. The curving railstones are possibly of the Rastrakuta period. This stairway is roughly a third the width of the facade.

The surviving set of Chalukya stairs most clearly comparable with those on the Durga and the Meguṭi is the one found on the Sarangi-math (Fig. 88).[27] Like them, its steps are fronted by a low screen wall articulated at the centre, and like the Meguṭi's, the steps here fit indifferently against the finished mouldings of the facade. In contrast, however, the screen here is topped with a large *candrasala* arch, bearing an image of Gaja Laksmi.[28] The steps here are of the same width as the remnants on the Bhagavati and, like them, span about a third of the facade.

Thus of 150 known early Chalukya temples, only two apart from the Meguṭi have twin lateral staircases like those on the Durga temple. And all four are found at the same site, two of a grand, facade-spanning variety and two in a more modest form. The relative uniqueness of the type within the Chalukya tradition and their similarity may suggest related authorship, but the similarities are not close enough to demand it.

If we step back and view their physical contexts, the porches to which these stairways are connected, we find ensembles of elements with a good deal more in common. The Meguṭi and the Durga temple porches have similar sizes, decoration and, more significantly, architectural purposes. They are both open, nine-bay (*navaranga*) halls, about eight metres square, enlarging and ennobling the structures to which they are attached considerably more than the usual four-pillared porches. They are each edged with *kaksasana* benches, whose backs are decorated with mouldings and friezes complementing the basements below. On the Durga temple these are particularly fine, with exceptionally engaging elephants, lions and sprightly *bhūta* (dwarfs) in high relief (Fig. 59). On the Meguṭi, the benches are placed between undecorated pillar shafts, whereas on the Durga temple the decoration of the pillars and benches are united by a single continuous frieze, as on the dynasty's latest temples at Pattadakal. The Durga temple's pillars are further enhanced by the presence of large *mithuna* couples. Like its stairs, the Durga temple's porch was thus not only the more comprehensively planned but also the more richly embellished of the two.

The Sarangi-math is closer to the Durga temple than the Meguṭi. Like the Durga temple, its porch pillars bear *mithuna* sculpture and continue the architectural imagery on the *kaksasana* backs, although its friezes are of the simpler sort. If we were to line the three temples up by complexity of conception, or development of imagery, we would read from the Meguṭi to the Sarangi-math to the Durga temple. Although presumptuous to date the temples from such a narrow range of information, it would be fair to state that the Durga temple's porch seems more developed, not merely more elaborate, than the Meguṭi's.

Because of its alterations the Bhagavati temple is more difficult to read, although its place in this series is clear. It is a simpler version of the Sarangi-math. Its basement mouldings and the size of its intended stairs are equivalent. However, its pillars are without couples. Confusingly, its *kaksasana* run in a continuous slanted panel, covering the pillars that stand behind them. But once we recognize their repetition of *purna ghata* vases on a slanting frame as a late Chalukya or early Rastrakuta motif, we can see that these bare pillars originally stood separate like those of the Meguṭi.[29] Both the Sarangi-math and Bhagavati stairs are placed against open three-bay *mandapas* lacking discrete porches.

The last significant element to be considered here is the relation of the Meguṭi's porch and stairway to the rest of its structure. They are an addition to the temple whose hall carries the dated inscription. The original Meguṭi was composed of the inner sanctum with a surrounding *sandhara* hall, a forward *mandapa*, and an open porch—marked on the plan by a short staircase with a moonstone (p. 68, diagram 2a).[30] Ravikirti's beautiful inscription, now roofed by an Archaeological Survey slab, is embedded in the wall of the original *mandapa* (Fig. 86). The difference between the original structure and its added porch is visible in the details and cutting of its basement friezes, the desultory walls connecting the *mandapa* with the porch, and the doubling of the pillars, where the older porch is extended by the later one. Thus, though the Meguṭi and the Durga temple staircases are fairly close in conception and execution, neither can be dated to the 634 inscription on the original Meguṭi. They are both of a later date.

THE GATEWAY

Our discussion of the Durga temple will more or less follow the path of the pilgrim or worshipper, from the entrance gateway to the temple, around the platform on the exterior, up onto the platform, around the inner temple and then inside.

One of the most prominent elements of the Durga temple's design has also been one of the least noticed—its gateway (Figs 26 and 27).[31] There is no way of knowing how many early

Chalukya temples had gateways or surrounding *prakara* walls. But gateways in stone were undoubtedly rare. Only three temples have come down to us with independent gateways: the great twin, climactic temples of the tradition, the Virupaksa and Mallikarjuna at Pattadakal, and the Durga temple. Aside from these, only four or five other early Chalukya passageways can be traced, and only one is fully developed: the entrance to the ritual tank at Sulebhavi, five miles east of Aihole and closely related to the Durga temple's. The others are modest passages, set into other structures, and not discrete *pratoli* or gateway structures.[32]

The Durga temple's gateway has an oblong plan. On the exterior its pilasters portray it as three bays across and two deep, though its interior is three bays each way. Its interior fits the long established pattern for entrance passages, with column-screened chambers on raised platforms to either side (Figs 26 and 52).[33] Though damaged on the north, most of it is still in a good state of preservation. It is a typical early Chalukya sandstone structure, finished with a crisp relief depiction of the pillar and lintel (wood) construction that seems to have been the ideal model for all stone buildings.

Though it is not obvious without careful measurement, the *pratoli* is carefully positioned and proportioned in relation to the temple. It is lined up within the same compass-controlled grid as the temple itself. Its location is precisely one-half the temple's width (the radius of the apse) to the south, its western edge lined up with the point at which that same radius cuts through the centre of the closed *mandapa* (diagram 1). The structure's area is roughly the same as that of the nine-bayed entrance porch on the platform.

Like the temple's stairways the *pratoli* approaches it obliquely. Worshippers are required to enter the temple's compound from the side. Proceeding through the gateway they emerge to find themselves facing the *mandapa* across the colonnade at its entrance, but before they reach the *mandapa* they still have a way to go. They have a choice of proceeding in the standard ritual circumambulation of *pradaksina* to their left, or going more directly to the stairway on the right. Either way the oblique positioning of the gateway complements the lateral orientation of the stairs. As the measurements of its location fit the gateway into the geometry of the temple's layout, its lateral situation fits it to the temple's scheme of approach.

The ceiling over the passageway is stilted above the slanted ceilings of the side chambers, so the structure has the clerestory section of the usual early Chalukya *mandapa* (e.g., Fig. 47). Such a broken roof line is incompatible with the possibility of the multistoried tower, characteristic of the mature southern *gopura* (Fig. 89).[34] Instead of a tower, it is capped by a trefoil *candrasala* arch, over the raised roof (Fig. 53). Though this is a unique survival and a fragile one, it seems to be an original element of the gateway's design. It is undoubtedly of early Chalukya manufacture; it fits well, and adds a satisfying finish to the design.[35] A twin piece, presumably from the broken, northern facade, was found nearby. The figure within each is a two-armed male, seated cross-legged, in what may be the pose of a charioteer, with its arms symmetrically splayed. It is most likely Aruna (dawn), who drives the Sun's chariot, though it could be Aditya, the Sun himself. A similar figure holding lotuses occupies the trefoil *candrasala* above the sanctum doorway of the nearby Surya (or Suryanarayana) temple, an early Chalukya structure connected in several ways

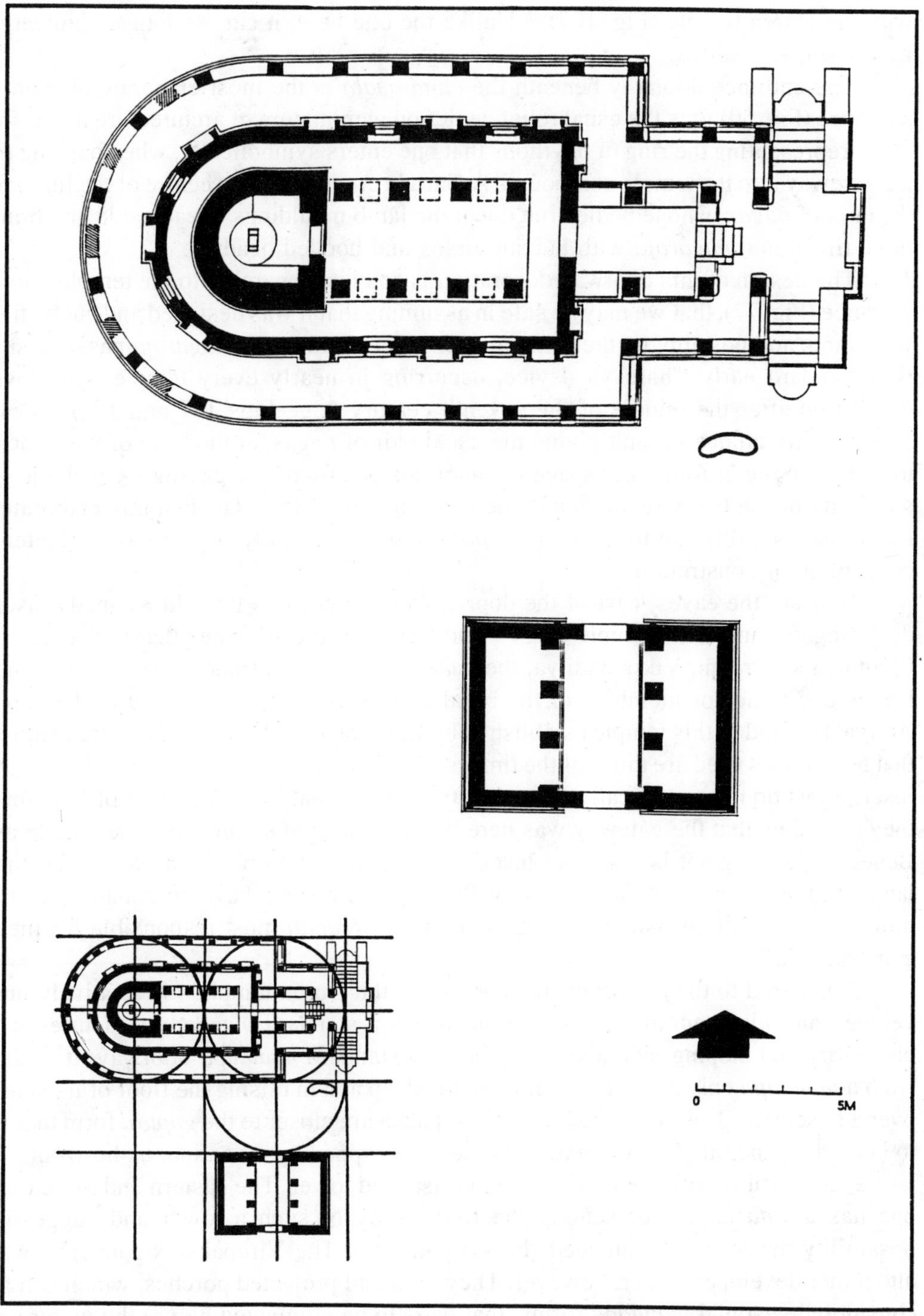

Diagram 1: The Durga temple and its gateway, after George Michell's Drawings 23 and 24.

with the Durga temple (Fig. 107).[36] Unlike the one here, it carries lotuses indicating that it is definitely Aditya.

The entrance doorway beneath the *candrasala* is the most elaborate element of the structure (Fig. 50). It is the usual relief depiction in miniature of architecture in the southern style, representing the ring of pavilions that one enters symbolically, when passing through the gateway into the temple compound. A Garuda crouches in the centre of the lintel holding the tails of *nagas*, whose bodies run down the jamb mouldings to each side and branch off three times into *nagaraja* with human torsos and hooded heads.

The design of this doorway decoration is so close a parallel to the temple's *mandapa* entrance (Fig. 77), that we may be safe in assuming that it was designed and cut by the same workshop, and possibly by the same masters. The Garuda and *nagaraja* passage-surround is a standard early Chalukya device, occurring in nearly every temple with developed decoration after the middle of the seventh century (e.g., Figs 107 and 108). These two, however, are unique in multiplying the usual pair of *nagas*, at the base of the door jambs, to a set of three or four pairs spaced at intervals all around the passage. Given the general similarity of the two structures and the coordination of their layouts, this elaborate decoration makes it difficult to think of the *pratoli* as significantly separate from the temple in conception or construction.

Beneath the eaves, east of the doorway on the north is the Old Kannada inscription declaring a grant to the temple (Figs 9 and 52). This record states that in the reign of the Chalukya sovereign, Vikramaditya, the *vaddaravula* tax on trade in certain oils and betel leaves due to senior members of the royal court was being transferred to the support of Aditya, the God of this temple established by Komarasinga.[37] Epigraphers are in agreement that letterforms used are those of the time of Vikramaditya II (733/4–744/5).[38] Though these inscriptions do not specifically refer the structure's creation to the reign of Vikramaditya, they do tell us that the gateway was here by his time, and so probably the temple as well. Beneath the tax grant is a second inscription of the same era, in Old Kannada (the local language), naming Savitara, the son of Pirireyya. Since we have no donation ascribed to him, it seems quite possible that this man is the *sthapati* most responsible for the gate's construction.[39]

Compared to the *pratoli* of the Virupaksa, the Durga temple's is relatively underdeveloped and idiosyncratic in conception. It has a standard *mandapa* structure, of raised clerestory and sloping side aisle roofs, plus a standard *mandapa* doorway. It is different from a *mandapa* only in being wider than it is deep and in raising the floor of its side aisles over a basement. The two *pratoli* of the Virupaksa are closer to the *gopura* form that is soon to become standard. On their exteriors they are capped by a continuous horizontal entablature, compatible with the raising of a multistoried tower. The eastern and more complete one has a *kuta hara* representing the first storey of such a tower and suggesting the possibility that one was intended (Figs 89 and 90). The Virupaksa's gateways were not altogether developed either, however. They both had projected porches, which can also be considered vestigial *mandapa* forms, that were to be eliminated before the mature *gopura* form was reached (Fig. 92).[40] Like the *gopura*, the passageways of the Virupaksa *pratoli* shift the entrance *kuta hara* from the doorway architrave to the parapet of the roof.

The Sulebhavi gateway lies conceptually between these two.[41] It shares *mandapa* elevation and doorway decoration with the Durga temple's *pratoli* (Fig. 91), and its projected northern *catuski* porch with the Virupaksa's. This rather unusual structure also has doorway articulation and Trimurti ceiling panels typical of the early Chalukya *mandapa*. What is more interesting, some artists who worked on the entablature of the Sulebhavi's southern doorway also seem to have been involved with similar decorative details on the Durga temple's *mandapa* doorway and on at least one of its *kostha* niches.

A neat vernacular wall of broken stones (visible in Fig. 52) surrounded the Durga temple and the other structures of its complex, at the time that the first antiquarians arrived to record it (Fig. 3).[42] Its age is difficult to guess. The Durga temple and its stone *pratoli* conceptually required a wall as refined as they are. But no trace remains of such a wall, though equivalents are found at the Mallikarjuna and Virupaksa of Pattadakal (Fig. 92), the Kudaveli Sangamesvara, near Alampur (Fig. 102), and the ruined temple on the hill at Panyem.[43]

The existence of the Durga temple's gateway marks it as the most prestigious and developed structure of the early Chalukya period at Aihole. The fact that only two other temples in the entire tradition seem to have had such significant gateways, and that they are among the latest and most developed structures of the tradition, suggests that this gateway and its temple are among the dynasty's later and more developed creations. Though not quite so developed as Vikramaditya II's climactic Virupaksa and Mallikarjuna, of 733–45, the Durga temple was not far behind.

THE LAYOUT

It is the apsidal curving of the Durga temple's plan that first attracted the interest of the European historians, at a time when few such plans were known to them outside of the striking, rock-cut *caitya* halls in the vicinity of the British enclaves of Bombay and Pune. And, as those monuments were Buddhist creations of the early part of the first millenium, they associated the Durga temple with the same religion and era. Subsequent research, however, has revealed quite a different picture, one in which apsidal shrines are a standard if relatively uncommon form, used significantly by several Indian communities. We now know they were employed by the Ajivikas, the Jains and Brahmanical Hindus as early as by the Buddhists.[44] Jains, Brahmanical Hindus and secular builders have continued to employ round-ended layouts ever since.[45] Among the early Chalukya remains, four temples are found in this form, as are two roughly contemporary Pallava temples.[46] Apsidal structures are found regularly among the miniature votive shrines at Karnataka and Telingana sites like Mahakuta, Mahanandi, Cejerla, and Yelleswaram.[47] This should be no surprise, since they are an ubiquitous element in the miniature architectural detailing that fringes the roof lines of nearly every developed structure of the Dravida style: the *panjara*, which appears between *sala* and *karna kutas*, as established in the temple texts (e.g., Fig. 101). It would not be unrealistic to suppose three to four percent of all temples of this period in South India were constructed on this 'two-sided' plan.

The fourth apsidal Chalukya temple—along with the Durga temple and those at Satyavolu and Cikka Mahakuta—is a fragmentary ruin just north of the Cekki (Star) gudi (Cousens' temple 15), 250 metres north-west of the Durga temple (Fig. 94). Although little more than its basement survives intact, there are enough fragments to reveal a good deal of interesting information. Fifteen metres long and eight metres broad, its hall is a good deal larger than Cikka Mahakuta and more or less equal to the Durga temple's inner hall.[48] Like the Cikka Mahakuta temple it has fewer *kostha* offsets than the Durga temple. Like both its altar is circular. Its surviving Linga and Nandi indicate that like Cikka Mahakuta its dedication was Shaiva. It is a variation on patterns found in the other two.

More important and telling than the fact of the Durga's apsidal plan is the specific form that it takes. The Durga is a rare example of an apsidal temple with an open veranda on all sides. Such forms go back about as long as the type. They can be seen almost a millenium earlier, in the Naga temples of Sonkh (Mathura),[49] and subsequently at Nagarjunakonda.[50] But temples with surrounding open verandas are not at all usual in later temple architecture. Only one other Chalukya temple, the nearby and rectangular Bhagavati (Fig. 87), has a surrounding gallery of this type.[51] Other Chalukya temples such as the Huccappaya-math and the Sarangi-math have open colonnades, but these are found on their facades only. What is interesting about the encircling galleries of the Durga and Bhagavati temples is the way they are used, like the minars of the Taj Mahal, to expand the size of the structures they surround.

There is a regular pattern of growth among the early Chalukya's major structures, which continues through the length of the tradition. This seems to be true of both the rock-cut and the structural monuments of the first century of Chalukya art,[52] and of the following century as well. The inscription in Badami's Cave III is of relevance to this issue as it says that the Chalukya king, Mangalesa, 'erected a temple, an abode of the great Vishnu *surpassing everything which is celestial or human*, fashioned with the most curious workmanship, and worthy to be looked at.'[53] All temples do not grow progressively larger. Temples are found in a variety of shapes and sizes and scales—from simple sanctum and porch arrangements to more elaborate sanctum, hall and porch combinations—throughout the tradition's development. But the maximum size of the largest and most lavish temples is continually extended as time goes on. The eighth century witnesses the development of a variety of devices in a continuing attempt to extend the size of these more regal monuments.

For early Chalukya temples of the late seventh and early eighth century, there is a standard large-scale *mandapa*-temple eight to eleven metres wide, and sixteen to twenty metres long, seen in examples such as the Tarappa at Aihole and the Makutesvaranatha at Mahakuta. This size is maintained throughout Vijayaditya's and Vikramaditya II's reigns, while only five more lavish structures are expanded beyond it. The climax of this development is reached at the end of Vijayaditya's time when a new synthesis was achieved in the three great temples of Pattadakal, which were constructed on a super-scale, twice the length and width or four times the area of the standard *mandapa*-shrines.[54] Thus succeeding imperial rulers strove for ever more splendid glorification of themselves and their personal deities. This continued with the even greater size of the Kailasa at Ellora, the triumphal temple of the Rastrakutas, who conquered the Chalukyas.

The design of the Durga temple is one of the most advanced of these efforts to establish ever greater *size*, in an extended large-scale temple, before the leap to the super-scale taken with the Sangamesvara, Virupaksa and Mallikarjuna.

The standard *mandapa*-temple is composed of a sanctum fronted by a hall three bays wide and three bays long, approached by a one-bay (*catuski*) porch. As seen in the Malegitti the sanctum is attached to the *mandapa* in *nirandhara* fashion (diagram 2d), but it could be included within it in *sandhara* fashion, as seen in the Makutesvaranatha. Growth from this ideal was accomplished by the simple process of adding bays without any change in scale. This can be seen first in the Jambulinga at Badami of 699 (diagram 2b), where three sanctums are accommodated around a single *mandapa*, which has been expanded by an aisle on each side. The Jambulinga's porch is also expanded on each side, from a single bay to three bays by three. The result is a twenty-two metre temple. The Lad Khan was the largest temple at Aihole before the Durga temple, but because of its even more unusual plan it is difficult to compare with others (diagram 2c). It achieves a larger interior space and height than any of its predecessors by adding a bay on each side, to reach a length of nearly twenty-two metres. In its interior the Lad Khan makes use of a pair of pillar types unique to it and the Jambulinga, which seems to link it also to the period of around 700.[55]

A consideration of the Durga temple's layout reveals refinements on the pattern of expansion used in the Lad Khan. What we see in the Durga temple is a large-scale *mandapa*-temple that has been expanded by the addition of an open veranda on all sides. Both the 'inner temple' and its porch are a bay longer than usual. Together they extend to over nineteen metres. By adding the gallery and the embedded regal stairway the full structure is extended to over twenty-six metres. The Durga temple is the only early Chalukya temple with two internal ambulatories, and the largest Chalukya temple before the end of Vijayaditya's reign.

The Galaganatha temple at Pattadakal, and several of its cognates at Alampur, have unusually extended platforms that may have been intended to carry surrounding colonnades, though nothing above their platforms remains. Since all these stone temples were intended to be completed with elements and accoutrements in ephemeral materials—such as plaster and paint on sculpture, and banana tree and mango leaf *toranas* applied to doorways—temporary wood or brick galleries are not out of the question here. The stone skeleton of the Galaganatha is roughly twenty-seven metres in length; with its platform it would be thirty.[56]

An interesting late attempt to extend a temple through the addition of elements is found in the Papanatha at Pattadakal, a structure begun before the Durga temple and finished after it. In the Papanatha we see a large-scale *mandapa*-temple of Vijayaditya's reign, with measurements similar to the Durga's 'inner temple' extended during the following reign by

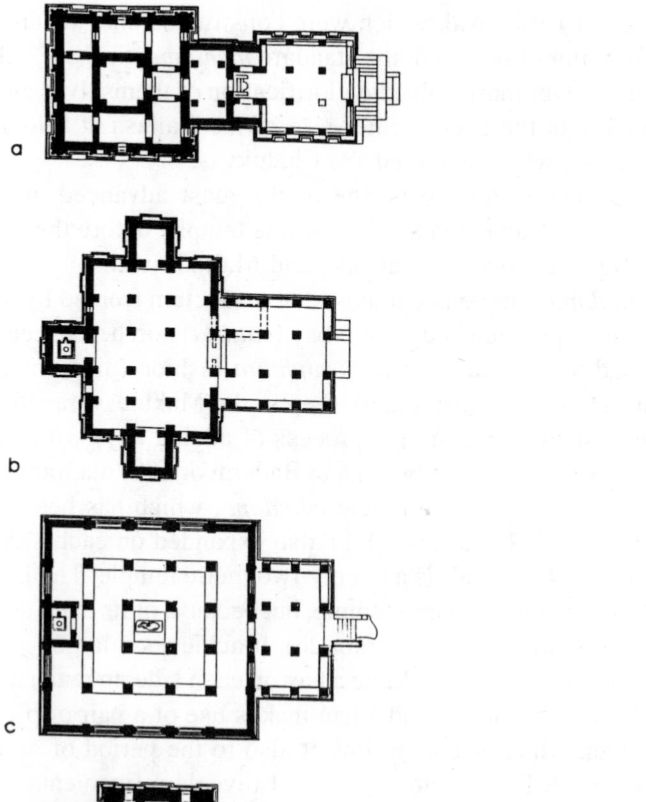

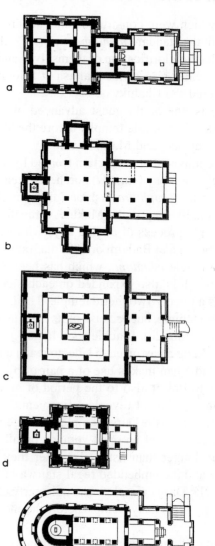

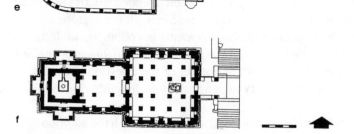

Diagram 2: Early Chalukya plans to scale, after Michell: (a) Meguti, (b) Jambulinga, (c) Lad Khan, (d) Malegitti, (e) Durga temple, (f) Papanatha, and (g) Virupaksa.

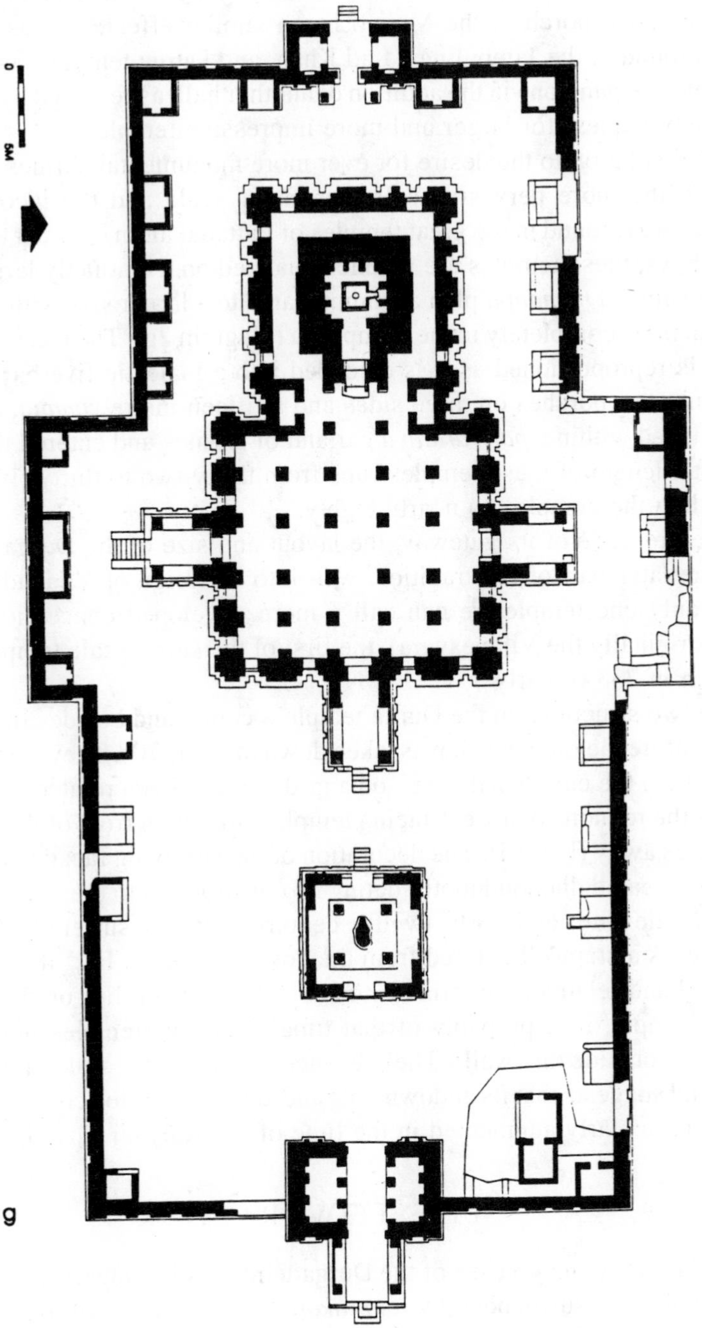

g

Diagram 2 (*cont.*)

the addition of a second *mandapa* to attain a total length of twenty-eight metres (p. 68, diagram 2f). The added porch of the Meguṭi has a similar effect. Just as growth by the addition of bays found in the Jambulinga, Lad Khan, and Durga temple was not satisfying enough, neither was expansion via the addition of another hall, as revealed by the next major step in the dynasty's quest for larger and more impressive temples.

The eventual solution to the desire for ever more monumental shrines seems to have been achieved in the more pervasive enlargement of scale and the incorporation of a courtyard and gateway, found in the great temples of Pattadakal. In contrast to the rudimentary addition of bays, these temples are reconceptualized on a distinctly larger scale, with a significantly revamped *mandapa* plan accommodated to a larger size with a more unified aesthetic, as seen most completely in the Virupaksa (diagram 2g). The usual three-bay, ten-metre *mandapa* is reproportioned as it is extended into a majestic five-bay twenty-metre *mandapa* with entrance porches on three sides and a fifteen-metre *vimana*, all surrounded by a courtyard closed within a *parivaralaya* garland of shrines and entered through a great gateway. The total length of these temples runs from thirty-two to thirty-five metres, in a courtyard extending the complex to nearly eighty.

As with the presence of its gateway, the layout and size of the Durga temple locate its creation in the later part of the tradition, well into the reign of Vijayaditya, who was responsible for only one temple we can call a more developed conception. That is the Sangamesvara (originally the Vijayesvara), the first of the super-scale temples, left unfinished at his death in 733 or early 734.

There were two structures in the Durga temple's compound besides the temple itself and its gateway, before the rubble wall was taken down in the 1970s. They were both created a good deal later than the early Chalukyas, on a grid that has been rotated by about twenty degrees.[57] One is the remains of a west-facing temple, directly in front of the Durga temple about fifteen metres away (Fig. 85). The decoration of the surviving facade of this structure is composed of a repeated diamond motif, dating its construction to the time of the Kalyani Chalukyas, of the eleventh and early twelfth centuries. It has suffered a good deal of damage. The other is a stepwell entered from the north (visible in Fig. 48). It was created out of undecorated and relatively unrefined stone blocks. Since it lies on the same rotated grid as the later temple, it is probably of that time. (The two temples numbered 19 on Cousens' plan were outside this wall.) The presence of these later structures in the Durga temple's compound suggests that its endowments and active operation continued for several centuries, being particularly augmented in the time of the Kalyani Chalukyas.

THE TOWER

From a distance the first thing you see of the Durga temple is its Nagara *sikhara*. This was true when the temple was surrounded by its *prakara* wall and it is still true, whether you come on it from the village to the south or from across the fields. First you see the crystalline geometry of the tower, now ragged at the top, and then its dramatic transition to the curves of the hall (Fig. 49).

There are five distinct substyles among the early Chalukya's Nagara (or 'northern') style *sikhara*. Each is a variation on the *latina* tower: a single spire with an essentially square plan, composed of a vertical piling of miniature stories curving in at the top, where they are capped by the cogged-wheel of the *amalaka* and a *kalasa* vase. Damaged though it is, the style of the Durga temple's tower reveals a quite specific provenance within the geography and chronology of early Chalukya traditions.

The most familiar of the five varieties is what we may call Karnatak Nagara, seen on the Huccimalli-gudi at Aihole (Fig. 47), the Sangamesvara temple at Mahakuta (diagram 3a)[58] and Papanatha temple at Pattadakal. This seems to be the earliest and most common Nagara type found at the dynasty's Karnatak sites and standard on their large-scale temples at Aihole. The key formal characteristic of the Karnatak Nagara is its clear articulation into broadly discrete horizontal and vertical divisions. Horizontally it has nine clearly distinct *khanda* (layers),[59] with relief decoration in discrete units at the centre and corner of each side. Structurally each of these units is a separate stone block. Vertically this decoration appears as three raised *lata* (ribs), called *venukosa* at the corners and *madhyalata* at the centre. The *madhyalata* is wider and more prominently projected over the *bhadra* offset in the sanctum wall below. It carries a *surasena* motif (an arch flanked by half-arches), repeated at each level. Symbolically it serves as a crown to the *bhadra*. The *venukosa* are gathered in three-layer combinations, two of repeating *surasena* topped by one with a *bhumi* or *karna amalaka* (a relief depiction of the cogged wheel that caps the whole tower). The combination represents a miniature tower, so that each full *sikhara* is composed of three *bhumi* (stories) of miniature *sikhara*.[60] At the top are one or two continuous mouldings that run above the *lata* and unify the whole.[61] On the front of the tower is a large circular *nasika* medallion displaying an image of the god found within the temple (e.g., Fig. 47).

The second Nagara style found among the early Chalukya monuments is a highly schematic form seen in the Aihole's Mallikarjuna[62] and Galaganatha[63] (p. 72, diagram 3b). It is also found among the smaller temples at Mahakuta and Bhadranayika Jalihal.[64] This is an abridged version of the Nagara, maintaining the silhouette and *khanda* levels that underlie the more elaborate standard forms, but replacing the richly varied articulation of arches and *amalaka* with repeated layers of continuous *kapota* mouldings. Its layers are usually stacked, as they are here, with intervening courses of miniature pilasters, though sometimes these are omitted.[65] The representation is the same in either case, storey upon storey of dormered roofs, but the poetic richness of the miniature towers and the more elaborate detailing is lost. Though many writers have missed the Nagara essence of these towers, the gentle curve of vertical silhouette and culmination in the *amalaka* are unmistakable. The regular association with *purnaghata* pilasters, Nagara *udgama* pediments, and *bhadra* offsets as well as the existence of *bhumi amalaka* on some examples such as the Galaganatha confirm this identification. Ramachandran and Gravely called this the Kadamba Nagara, following Moreas' belief that its simplicity marked it as the style of the dynasty that preceded the Chalukyas in Karnataka.[66] But, since the earliest examples seem clearly to be Chalukya, and they occur later than the Karnatak Nagara, that is misleading. Dhaky and Meister propose to call it *Phamsana*.[67] I would call it the *rucaka*, or 'plain' Nagara. This

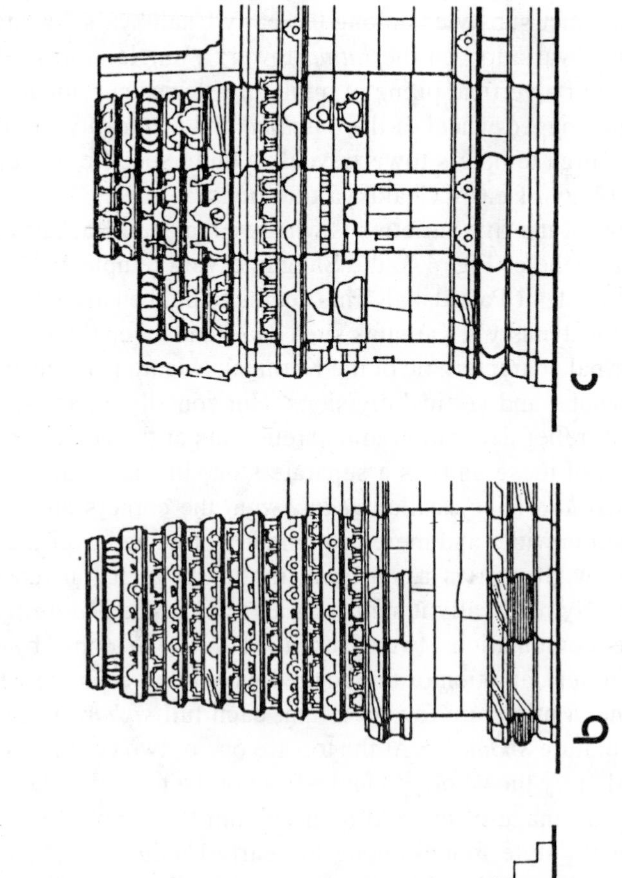

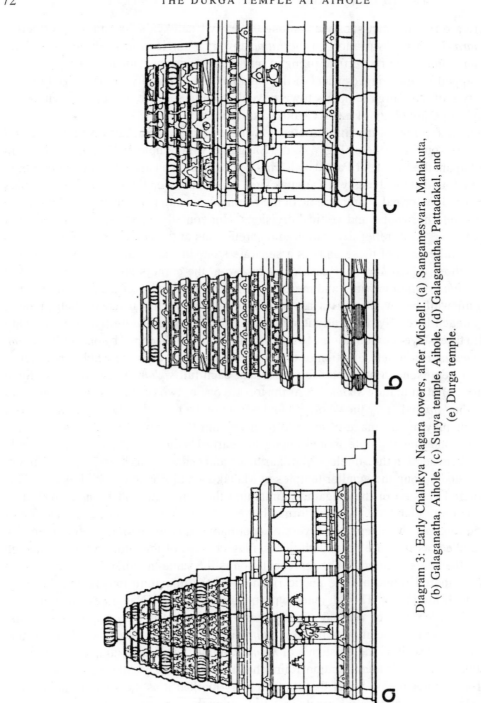

Diagram 3: Early Chalukya Nagara towers, after Michell: (a) Sangamesvara, Mahakuta, (b) Galaganatha, Aihole, (c) Surya temple, Aihole, (d) Galaganatha, Pattadakal, and (e) Durga temple.

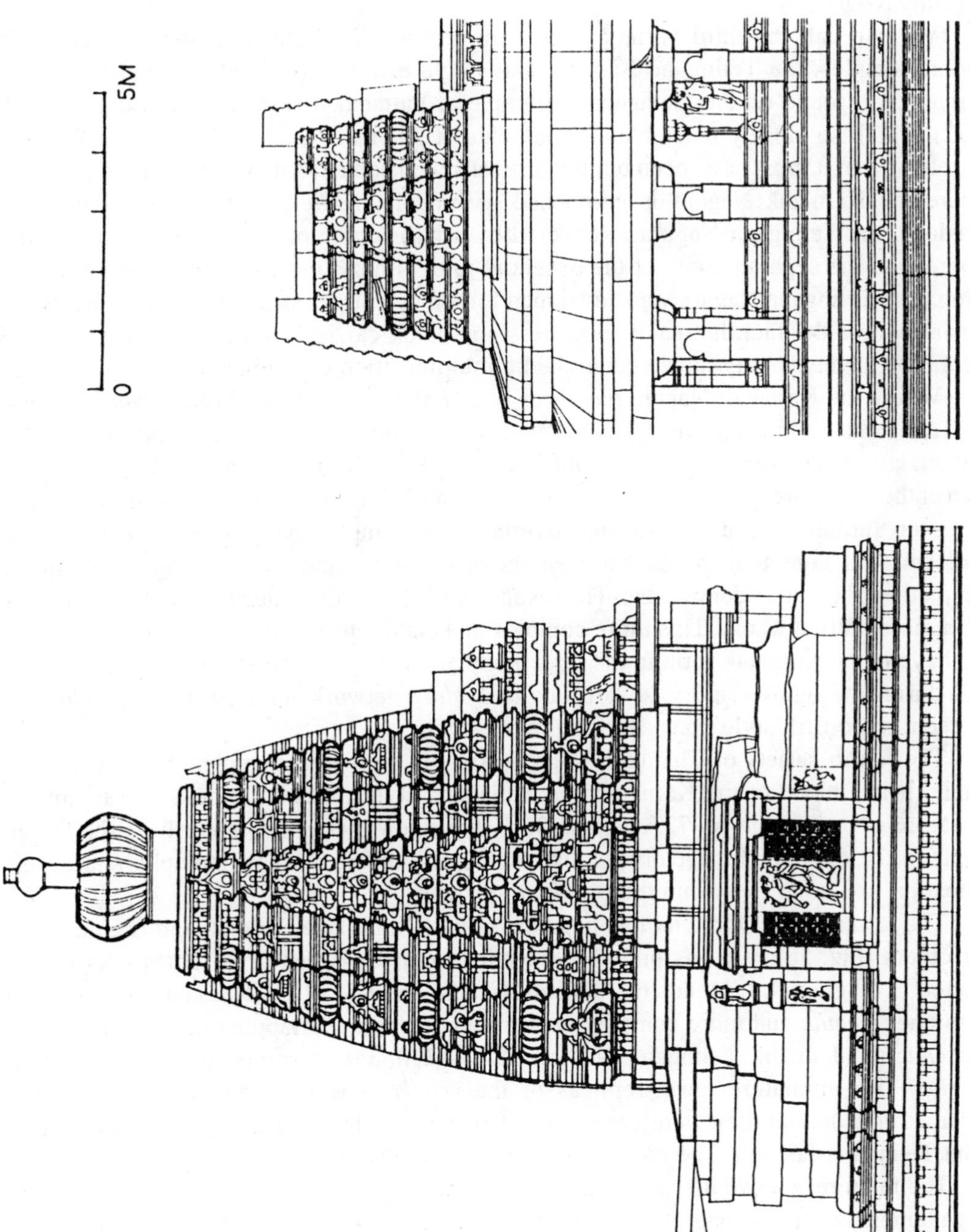

Diagram 3 (*cont.*)

form is also found in the Chalukya's Andhra sites, such as Mahanandi, Kadamara Kalava and Satyavolu.[68]

We can call the third variety of Nagara *sikhara*, characteristic of the Chalukya's Andhra temples, the Telingana Nagara. The single example of the Telingana Nagara in Karnataka is found on the Galaganatha temple at Pattadakal (Fig. 103, and diagram 3d, p. 72), which so closely resembles the temples of Alampur, such as the Svarga Brahma (Fig. 104), that it must have been built by artisans who came from that site for the purpose. Where the Karnatak Nagara is composed of broadly discrete, horizontal and vertical divisions, the Telingana Nagara is covered by a burgeoning of decorative elements that subordinate the separate units of the essential grid within a more diffused web of articulation. The Telingana Nagara was developed for a much larger structure than the Karnatak Nagara, where the fact that each separate stone block carries a separate combination of decorative elements may have encouraged a multiplication of elements.

Where the Karnatak Nagara has three *bhumi*, depicted on nine broad *khanda* layers, the Telingana Nagara has four *bhumi*[69] crossing some twenty narrow, and not always distinct, layers. The *surasena* of the *madhyalata* band overlap across pairs of *khanda* layers. Each of the miniature corner temples is composed of five differing layers, whose *candrasala* go a step further to interconnect and overlap in a complex pattern below each *bhumi amalaka*. And here the spaces between the *madhyalata* and *venukosa* are sometimes occupied by decorative details also. The result is a rich network of decoration that coalesces into a more unified whole. This more complex and elaborate Telingana design is a distinct step beyond the Karnatak form in the direction that the Nagara was developing throughout India during the eighth century, toward a unified *jalaka* network of interweaving *candrasala* (as seen in the fifth style considered below).

The fourth variety of Chalukya Nagara exists in only two examples, both of them at Aihole. It is a blend of the Karnatak and Telingana styles, found on the Surya temple in the centre of the village (p. 72, diagram 3c)[70] and a few metres to its north on the Durga temple (p. 72, diagram 3e). Otherwise distinct in every detail, these two temples share their dedication to a solar deity and their *sikhara* designs.

The tower of the Durga temple has nine of its *khanda* layers intact, and fragments of four others (Fig. 56).[71] It was probably intended to have sixteen or seventeen, as reconstructed in diagram 4. It blends the discrete *khanda* and *lata* of the Karnatak Nagara with the thinner *khanda* and more complex interconnection and overlapping of *candrasala* and *surasena* found in the Telingana Nagara. Its *madhyalata* is composed of overlapping *surasena*. The miniature tower-replicas of the *venukosa* were three in number, in the Karnatak fashion, but they were composed of five interconnected and differentiated units in the Telingana fashion. The correct five-unit assembly can be seen on the rear.

The main reason we do not see the characteristic curve of the Nagara *sikhara* on the Durga temple is that its upper courses have been lost. It is only in the upper third of a tower that the curve is clearly manifested.[72] Here that would be above the second *bhumi amalaka*.

An arched emplacement for a *nasika* can be seen on the tower's eastern face (Fig. 55). The medallion itself is probably the unfinished fragment, showing a figure from the hips

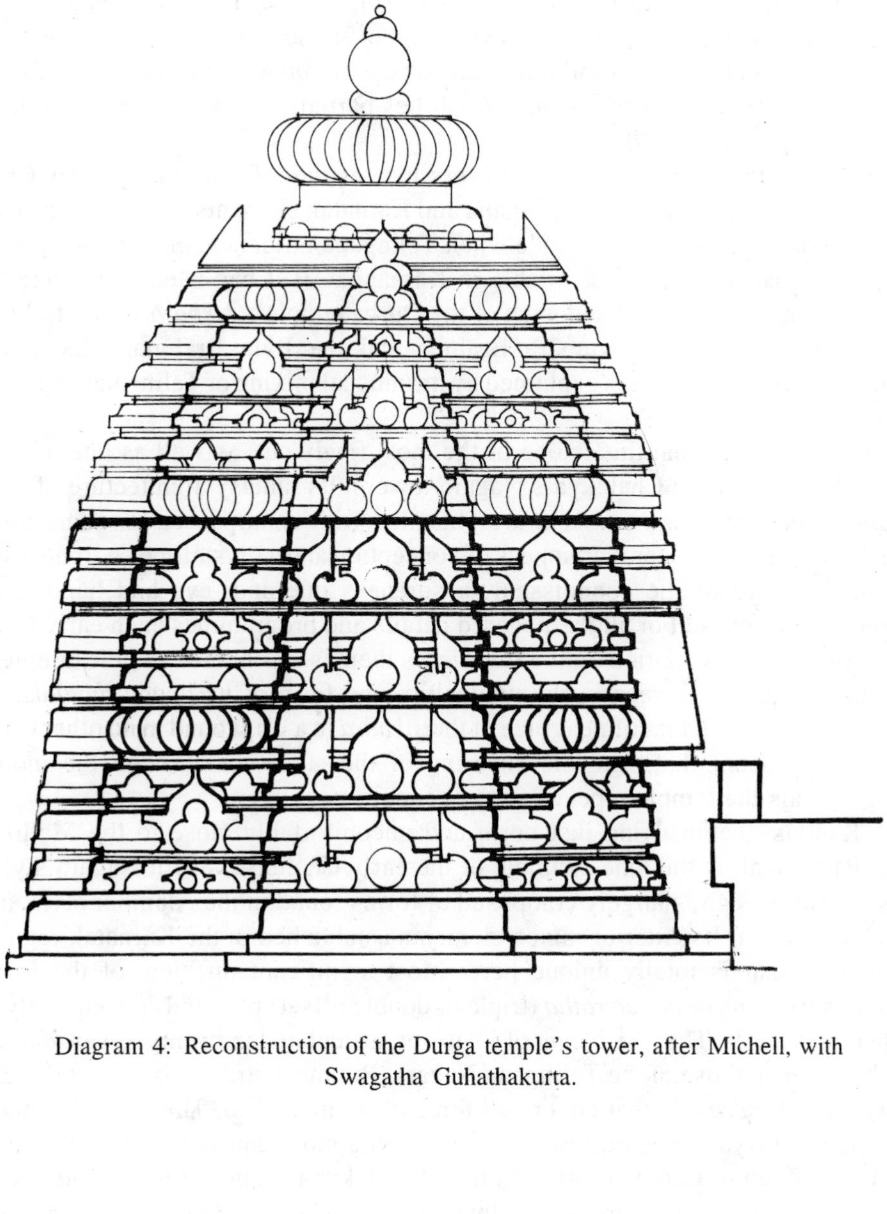

Diagram 4: Reconstruction of the Durga temple's tower, after Michell, with Swagatha Guhathakurta.

up (Fig. 54), which was found in the courtyard (Fig. 11). It has its arms splayed with matching attributes, like those in the medallions over the gateway.[73] Relatively similar figures are found on the rear of the miniature shrine atop the Lad Khan and in the *nasika* of the Surya temple. The tower's *amalaka* still lies partially buried where it has been cast on the south (Figs 15 and 49).

The style of the Durga and Surya towers locates them firmly in the early Chalukya tradition. Their unique blending of Telingana and Karnatak elements situates them at a point in the development of the dynastic style when Telingana influence, most likely in the form of artists from that region, was available in Karnataka. If it had been constructed in the Telingana region, at Alampur, the design of the Durga temple's *sikhara* would fall conceptually between those of the Kumara Brahma and the Bala Brahma.[74] Its somewhat anachronistic appearance here is explained by its unusual mixing of Telingana and Karnatak elements.

It should be noted that this is one of the most finely cut, as well as one of the most complexly designed of the Chalukya's Nagara towers. Its fantasy architecture of differentiated *candrasala* and *bhumi amalaka* are chiselled with unsurpassed care and precision (Fig. 56). Up close can be seen a crispness of conception and a crystalline sharpness of edge that catches the eye of the connoisseur, a sureness of mind, eye and hand that it is impossible not to admire. For all their shared details and programmes each early Chalukya temple is unique in its variation on the tradition's themes. A characteristic example of the Durga temple's quality is seen in the uniquely round form of its *bhumi amalaka*, which contrast and transcend the rectilinear face of the *sikhara* in a way found in no other Chalukya temples. It is a detail that, like the shearing of the stairways through the mouldings basement, reveals the temple's peculiar eloquence.

The Kasivisvanatha, lying just north and uncomfortably close to the Mallikarjuna temple at Pattadakal, is the lone example of the early Chalukya's fifth Nagara style (Fig. 36).[75] Its interior design is largely composed of forms found in the Alampur style, as seen in the Visva Brahma. Its exterior mixes elements established in the Karnatak region with a Nagara form that is totally unique here. Most significant, in view of the foregoing discussion, is its *sapta* or *panca ratha* (triple or double offset) plan and consequently triple-to-double offset tower. The five *bhumi* of its tower, articulated in twenty-seven *khanda*, are more elaborate than those of the Telingana Nagara. But most striking is the *jalaka* network of interweaving *candrasala* that covers all three of its inner *lata*. This is undoubtedly the latest of the Chalukya's Nagara tower styles and the most unusual. Unlike the temple's interior it is difficult to find its roots within the Chalukya tradition. And indeed, its source is more likely found in western India, in traditions related to those found at Roda or Ossian.[76] We know that Chalukya vassals such as Jayasraya Mangalaraja and his younger brother Sryasraya ruled in sections of Gujarat.[77] Exactly how architectural patterns, so closely related to western India, came to appear at the Chalukya's royal capital is not clear. It is not beyond the realm of possibility, however, that artists were sent (or called) to Pattadakal by these regional feudatories desiring to share in the glory of their liege as did those of Alampur on the east.

For modern observers, the Durga temple's uniquely fascinating aspect has been its seemingly inexplicable combination of a square tower and a round hall. No one since Cousens has failed to notice it, and few have failed to base their essential interpretation of the temple upon its signal deviation from common expectation. This is as true for the history text used today in the public schools of Bijapur, seventy miles away, as it was for the professor of European Renaissance art history teaching in Des Moines, Iowa, who took a course in Indian culture as a graduate student in the United States.[78] The Victorian vision of India as a place seen from Bombay through the sights of Thana Ghat, judging all by what was available and convenient to the first antiquarians, has left its legacy for all of us. It is this that led Brown, Soundara Rajan and so many others to question the tower's appropriateness to the structure's original conception.

Unusual as the feature is in the whole of South Asia, within the local Chalukya tradition it is less so. Three of the four known apsidal Chalukya temples were in this region. And all three, the one at Cikka Mahakuta, the Durga temple, and the ruined temple in the Cekki group, seem to have had Nagara towers. The *sikhara* is missing at Cikka Mahakuta, but the modified square of its *bhadra-ratha* base is fit for a Nagara tower (Fig. 40), and the temple's sanctum doorway with its *amalaka* detailing is clearly northern (Fig. 93). The ruined temple in the Cekki group is survived by little more than its neatly finished basement of *jagati* and *khura-kumbha* courses. But these fragments include pillars with *talapatra* corbels, plus *sikhara* elements of *surasena*, *amalaka* and *bhumi amalaka* belonging to the Chalukya's Nagara styles (Fig. 94).

Though the Durga temple's rectilinear tower does not fit as comfortably as one might expect on the curving outline of temple's roof, it is set there quite as neatly as any other tower in the tradition at Aihole. There is no hint of alteration from another design, or lack of planning. So as George Michell, the architect who measured and drew almost every early Chalukya temple, has said, 'Though awkwardly placed on the apsidal-ended roof, [it] appears to be original.'[79] To which I would add: it also fits well within the tastes and standards of this tradition. There is no reason, apart from it being a unique combination for the early Chalukyas, to suggest that it is inappropriate. Rather it is a striking example of the mixing of styles—Nagara and Dravida, Telingana and Karnatak—that is a hallmark of early Chalukya tradition,[80] and as we shall see, a particular penchant of the designers of this temple.

The towers of the Aihole temples are generally built as discrete physical entities over flat ceilings, without any interlocking stones that could prove them integral. Indeed, a good number have lost their towers, though their surviving decoration implies their former existence.[81] Consequently the flatness of a roof is no proof that any temple lacked a tower. On the contrary, there is remarkably consistent evidence in the record that there never was a flat-roofed temple style, here or anywhere else, and that the temples that appear towerless today are all actually structures whose original towers have been lost.[82]

There are other problems with the charge that the Durga temple's *sikhara* is inappropriate: first, the presumption that the tower is wrong, and second, the fairly outlandish proposition that recent Western observers are wise enough to recognize this while those who put it there were not. Though the suggestion of a gross aesthetic mistake may have seemed plausible to those who thought of it as a primitive, early attempt at a temple tower or a recent restorer's transfer from another structure, neither of these propositions has proved to be true. Now that we know it to be a mature example of the best early Chalukya workmanship on a carefully conceived monument, we have to assume that it was the conscious choice made by legitimate *acarya* and *sthapati* designers. To call it wrong now is to presume, with remarkable arrogance, that the legitimate practitioners lacked the aesthetic or ritual understanding available to the later critics. The most we can say in this regard, as with the tower's mixing of Telingana and Karnataka styles, is that it was an aesthetic choice more or less unique to the early Chalukyas, and one that did not suit the taste of later designers.

Few serious scholars support Cunningham's theory today. The careful depiction of temple towers throughout the Durga temple's narrative and decorative schemes indicates well enough that its designers knew about such things (e.g., Figs 68 and 75). Neither here nor among any of the known depictions of temples in India's vast store of visual imagery are there any temples shown without towers.[83] As surely as the temple's broken Nagara tower required upper courses and the *amalaka* that now lies on the ground beside it, so the temple's body required a tower. And just as surely, what we see today are the remains of a *sikhara* that was uniquely original in its conception and brilliant in the quality of its execution.

And, it is now time to add—since the reader of this essay has had the opportunity to see the tower in greater detail than usual, and to separate what it is from earlier stereotypes—this really is quite a nice combination of forms. Turn to plates of the tower (Figs 55 and 56) and its situation on the temple (Figs 48 and 49). As the round geometry of the *bhumi amalaka* contrasts elegantly with the angularity of the tower's outline so the tower's rectilinearity plays a satisfying staccato against the slow curve of the temple's west end. It will not be too far into the future when those not introduced to the tower as a mistake will see it for the successful originality that it displays.

THE BASEMENT

The Durga temple's basement or *adhisthana* is one of its most analytically accessible aspects. It is composed of a series of discrete mouldings, traceable in other structures in relatively clear variations on a limited set of alternatives. There are six key, dateable temples at the Chalukya's Karnatak sites, and the basements of these buildings form a consistently developing series (p. 79, diagram 5). Though most temples throughout the early Chalukya tradition had basements composed of a standard set of four courses, the more lavish temples grew by addition and elaboration of courses from the four-element combination found in the great Vaishnava cave of 578 to the seven-element combination of the Virupaksa, with only the abbreviated platform of Badami's Jambulinga failing to increase beyond its predecessors. The sequence offers progressive refinements that allow us to locate the Durga temple's basement with some clarity.

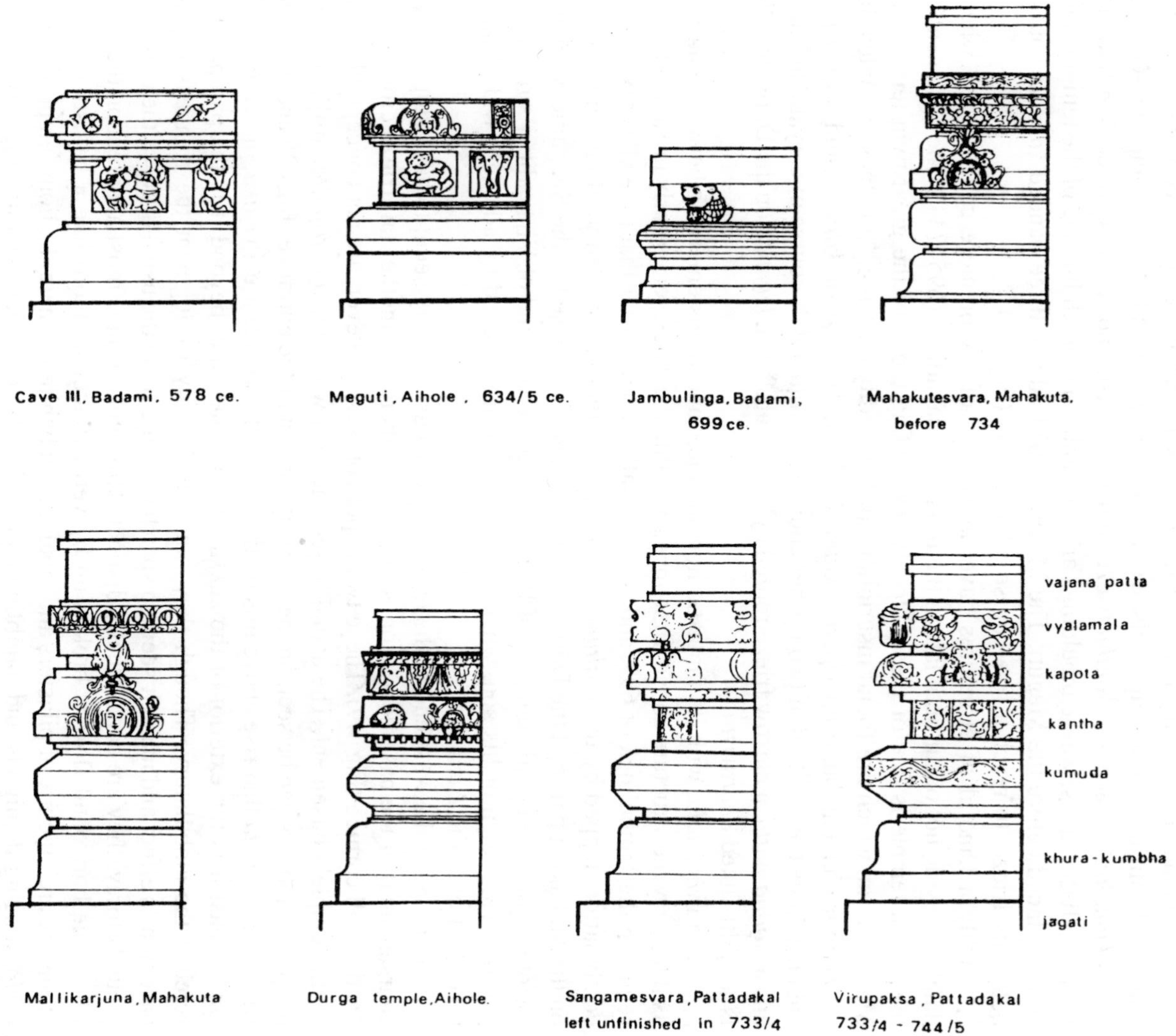

Diagram 5: Early Chalukya basements, after the *Encyclopaedia of Indian Temple Architecture*.

The standard *adhisthana* of the Chalukya's Karnatak region is composed of four courses. From the ground upwards we see a plain *jagati* (plinth), a compound-curving *khura-kumbha*,[84] a recessed *kantha* frieze, and a quarter-round *kapota* cornice. We find this form on all the caves, where mouldings are traceable, and on all but one of the temples that can be placed before the Meguṭi. The Meguṭi of 634 adds a three-banded *kumuda* course below its frieze, to reach a five-course combination (Fig. 86).[85]

Only a handful of structures have *adhisthana* of six or more courses, and where datable they do not occur until late in the reign of Vijayaditya (695–734). The basement of the Durga temple is one of these, closely resembling those of the great twin temples at Mahakuta, on which are found inscriptions of Vijayaditya's reign.[86] On these temples the usual four-element build-up (*jagati*, *khura-kumbha*, *kumuda* or *kantha*, and *kapota*) is augmented by the addition of two further courses: a *vyalamala*[87] course of caryatid animals and a *vajana-patta*, a narrow frieze roofed by a flat slab.[88] The *kumuda* on the Durga temple is a multi-fluted *dharavrtta*.

The *vyalamala*, with its fantastic lion and elephant torsos emerging between courses as if to carry the structure above, first appears within the dated series early in Vijayaditya's reign, on the Jambulinga of 699, and is universally popular after that time. The six-course combination, topped by the *vyalamala* and *vajana-patta*, is not seen until late in the reign on the Mahakuta pair and the Durga temple. It is only surpassed in the Sangamesvara and the other two super-scale temples of Pattadakal, at the very end of Vijayaditya's reign and the following reign of his son, when seven courses are reached by adding a wide *kantha* (necking) over the *kumuda*.[89]

Looking at the west end of the temple this discussion may seem to have stopped two courses short of the basement's top, since we see there yet another tall frieze crowned by another roll cornice (Fig. 49). These two upper courses, however, are not conceptually part of the temple's basement. The actual basement ends with the *vajana-patta*, at the level of the porch floor, as can be seen on the stairway-screen of the entrance (Figs 25 and 57). The *kantha* and *kapota* that rise above this on the rest of the facade are a *vedika*, or screen wall. On the east it is the exterior of the *kaksasana* benches, and beyond it is the parapet that screens the ambulatory. Though they function visually to augment the richness of the basement's effect and make it seem to span half, rather than the usual third, of the temple's ground storey, they are conceptually distinct. This separation is most apparent on the east, where the horizontal flow is broken up by vertical accents more like a balustrade, in a miniature architecture of pilasters and mouldings inhabited by heraldic lions, elephants, and *vyala*, lunging demigods and gambling *bhuta* (dwarfs) of superb quality (Fig. 59).

The 'Sri Jinalayan' inscription (Fig. 6) is located on the *kapota* directly opposite the entrance gateway (Fig. 50). Ending with an 'n' as it does, it may be most reasonably interpreted as a personal name, not a description of the temple. Growing agreement now holds it to be the name of one of the structure's master artists.[90] The same name occurs on the Parvati temple at Sandur, on a pilaster flanking its entrance. Unaccountably no one who has written on the temple at Sandur has found much in common between the two structures.[91]

Like a significant number of the larger early Chalukya temples, the Durga is not entered directly by a stairway on its longitudinal axis, running straight towards the god on the altar of the inner sanctum. Instead it is approached by lateral staircases, set into the platform on the east. This means that worshippers need not face directly towards the deity before they have completed a circumambulation, and that they need not turn away from it before they depart. A detail reinforcing the idea that a circumambulation of this temple was encouraged comes from the great lion that stood by the southern stairway (Figs 2 and 58).[92] This life-sized beast is posed in a heraldic stance, with its head turned to the side and one paw raised on the back of a miniature elephant, in a manner that gained great popularity in later times as the animal-half of the cognizance of the Hoysalas and other dynasties. From the *pratoli* passage the lion, with his somewhat averted gaze, visually blocks the approach to the stairway (diagram 1). Being sculpture it cannot force anyone to turn the other way, but the psychological effect of its imagery and position encourages that course, as do other details I will discuss below.

The embedding of the staircases within the *adhisthana* creates a situation found nowhere else in India, to my knowledge, and the *sthapati* used it well: shearing the lower mouldings in a way that accents the continuous flow of the courses at the same time as it cuts through them.[93] The lower four mouldings are cleanly sliced through, as if by a single stroke, leaving a flat plane where a section of the basement seems to have been removed (Fig. 57). This provides at once an elegant display of the *sthapati*'s technical finesse and an accented change of psychological as well as physical attitude upon the worshipper, who cuts through the basement to rise up the stairs to the level of the platform. The upper courses break the plane of this cut to run above the stairs on both sides. The *vyalamala* here is turned into a *kapota* above the stairs.[94] Abbreviated versions of the temple's main patronage inscription are repeated below this *kapota* on both the left and right walls of the stairway on the south. This is where worshippers would see them as they left the temple, in the direction of the gateway, where the full announcement of Komarasinga's patronage and Vikramaditya II's donation is displayed.[95]

THE COLONNADE

Between the tower and the *adhisthana* runs the colonnade of the temple's surrounding ambulatory. The spartan repetition of plain, square pillars that dominate the colonnade on the west has been used to put a stamp of underdevelopment on our historical vision of the temple's exterior (Fig. 15). But this is not the whole story. There are, as we shall see, only one of the four pillar types found on the temple, and their apparent austerity may be better understood when we realize their function as a foil for the decorative splendour added to the pillars on the eastern facade. Even so, these pillars are not totally plain; their shafts bear the dynasty's typical raised rectangular bosses and three-quarter rondels, and carry bracket capitals. Painted, as they most likely once were, the bosses probably produced a much more decorative effect.

The integration of these pillars into the architecture of the gallery is significant. Unlike most previous Chalukya porches, the Durga temple's was intended from the start to have *kaksasana* benches on its periphery. As standard up to this time, the pillars stand on the porch floor between separate lengths of *kaksasana* or *vedika* parapet. But unlike the porch pillars of the Meguṭi (Fig. 86) and the Huccimalli-gudi (Fig. 47), whose pillars bear no particular relation to the *kaksasana* later inserted between and around them, the Durga temple's pillars carry bands of the *kapota* moulding matched to those found on the backs of the *kaksasana*, tying the two elements together in a unity that reinforces the horizontal continuity of the base.

From the front the Durga is quite a different temple than the severe assembly of blocks seen from the west (Fig. 49). On the entrance facade the rhythmically piled basement and ceiling courses frame a gallery of three dozen, nearly life-sized figures, over a rippling dado of deities, scrambling dwarfs and leaping animals (Fig. 57).

Emerging from the gateway worshippers meet the temple at the point where the colonnade divides, figure pillars to the right and plain shafts running toward the apse (p. 83, diagram 6). To do the ritual *pradaksina* (circumambulation), they would turn left to circle around the deserted colonnade with the temple on their right (Fig. 49) before they reached the densely populated gallery of the entrance (Fig. 62). All twelve pillars on the west of the facade carry figure sculpture, most of them loving couples in three-quarter relief.

The handsome couple facing out from the pillar to the right of the entrance is typical enough of the style (Fig. 65, located at 12 on diagram 6). Unlike James Harle, who sees this pair exemplifying an imported northern style,[96] I see it as representing an evolving local tradition, produced by a particular master or workshop, whose work can be traced on a number of structures. On the Durga temple this work is found throughout the north side of the porch (Fig. 60). The style includes a regular appearance of buttressing attendant figures and sheltering trees acting as canopies. It contrasts with the more slender, oval-faced, style of the *mithuna* on the south of the porch, that employ neither attendants below nor trees above (Fig. 59). (In Karnataka it was common practice to divide work on temples in this manner, with different masters on different sides).[97]

The figure-bearing pillars decorating the entrance porch are a feature shared by many eighth-century Chalukya temples, but unknown in the monuments before the reign of Vijayaditya. They appear only after the Jambulinga of 699, and they undergo a quite clear development. They are first seen on Chalukya temples in Karnataka in the static *mithuna* couples, which appear on the porch pillars of the Naganatha at Nagaral (Fig. 95),[98] and then on the Lad Khan (Fig. 96).[99] The pillar figures of Lad Khan's porch are cut in a somewhat higher relief and a more fully realized style than those of the Naganatha. Though still attuned to the planar surface of the block they show figures moving gracefully in space with carefully measured foreshortenings. The work we see in the *mithuna* of the Sarangi-math (Figs 88 and 97) could easily be later work from the same workshop. The sculpture of the Sarangi-math masters is more plastic and free of the pillar than that found earlier, but the usual—if not universal—use of the overhanging tree and buttressing figures is similar. The Durga temple's pillar figures are very likely by the same hands. All these sets of figure pillars are located on open porches. As we have already seen, those of the Sarangi-math and the Durga temple are closely related by their lateral stairway arrangements.

The sculptural style and decoration of these figures on the Lad Khan and the Durga

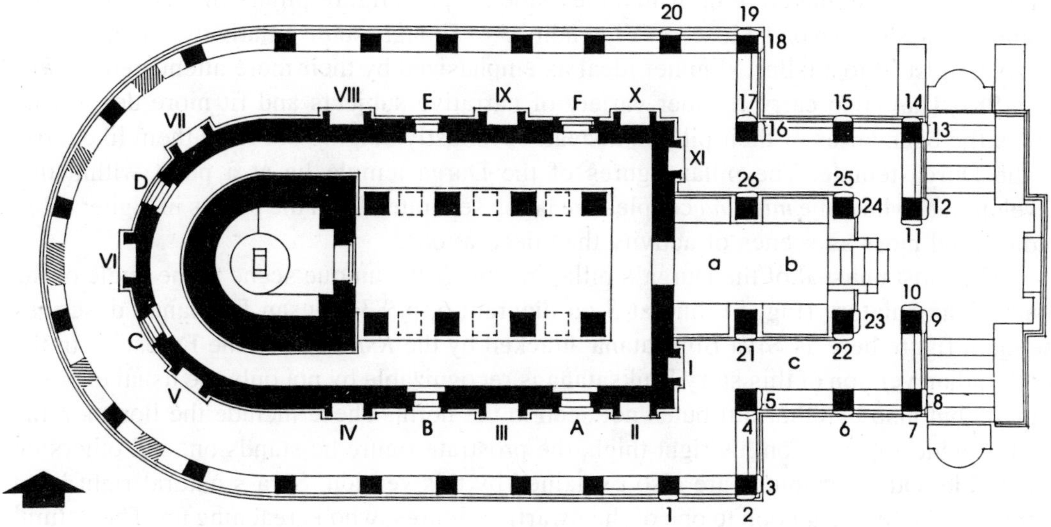

Diagram 6: Guide to the imagery of the Durga temple, after Michell 23.

Pillar Figures

1 Mithuna under a tree, with child (u)*
2 Mithuna under arching tree, snout-faced female with child
3 Urdhavalinga Siva - Surya
4 Mithuna, babe in arms
5 Mithuna, tweeking
6 Mithuna, faceless
7 Mithuna, Asvamukhi noosing a shaven-headed(?) male
8 Mithuna, legs entwined
9 Mithuna, female pulling back a Brahmachari(?)'s head
10 Dvarapala with Chastisement of Chaya
11 Dvarapala
12 Handsome Mithuna
13 Mithuna (u)
14 Mithuna under a tree leaning on a child
15 Mithuna under a palm (?)
16 Mithuna under a tree, female with a broken face
17 Mithuna under a mango tree
18 Mithuna with child, she throwing out her hip, lower faces broken
19 Mithuna under arching tree with a child (worn)
20 Mithuna (much worn) with a child
21 Mithuna, her face and his leg broken
22 Mithuna, she collapsing drunk
23 Narasimha disembowelling Hiranyaksipu
24 Ardhanari Siva
25 Mithuna with pearls
26 Mithuna catching pearls

Major Niches and Figures

I (empty)
II (empty)
III Siva Vrsavahana
IV Narasimha
V Garudavahana Vishnu
VI (empty)
VII (empty)
VIII Varaha
IX Mahisasuramardini
X Harihara
XI (empty)

Ceilings

a Nagaraja
b Matsyacakra
c Gandharva-Apsaras

Windows

A Nandyavarta
B Diagonal Lattice
C Lotus Cakra
D Petal Cakra
E Grid Lattice
F Grid Lattice

(The twc unfinished figures standing in the rear of the colonnade, and the three accompanying slabs alternating with the finished columns, are all structural additions to the original concept.)
* (u) significantly unfinished

temple led Harle to date them to the eighth century, even when he had trouble accepting that date for the architecture on which they stood.[100] The figure-pillars of Vikramaditya's reign take a step beyond those of Vijayaditya's. Though some relatively squat figures survive, most fit to a taller, slimmer ideal as emphasized by their more attenuated crowns (Fig. 98). They also carry a wider variety of narrative subjects and fit more decorously within the boundaries of their pillars, instead of robustly bulging out from them like those of the Durga temple. The pillar figures of the Durga temple lie at a point within this development where the *mithuna* couples are being separated from the pillars in higher relief and offered more as scenes of activity than decorations.

The most unusual of the Durga's pillar images is the unique scene at the angle of the southern ambulatory (Fig. 51, and at 3 on diagram 6, p. 83). Susan Buchanan describes the main figure here as Siva Bhiksatana attacked by the *Rsis* of the Pine Forest.[101] In the south Indian version of this story Bhiksatana is recognizable by not only the usual exposed genitals but also by other attributes not seen in the north. These include the lion skin the head of which appears on his right thigh, the prostrate figure he stands on, and others on either side. Other attributes are also explained by this version. Siva's natural right hand seems to be granting a boon to one of the dwarfish figures, who is reaching up. The natural left seems to hold a *kamandalu*, water jug. The two upper arms end in symmetrical masses that could be an axe and a snake. A pair of *bhuta* seem to be flying behind these. I think I also see a fifth arm on the proper right and attributes I cannot read on the left. The small figure lunging to the lower left complements the one who seems to be accepting the boon. The God wears head jewellery so full it appears to be a crown, rather than the ascetic Siva's usual pile of matted locks. This is quite an unusual Bhiksatana from the north Indian point of view, though one appropriate to the south.

As *pradaksina* leads worshippers around the north of the temple beneath the colonnade to the point where they turn right and ascend through the basement courses to the platform (Figs 62 and 61), they walk directly up toward two unusually personalized couples (at 9 and 10 on diagram 6, p. 83). In one is shown a richly crowned woman turning out from the neutral space of the pillar, holding a kneeling male by the topknot of his otherwise clean shaven head (Fig. 63). What is stressed is the tension in the man's head, as he strains against the woman behind him and clutches his rosary to his chest. The weight of the woman's shoulders, breasts and hips have a massive presence that characterizes the style. A simple detail that epitomizes it is found in the thick rhizome of the armlet wound in a tubular spiral around the trunk of her arm, curling up at one end and down at the other, as thickly sensuous as a pair of thumbs. This is the style of the southern pillar figures.

Facing each other across the entrance to the porch at this point, between the Brahmachari *mithuna* (Fig. 63) and the handsome *mithuna* with which I began this discussion (Fig. 65), are an unmatched pair of *dvarapala*, (door-guardians). The more standard of the two is the figure on the north (Fig. 66).[102] It is a classic of the genre in a *tribhanga* (triple-bend) stance: the axis of his crowned head counterpoised against the axis of his torso, which is counter-poised against the axis of his hips and legs. He is dynamically poised against his emblematic club and buttressed by a dwarf. In spite of the iconoclastic damage, the skill of the rendering and the strength of the form is emphatic in the clean lines of the silhouette and the contrast of the axes and planes. The cylinder crown sits on a squarish face over the flattened torso. The slab of the original block is subtly confirmed by the invisible plane of the shoulders and splayed arms. A bit slimmer and more plastic, a bit more dynamically poised than its ancestors in the Badami caves (Fig. 83) a century and a half earlier, it is cut from the same local cloth.

Facing across the entrance is not the usual matching figure but another of the south side's dynamic couples (Fig. 64). The male, the complementary *dvarapala* in identical dress, leans with his left knee upon a small and very damaged female with a human torso and horse's hind quarters. Gently but firmly he holds her back. This is the scene that Srinivas Padigar has identified as the chastisement of Chaya, the arrest of Shade, the maid servant of Aditya's chief queen, who impersonated the queen when Aditya's heat became unbearable. The comparable scene in the contemporary Aditya temple at Badami, the Malegitti (Fig. 41), was also placed to the right (or south) of the path leading to the sanctum.

The stylistic consistency linking these pillar-figures to the niche figures of the *mandapa* within is unmistakable.

THE VERANDA

The study of the Hindu temple was for its first century or so largely confined to exteriors. This was not true of rock-cut temples, in which interiors had received the artists' main attentions, and where abandonment had left them conveniently accessible. But for the structural temples, flashing so splendidly in the open light, there seemed little need to penetrate beyond the richness of the surface. Of the twenty-three illustrations of the Durga temple published before 1955 only four dealt with the structure's interior—a pillar, a doorway, a plan and a single view within the veranda.

Only with the burgeoning of historical study that accompanied Independence did scholars seriously begin to move inside. As the archaeological surveys and academies came into Indian hands there was both greater interest in and access to the interior of the temples, which now were recorded by photographers. The simultaneous rise of the art book market in the 1950s created a demand for new photographic imagery and possibilities for aesthetic photographers seeking new imagery. Eventually, lighter cameras and faster film made it possible for the scholars to join them. In the case of the Durga temple the magnificent icons located within the veranda were a particular spur in this direction. Between 1955 and 1967 all the major deities of the interior leapt beyond the opacity of the printed word into photographic clarity. A wealth of interesting detail has continued to pour forth in the years since.

The Durga temple has four distinct interior spaces. We will examine them one by one, in the order of ritual progress. Worshippers move through the temple along a spiritual as well as a physical path. Simultaneous with the steps that lead them by stages inward towards the sanctum, contemplation also turns inward towards the deity that lies within, mind and body coming together in a single focus as the devotee comes face to face with the image on the altar. We will pass first around the ambulatory of the encircling veranda with its view of the *mandapa* wall and surrounding deities, then up onto the inner porch that faces the splendid entrance to the inner hall, and finally through the hall to the sanctum. Each of these spaces has its own distinct decoration, indicating its unique ritual situation in the worshippers' progress.

The architecture's details orchestrate the worshippers' passage, enunciating the stages of their progress as they circle the temple and approach the entrance. From the outside, the columns of the gallery all repeat the same simple design until the east is reached, where the auspicious figures are added around the entrance to the shrine and the quarter-rounds of the bracket capitals are cut into a series of smaller rolls to enrich their effect (Fig. 61). At the centre of the facade, which is the temple's entrance, a special accent is provided by a pair of brackets angled in front of the corbels.[103]

On ascending the stairs to the platform, worshippers must turn to enter the *pradaksina patha*, between the pillars with the doorguardians and the chastisement of Chaya. The choice at that point is either to climb another set of stairs to the porch of the inner temple and move directly toward the sanctum, or to take the second left turn into the *pradaksina* path, where another, higher circumambulation will allow experience of the rich wealth of ritually significant imagery already glimpsed through the colonnade. As they turn the first corner, worshippers find themselves accompanied by heavenly *vidyadhara* couples on scudding clouds overhead (Fig. 67). Only one of the original quartet of these couples remains in place. Another now lies in the site museum and the other two are the famous pair now in Delhi (Fig. 6). Ahead lies the architecture of the hall (Fig. 68).

Though seldom illustrated or considered as a unit, the veranda gallery is a remarkably distinct architectural and ritual ensemble. Its continuous passageway runs all the way around the temple beneath a sloping roof on a plain colonnade, the angles and curves of which contrast with the richness of the hall within and guide the worshippers' approach to the God. The outer colonnade of twenty-eight square pillars, linked by a waist-high parapet, gives the space a psychological closure (Fig. 68). The series of deities set in the elaborately articulated wall of the hall provides the focal point. The textual term for such an ensemble is *pradaksina patha*, the path of circumambulation, where the worshipper goes respectfully around the God who is kept throughout on the ritually purer right.

The eleven niches of this hall represent a *parivaralaya*, a garland of miniature pavilions surrounding the central pavilion of the inner sanctum. They housed the temple's sculptural glory, its *parivaradevata*, the inner circle of deities attending Aditya. This was, in its time, the most ambitious sculptural ensemble in Karnataka and possibly in all India, composed of figures whose size, richness and quality were among the most impressive anywhere. When Vijayaditya's death caused his last great temple, the Sangamesvara at Pattadakal, to be abandoned before completion, the Durga was left the most developed temple in the Chalukya heartland. Only the creation of Vikramaditya II's twin masterpieces of the following reign, the Virupaksa and Mallikarjuna at Pattadakal, have more developed image programmes.

The richness of the architectural framework housing these images is impressive. The eleven *deva kostha* niches and the four smaller window entablatures of the *mandapa* are superb, individually and as an ensemble. The animation and variety of their designs and the quality of their finish is exceptional, each one a totally distinct composition. Multiple *kostha* temples are found in both the Chalukya's southern and northern styles. The usual pattern of these designs requires the repetition of uniform entablatures. The Mahakutesvara temple at Mahakuta and the other large southern-style temples of Vijayaditya and Vikramaditya II's reigns transcend this normal regularity with a variety of individually unique entablatures, but no other early Chalukya structure has as varied or finely wrought a combination of designs as those found on the Durga temple.

The *mandapa*, and so the veranda interior, is essentially southern in style, composed mostly of entablatures and pilasters with *ghata* capitals. The niche and window crowns are also predominantly Dravida in style. Six of them represent square *kuta* domes, like those beginning and ending the series on the east (Fig. 68). One is an oblong, vaulted *sala kuta* (Fig. 72, right) and one is a miniature *hara* (combination) of southern elements, with square *kuta* and oblong *sala* elements (Fig. 72, left). There is also a *makara torana*, an alternative crown associated with the southern style. Four, however, have northern-style crowns or *udgama*, composed of combinations of *candrasala* and *surasena* arches over multiple stories (e.g., Fig. 69). The remaining two are southern *hara* combinations which mix in northern elements.

The ensemble of these niche frames is one of the most splendid creations of the early Chalukya tradition. The Chalukya were the first in a long line of royal Deccan patrons to sponsor a blending of the northern and southern styles, expressing both the natural tendency to take advantage of the different traditions existing in the lands they ruled and a conscious desire to declare in art the grandiose claim of their inscriptions: that they were rulers of both north and south India.[104] From their inception the early Chalukyas mixed the two normally distinct styles with freedom and relish. This can be seen in their earliest work at Badami, where Cave II has southern-style pillars and a northern doorway,[105] and in the ruined *vimana* of the north fort where its Dravida-style dome is crowned by the Nagara style's signature cogged wheel (*amalaka*).[106]

It is a characteristic of most of the major Dravida-style structures of Vijayaditya's reign to mix distinctive Nagara elements into their designs. All but two of the wall entablatures of Badami's Jambulinga have modest northern crowns, the two exceptions being the long *sala kostha* of its facade. The Naganatha has northern *amalaka* mixed into one of its southern *hara* entablatures and one that is fully northern. The Mahakutesvara has the combination closest to the Durga temple: three southern style, three northern (e.g., Fig. 100), one abraded and one mixed.

The Durga temple offers a diverse and elaborate climax to this development, mixing single *kuta* entablatures with *kuta hara*, exhibiting the different types occurring elsewhere, and adding some eloquent variations of its own. The size, quality of execution and elaboration of detail found in the Durga temple's series establishes a distinctive level of sculptural quality. What are conventional phrases in the decorative schemes elsewhere, reach the level of high oratory in the *kostha* frames of the Durga temple's gallery.

The contemporary structure most like the Durga temple in its mixture of unique elements and exceptionally fine architectural detail, going beyond the established standards of the large-scale Chalukya temple, is the Papanatha at Pattadakal. Like the Durga temple the Papanatha's conception involves increased size and richness. In its final form the Papanatha is a large-scale structure extended to the super-scale size by the addition of a second *mandapa*. And like the Durga temple, it puts on a prominent display of mixing northern and southern elements. The Papanatha is the unique example within the Chalukya's Karnatak tradition where an essentially northern-style structure introduces highly prominent southern features. Its otherwise consistently Nagara exterior features a striking Dravida *hara* entablature (Fig. 101). A few select Dravida elements crop up on its interior as well. Unlike any other Nagara structure it brings a distinct set of variations to its *udgama* entablatures. The variety of the Kudaveli Sangamesvara makes it the only comparable structure in the Andhra region, although the quality is more limited (Fig. 102). Like the Papanatha it is an essentially northern structure with significant southern elements, including its niche crowns and its *parivaralaya* courtyard wall. The three great super-scale temples of Pattadakal are consistently Dravida in style, with little mixing-in of Nagara elements.

The architecture of the veranda is marked uniquely by the elaborate decoration of the inner porch that raises the expectations of the worshippers at the beginning and end of their circumambulation. On its exterior this porch is part of the veranda, presenting an impressive array of finely finished sculptural imagery. On passing into the veranda the worshipper confronts pillar images of Narasimha disembowelling Hiranyaksipu (Fig. 61) and Ardhanari. On either side they find the pillars above carrying *mithuna* and the mouldings below narrative reliefs of the *Ramayana* (Fig. 68). The epic runs in the direction of circumambulation, from the Ayodhya Kanda on the north to the Kiskindha on the east and Sundara on the north. Two fragments of relief on the temple's exterior suggest that the tale was intended to continue there, though it could only have been finished in plaster or paint.

THE DEITIES OF THE MANDAPA WALL

Seven of the hall's eleven *parivaradevata* (circle of Gods) survive, six in place. This is neither enough to fully clarify the temple's iconographic programme nor to indicate its main deity. They are reasonably well preserved, however, to give us a good idea of the intended style and level of quality. In the order of *pradaksina*, they are Siva, Narasimha and Vishnu on the south, Varaha, the Goddess Durga and Harihara (Vishnu-Siva) on the north. Another Siva was found outside at the time of Burgess' visit and at least one figure of comparable size has lain in the compound in recent times. It is not clear which of the five empty niches these two may have filled.

The image in the third *kostha* of the gallery is a magnificent eight-armed Vrsavahana: Siva leaning upon his vehicle and alter-ego, the bull Nandi, flanked by a dwarf holding Nandi's tail (Figs 20 and 69). The God stands in a sinuous triple-bend stance with eight arms radiating comfortably from his torso. Unusually, he wears a jewelled tiara, similar to that on the nearby pillar-figure (Fig. 51). Like the northern *dvarapala* (Fig. 66) which it also resembles in its jewellery and dress, the supple body seems to be completely lacking in muscle. The piece is cut from a single block which was set into the *kostha* and locked there by the pilasters, one of which is missing. The surviving one shows how they covered the figure at the base, and were themselves cut out above so as not to obscure its symbols.

The image in the next niche is Vishnu in his main-lion incarnation, Narasimha (Fig. 70). Even discounting the damage the figure has suffered, it is clear that this image was less suavely finished than the Siva. Its benign lion head is robustly bulbous and relatively caricatural, with round eyes and a wide grin. Long locks of hair run down on to his shoulders. The image is a bit less naturalistic, but otherwise not unlike its magnificent forerunner in Cave III at Badami (Fig. 43), which like it bears a lotus on its head, a feature peculiar to the Chalukyas. It has a halo created by the half-round frame of its block and a cutting for it on the wall behind.[107] It is located into its *deva kostha* in a different way than the Siva. Its block is sunk neatly into the shelf of the niche. The strongly fluted *ghata* pilasters here stand nearly free, one not quite finished.

The next image in the passage is a quite marvellous Vishnu striding over a human-headed Garuda in the company of a small female (Fig. 71). In this figure we return to the style of the *dvarapala* master seen in the Siva. The figure form and body jewellery are equivalent. The God's bulk is forcefully present, three arms and a leg projected out fully free of the block in a manner that left vulnerable the leg below the thigh, as well as two arms. As in the Siva *kostha*, the pilasters lock the figure in place, overlapping the panel with the *malasthana* bands on the left and *ghata* cushions on the right.

Around the apse and past two empty *kostha* on the north is the Varaha (boar) incarnation of Vishnu (Fig. 21), which may be the work of the same master responsible for Narasimha, on the opposite side of the *mandapa*. In both these figures we get a relatively slight human body supporting an enlarged animal head. The God is shown striding victoriously over the supplicant Nagaraja and Nagini representing the flood from which he is rescuing the earth Goddess, who he raises up on his left arm. Its slab is sunk into the base of the niche. The *pranala* of the shrine run-off is set in the basement just west of this niche, reinforcing the need for the worshippers' circumambulation in the veranda.

The next figure in line is the Goddess Durga, as Mahisasuramardini, the slayer of the demon buffalo (Figs 22 and 72). She is eight-armed, in the manner of the Siva directly opposite on the south. Her position here on the temple's north side is where we would expect to find it in a temple of Siva, and it brings up the significant point that there is no balancing image of Ganapati.[108] The Mahisasuramardini is the baroque gem in this superb collection of sculpture, and it too is most likely the work of the *dvarapala* master. Her crown is piled as high as Vishnu's and Siva's, and her decoration matches theirs, with the exception of the feminine wristlets, necklace and *channavira* beads falling between her breasts. Her slab is set into the niche by a shallow inset at the bottom and a slight overlapping of the upper edges by the pilasters on each side.

The last of the *parivaradevata in situ* is Harihara, the unity of Siva and Vishnu (Fig. 73). It is a curiously static, eight-armed figure that has been likened to the Vishnu on the Malegitti (Fig. 42).[109] This image appears to have come from other hands than those we have seen up to this point. It is a stocky figure standing full front and severely symmetrical. With its right hands vandalized, the Shaiva nature of that side is only subtly distinguishable from its Vaishnava left by the split of the crown that turns one side into Siva's *jata* (hairlocks). The only other sculptural hint of the split on the body is in the off-centre placement of the rosette in the necklace.[110] Here too the panel is secured in place by the upper elements of the pilasters and their corbel brackets.

There has been speculation that some of these images were created later than the temple and set there as replacements of other supposedly original figures. There seem to have been two impulses behind these suggestions. One was James Harle's attempt to explain what he saw as distinctly eighth-century sculpture on the Durga temple, whose architecture he believed to be earlier.[111] The other was Aschwin Lippe's attempt to demonstrate a Pallava style at the early Chalukya sites, to correspond with the Pallava defeat of the Chalukyas in 642. Lippe contended that a selection of images among the Chalukya sites of Aihole and Badami were essentially Pallava, and the result of what he called 'additions and replacements' undertaken by Tamil artists or Karnatak artists following Tamil, 'Pallava', models. On the Durga temple, he said, '[a]ll the gallery panels appear to have been inserted after construction'.[112] Unlike Harle, however, Lippe believed the temple itself to be eighth century, and the Harihara and Varaha images to be original. For him it was the Narasimha that seemed a definite addition, though possibly the Vishnu and the Durga were as well.

It is not absolutely certain whether or not the sculpture could have been inserted much after the construction of the temple. But it would have been exceedingly difficult to manoeuvre such large stones, finished with delicate and vulnerable details, through the path necessary to get them there (Fig. 61). And one must ask why anyone would bother. Lippe's suggestion that the Pallavas did their supposed recutting in an attempt to humiliate the Chalukyas seems unlikely. Vikramaditya II did leave an inscription on a pillar in the Kailasa at Kanchi claiming to have defeated the Pallava king and then to have returned the gold to his God's temple. But this humiliation was accomplished through gifts to the God, not vandalism of its temple. Images are sometimes added to temples after their completion, but there is nothing about these to suggest that they are any later than those carved on the pillars *in situ*. On the contrary, these seem clearly to be early Chalukya sculpture at its best. If the temple is early eighth century there is no reason to suppose the images are not contemporary with it.

It is apparent that rather than being carved *in situ* from blocks tightly fitted in their structures like some Chalukya temples (e.g., Fig. 42), the *parivara* images of the Durga temple were inserted in fairly complete condition, into spaces prepared for them. But it is not clear how late in the building process this insertion occurred. Their broad-based slabs were held in place like the rest of the temple by their vertical weight, but for added safety some were sunk in sockets and most locked-in by pilasters. Though not the tradition's most common method of setting sculpture, several other cases exist, and there is no reason to suppose that it was not the original intent of the temple's designers. It was employed on the Huccappayya-gudi, for instance (Fig. 99), and in the Kudaveli Sangamesvara. There is, contrary to Lippe's suggestions, no evidence of any previous images or of an alteration of the structure necessary to fit images of one size into spaces made for images of another size. Where the pilasters have been adjusted to fit the sculpture, it is reasonable to see that as part of the process of setting, but there is no reason to suppose the process was later than the original construction. It was used in precisely the same way for the Varaha and the Harihara which Lippe supposed were original, and also for the Narasimha he supposed was an addition. Though the Narasimha image does share features with the one in Badami's Cave III (Fig. 43), there is no reason to see it as copied from it. Neither has it any characteristic particularly related to Pallava imagery.

Five niches of the veranda are empty today. At least one of the sculpture for these can be identified with some certainty; another seems possible. The unquestionable candidate is the Bhiksatana Siva photographed by Burgess on his first visit, and taken to be a Jina by Fergusson (Fig. 6). This image shows Siva as a naked beggar. The style of the figure and the outline of the block both accord with the Narasimha image.[113]

A much abraded, multi-armed figure found within the courtyard may be added to this set. Its pose is the bendless one found in the Bhiksatana and Harihara. It has small figures at its base: the one on its right is female and the other a male dwarf. The Vishnu of the Malegitti (Fig. 42) and a loose image at Badami have the same combination of attributes. It is possible that this Vishnu, matching the one on the north of the other Sun temple, once stood in one of the veranda's empty niches.

The fact is that the previous discussion not withstanding, there is nothing so uniquely distinct about the style of any of the temple's major figures to assure us that they were not done by a single workshop under the guidance of one great master.

The iconographic conclusions available from this ensemble are inconclusive. Shaiva temples regularly display a variety of deities as seen here, but there is no Nandi *mandapa* and so the presence of Siva seems out of the question. Nor is there any feminine imagery of the sort that could link the temple particularly with the Goddess. Early Chalukya Vaishnava temples, with the single exception of the Harihara (half-Siva) image in Cave III, are as exclusive in their display of Vaishnava deities as later Sri Vaishnava temples. So, the possibility of linking this Aditya to any of the major deities, including Vishnu, seems ruled out. The other known Sun temple with major *kostha* imagery is the Malegitti at Badami. It bears images of a door-guardian (Dandi?) and Vishnu's vehicle Garuda in front, Siva on the south and Vishnu on the north. On the inside it has a hall ceiling with Vishnu on Garuda, the chastisement of Chaya on the sanctum's right and Aditya in his chariot over the door. We cannot, therefore, see this Sun temple as a particularly Vaishnava one.

THE INNER PORCH

The inner porch is reached by a staircase, rising four or five steps above the floor of the gallery.[114] Beyond those stairs we enter an open interior whose refinement and elaboration is one of the richest in the tradition. It is a two-bayed space, with benches on each side.[115]

The four pillars are shorter than those outside, but more profusely decorated (Fig. 76). Unlike the exterior columns, however, these are finished with finely carved and polished decorative imagery. The wave corbels above carry leaping *yali* lions on their brackets. This motif appeared at the end of Vijayaditya's reign, becoming standard in Vikramaditya II's (e.g., Fig. 105) as an embellishment of the flat band in earlier corbels (e.g., Fig. 37).[116]

The lintels above carry a continuous Dravida entablature, a miniature architecture of pilasters and domes with occasional inhabitants. Over the entrance, facing in toward the shrine, is Aditya the sun with two attendants (Fig. 75). He is shown stiffly erect, with splayed arms holding lotus blooms. The miniature colonnade is carried over a *vyalamala* course, a *kapota* cornice and a *hamsamala* of geese.

The doorway to the *mandapa* is the climax of the porch (Fig. 78). It is an elaborate variation on the pattern we have already seen on the gateway, and the richest in the tradition before Vikramaditya's great temples at Pattadakal. It has a southern-style entablature supported by pilastered jambs and an elaborate complement of figurative imagery. At its centre is the image of Vishnu's vehicle Garuda, which convinced Burges the temple was Vaishnava (Fig. 77). Because of its association with *naga* circling the doorway, however, Garuda here should be seen to have an apotropaic rather than sectarian meaning. Aside from his guise as Vishnu's vehicle, Garuda is a remover of obstacles and sins, and a protection against snake bite, all of which have particular significance in this location on the temple. Here the sunbird holds the *naga* (his half-brothers) in check, surrounding the passageway in a halo of light and dark, flight and descent, encircling the site of transformation, where worshippers pass from the outer to the inner in their approach to the God. A Garuda grasping *naga* tails is a standard early Chalukya doorway imagery that can be found on many temples (e.g., the Cikka Mahakuta Apsidal temple, Fig. 93, and the Surya temple, Fig. 108), including distinctly non-Vaishnava ones like the Virupaksa at Pattadakal, where it has a place on the eastern gateway and southern *mandapa* entrance.

This Garuda passage imagery is the most elaborate of its type, with six waving *naga* torsos on the lintel and another eight weaving their way down the door jamb.[117] The normal formula in this case has a more modest Garuda holding a single pair of *naga* tails, their bodies circling the passageway and their torsos rising up at the top of the base boxes on each side (Figs 107 and 108). Here that motif is dramatically increased from one pair of *nagaraja* to four, with heads in Garuda's hands as well as below on the jambs. This expansion of the standard form occurs only on two other occasions in the tradition, and in both cases the work seems clearly associated with this design. We have already seen one, the entrance to the Durga temple's gateway where three pairs of *naga* appear on the jambs (Fig. 50). The other is the sanctum entrance of the Huccappayya-math, at Aihole, where the Garuda grasps the bodies of six *naga* on a lintel. The design and the cutting of the faces and other details are so similar that surely it is worked by the same hands.

Returning to the Durga's doorway entablature we see a highly plastic design like that on the *pratoli*, with three large *sala* and two intermediate *karna kuta*. There are figures inhabiting each of the miniature pavilions in the place where many early Chalukya sanctum entablatures carry images of their Gods, but these are very difficult to read. The figures on the outside are not symmetrical and carry no legible attributes. Still, because the one on the right is chubby and the other slim we may recognize them as Pingala and Dandi, Aditya's most common attendants and a rare combination of an attendant pair that is not symmetrical.[118] The inner pair are symmetrically posed women, lacking particular attributes. The central figure stands full front without a bend (Fig. 79). I can read this two ways, and in each interpretation the figure has a halo and may be identified as Aditya. In one it seems to have legs, in the other it seems to drive a two-wheeled chariot from a standing position. Either would seem to eliminate the possibility of it being Aruna. The figure in the storey above can be read without question. It is a two-armed Aditya with lotuses (Fig. 80).

Different hands did the cutting on most of the entablature over the Huccappayya-math's shrine entrance, but as the *design* there is a comparatively close variation on this one, it has similar architecture with a doubling of the upper storey and pilasters with square *ghata*-capitals beneath *yali* brackets. The Garuda holding twin *nagaraja* bodies twisting above the lintel may be by the same hands that worked those of the Durga temple, but the jambs and base figures are significantly different. Like many designs among the early Chalukya temples, this suggests that there were individual specialists or workshops specializing in particular motifs, who could be called upon for discrete elements of a compound design. The entablature of the *nandyavartta* window of the Durga temple's gallery may be by the same masters who did the one on the *mandapa* doorway. So too may be the south (entrance) doorway to the Sulebhavi gateway, which is close not only in its cutting but even in the existence of an image of Aditya in its upper storey.

THE HALL

The *gudha-mandapa*, or closed hall of the temple, is entered through the grand doorway, across a low sill. Its interior has been quite thoroughly damaged by the collapse of its roof and other calamities. Still, a good deal can be learned from it. It is a *sandhara* hall, one in which the sanctum stands free within its outer walls, so that worshippers may do *pradaksina* within it. The hall itself is unusually long. The normal arrangement of the Chalukya's large-scale hall can be seen in the Malegitti (p. 68, diagram 2d). It is three bays long with a central nave and clerestory[119] flanked by side aisles under lower, canted roofs. The search for a larger structure led the Durga temple's creators to add a fourth low bay at the front, so that nave and sanctum were joined inside a continuous outer aisle. This reinforced the concentric nature of the overall layout: sanctum and nave within the *sandhara* of the inner temple, and that within the outer gallery. If unusual it was closer to established patterns than the Lad Khan. Unlike the super-scale temples, there was no provision in this interior for independent subordinate shrines (e.g., p. 68, diagram 2g), or even for the relief depiction of these found in the contemporaneous, added *mandapa* of the Papanatha.[120] In contrast to its splendid exterior the inner side of the *mandapa* wall is totally plain, but for the *kapota* ridge that carries the rafters and a miniature *hara* over the entrance. The *mandapa* interior lies in shadow (Fig. 81).

Though they have all undergone some damage we can see the pillars are tall versions of the standard square Chalukya shafts, with raised horizontal bands and rondels, and decorative figures corresponding closely to those found outside in the porch and gallery. Archaeological Survey restoration of the 1970s has made it difficult to see how these pillars were finished, but earlier photographs give some idea. They were tall plain shafts with finely wrought details, as seen in the surviving fragments. There is no narrative imagery, vertical banding or large pillar figures such as seen in the succeeding generation at Pattadakal (Fig. 105). The original ceilings are lost, but enough of the entablature is left to show that it was a Dravida *hara* akin to those found in the inner porch. This *hara* was crudely reconstructed in the 1970s, in a way that covers and distorts its original form.[121]

The damaged doorway to the sanctum was related to the one at the *mandapa* entrance (Fig. 81). This was more obvious before the fanciful reconstruction of the 1970s, which is unlike anything in the tradition.[122]

THE SANCTUM

The sanctum, or *garbha grha* (womb chamber), has its inner floor raised above the level of the *mandapa*. Thus, when the *pujari* (ritual priest) was present he stood above the devotees, who advanced as far as the sanctum's doorway. From there the devotees made offerings for the *pujari* to convey to the altar. The round backed *garbha grha* is totally plain except for a circular altar whose image has been removed. At some point a shelf was added, connecting the altar to the rear and southern wall (Fig. 25). The altar contains a rectangular socket for the image that was once there. The oblong form of the socket eliminates the possibility of a *linga* denoting a Siva temple, as definitely as the mixed iconography of the *parivaralaya* eliminates the possibility of a Vishnu temple. The image it held may have been among the fragments found in the temple's compound before the removal of remains to the site museum, but if it was I cannot yet tell which one.

Characteristic of Karnatak temples before Vikramaditya II's reign, the sanctum of this temple has no antechamber or *antarala*. (I put that form's entry into the Karnatak region at this time because of its prominent inclusion in the super-scale temples of Vikramaditya II's time at Pattadakal and its equally prominent absence from the Sangamesvara.)

As the difference in shapes indicates, the tower does not fit exactly over the *garbha grha*. They are, however, closely connected and coordinated. Three of the shrine's walls coincide with the tower exactly, while the semicircular section lays within the tower's square and coincides at its centre. However irregular this may look to the aesthetic viewer, it is of little consequence to the worshipper. Contrary to some suggestions,[123] it is not a requirement of the *sastra* literature that the tower coincide exactly with the sanctum's walls, even though that was the usual solution and seems the most logical one. The Cikka Mahakuta apsidal temple seems to have had its tower stand totally inside its sanctum's perimeter. Though it is reasonable to see this as a highly irregular combination because it was not apparently used again, it is going too far to say that it was somehow wrong. If it was not ritually or aesthetically acceptable it would never have been built or allowed to stand.

The fascinating contrast of the jarring angles in the Durga temple's tower with the curves of its hall-end is best understood as one of a series of striking artistic leaps that characterize this unusually sophisticated and complex design, one that throughout delights in contrasts and polarities.

THE CURRENT VISION OF THE DURGA TEMPLE

It is my conclusion that the Durga temple is the penultimate example of a series of great temples built during the reign of the Chalukya's longest ruling sovereign, Vijayaditya, 696–733/4. A date of around 725–30 seems most appropriate.

This conclusion is based on a comparative stylistic analysis of the entire early Chalukya tradition and the hypothesis of a relatively consistent, if somewhat irregular, development of the motifs that I have analysed. That is, the temple design's relative place in the development of size, stairway programmes and basement mouldings, the place of its figure pillars in the progression of the type, and so on. In each of these evolutionary skeins the Durga temple's designers produced the most complex and sophisticated imagery to precede the super-scale temples of Pattadakal, created in the following reign for Vikramaditya II (733/4 to 744/5), the Virupaksa and the Mallikarjuna.

A key element in this scheme is the premise that Vijayaditya's own temple, the Sangamesvara (or Vijayesvara, as it was originally known), was left unfinished because it was created at the very end of his career and interrupted by his death in 733/4. Anyone wishing to place the Durga temple earlier would need to show that the Sangamesvara was earlier and explain why the two most developed temples of Vijayaditya's time were followed by so many less-developed structures and why it took so long before the monuments of Vikramaditya were to surpass the sophistication of the Durga temple with the further developments I have noted.

Early Chalukya studies are currently flourishing in the midst of attention from a growing pride of scholars.[124] There have been five serious art historical studies of early Chalukya architecture that considered the Durga temple since 1980, four of them by scholars having particular familiarity with the tradition. The first and most comprehensive is a doctoral dissertation by Carol Radcliffe Bolon,[125] expanded for its understanding of the Durga temple in an article comparing it with the Kudaveli Sangamesvara temple near Alampur.[126] Bolon's focus is on figure style and it is here that she finds significant similarities that lead her to compare these temples and date them to around 700, based on a pair of contentions. The first is a conviction that the Kudaveli temple is late in the Telingana regional series, which she sees confined to the seventh century. The second is a connection she draws between the sculpture of the porch of the Huccimalli-gudi at Aihole (Fig. 47) and the Durga temple. Bolon sees the Subrahmanya ceiling image in the Huccimalli-gudi (Fig. 106) as the work of the same artist who did the Durga temple's *nagaraja* ceiling (Fig. 74). A royal donation inscribed on the wall of the Huccimalli-gudi assures us that that structure, just across the fields to the north of the Durga temple, was in existence by 708.[127]

I agree that the Kudaveli temple and the Durga are of about the same time, but prefer to place both at the end rather than the beginning of Vijayaditya's reign.[128] The similarity of the two ceiling panels is undoubtedly strong, though I do not know whether or not we should consider them the work of one artist or workshop. If we do, locating the Subrahmanya early in that master's career and the *nagaraja* late would allow for the later Vijayaditya date I see for the Durga temple. Compared to the *nagaraja* ceiling, the Subrahmanya is more planar and less plastically massive, as one might expect earlier in the century, from the development of the pillar figures discussed above. It is also important to note that the Subrahmanya panel is most probably later than the Huccimalli-gudi as a whole, differing substantially from the ceilings inside and supported by pillars apparently recut to hold its distinctly later *purna ghata* bench-backs.

K. V. Soundara Rajan's discussion of the architecture of the early Chalukyas in the *Encyclopaedia of Indian Temple Architecture* sums up three decades of his writing on the subject. His analysis of the Durga temple there is once again focused on a detailed agamic delineation of its elements from which he concludes that it is essentially Dravida. He says that its apsidal plan 'should demand an apsidal superstructure', but he makes no further reference to his earlier suggestion that what we have today is a recent addition. In terms of date, he places it at the end of the seventh century, offering as his main evidence the opinion of the epigrapher K. V. Ramesh that the fragmentary undated inscription of the stairway walls have letter forms of no later than AD 700.[129] Not knowing more of the specifics it is hard to say what this letterform dating can be based upon. The only speculation by Ramesh that I know of regarding the date of the fragments to either side of the stairs is that they fit well with the gateway inscription, which he attributes to the time of Vikramaditya II (733–45).[130] Padigar agrees with that.[131]

Two recent surveys have dealt significantly with the Durga temple, in a way that takes advantage of recent advances. In her *Art of Ancient India*, Susan Huntington follows the contemporary vision, making no mention of supposed Buddhist origins or problematic tower arrangements, while praising sculpture and placing the date in the later seventh or early eighth century.[132] James Harle, who has done extensive research on Chalukya art, refers to the temple in his *Art and Architecture of the Indian Subcontinent*. Harle calls the temple a 'triumphant oddity' and the most splendid creation of the dynasty before their last great temples at Pattadakal. He dates it in the first quarter of the eighth century, and though he finds the tower unusual for the plan, he finds it usual for the Chalukyas.[133]

S. Rajasekhara's *Early Chalukya Art at Aihole* is the revision of a doctoral dissertation on the site that, despite its title, considers the other Chalukya Karnatak sites to some extent.[134] Rajasekhara sees the Durga temple as the culmination of early Chalukya art at Aihole, and its last major temple there. He describes the temple in great detail and pays some attention to its gateway. His conclusion is that its decorative development and sculpture are comparable to that found on the Mallikarjuna and the Virupaksa of Pattadakal and that it should be dated, with them, to the middle of the eighth century.[135] Along with Soundara Rajan, he recognizes it as an Aditya temple.

Though not entirely in agreement with my conclusions, these analyses are substantially similar. A century and two decades after Fergusson originated the Buddhist derivation theme and six decades after Cousens adapted the flat-roofed temple hypothesis, the Durga temple is finally being recognized for what it is rather than what it is not. Four decades after Independence recognition of the temple as a brilliant success of Brahmanical art has moved from the specialist literature into the survey literature. To reach the popular literature may take another generation.[136]

The Durga Temple in the Chalukya Tradition—A Summation

A COMPARATIVE STYLISTIC analysis of the entire range of early Chalukya temples provides a complex of developing patterns, anchored chronologically by those that can be dated by inscription. With over 150 temples and related early Chalukya structures identified, there are a number of elements that can be compared from one to the next. This has allowed a fairly extensive and detailed set of correlations ordering separate developments and combining them all to place most structures into a pattern of relations with the rest. After more than a century of study, a complex *indra jala* of interconnected details recognized by those specializing in the early Chalukya tradition has begun to overwhelm and replace the cruder analysis of one-point plots and point-to-point comparisons, based on a limited number of issues or based outside of the tradition. There are two major issues here for the study of Indian art. One is recognizing the value of a thorough analysis of the concrete form of the fullest range of available monuments. The other is the value of identifying the regional dynastic tradition as the primary context of the temple's material and social production.

Most survey writing on the Durga temple after Cousens repeated his estimate of the temple's age based on a pan-India perspective, linking the Durga temple's supposedly 'mismatched' tower and roof to Cunningham's flat-roofed temple hypothesis. A mid-sixth century date may reasonably fit the temple from that perspective if we limit our consideration to a particular selection of structures from among the early Chalukya corpus. Most of those who know of the temple have learned of it in this form. But only a limited view of the temple can be had from a limited view of the tradition, and only general aspects of the temple can be understood at the pan-India level. Compared with the Parasuramesvara at Bhuvaneswar and the Khandariya Mahadeva of Khajuraho, the Durga temple's tower, in the indistinct view of a photograph of the entire structure, is apparently simpler and less refined. A generally accepted seventh century date for the Parasuramesvara yields a reasonable acceptance of the Durga's sixth century association.

The coarseness of this pan-Indian explanation is revealed by any detailed study of the temple's actual tradition, the early Chalukya dynastic arts of the mid-sixth to mid-eighth centuries in Karnataka and Andhra. The Durga temple's tower in this context turns out to be a surprisingly independent and highly refined version of a fairly advanced Chalukya type belonging to the eighth century. Its unusually straight-sided outline is explained largely by the fact that its upper third is missing.

Detailed study of the temple from the perspective of its situation in its regional dynastic tradition yields a measure of understanding that is not visible from a pan-Indian vantage point. Nor can it be seen as well from similarly abstract sightings through textual, technical or site traditions. Confining one's perspective to the southern style in isolation, as seen in the *Encyclopaedia of Indian Temple Architecture*'s 'Upper Dravidadesa' volume, militates against an adequate appreciation of the unique quality and the sophisticated blend of sources found in the Durga temple, where that blend with the northern style is one of its most significant aspects. Soundara Rajan's article not only fails to consider the Telingana source of the tower's forms, it fails to point out the fact that the tower is in the northern style.[137]

By a similar token, restricting discussion to structural temples would work against consideration of the rock-cut monuments where the dynasty's art was first recorded in stone. It would have eliminated the beginning of our sequences of basements and ceiling panels, as well the only examples of corbel brackets to survive.

To focus upon one site alone also severely limits the value of a study. Rajasekhara demonstrates this when he extends his consideration of Aihole into detailed comparisons with monuments at all the other local sites. Regional discussions limited by modern linguistic or political divisions are as problematic. Michell's exclusive focus on Chalukya monuments of Karnataka and Prasad's complementary focus on their Andhra monuments forbids each of them from appreciating the major cultural sharing which existed between the two wings of early Chalukya temple tradition.[138]

What is important here is to realize that there is a concrete cultural tradition within which the Durga temple was created and to which any analysis of the structure must refer if one is to understand it: the regional dynastic culture ruled by the early Chalukyas. All other perspectives through which we may analyse it will have value only if they take that primary tradition into consideration. We may usefully study architecture in general or Indian temple art; we may study the art of a single site or even a single temple, and in so doing develop understanding about architecture or Indian temple art, the art of a single site or a single temple. But these are arbitrary and abstract perspectives that do not reflect the full concrete reality within which artists lived and worked. The monuments of Aihole, Pattadakal and Badami share too much to suggest that artists working at any one of these sites were unaware of the work being executed at another. This familiarity clearly spreads as far as the Chalukya's Telingana region, though as clearly it does not seem to extend to potentially contemporary structures of their Maharashtrian provinces. The same sharing existed between artists working on their Nagara and Dravida works. These style categories were not racially inherited nor caste restricted. They were simply alternative formal vocabularies within which a fine temple could be built. The same artists worked with elements derived from both styles. The Durga temple is not unique, but typical for its time in showing elements from both styles not only on the same structure but mixed within a single design element.

Visual imagery, like the verbal imagery of language, is produced in the social world within which its creators actually live and work. This is the concrete reality from which its creators draw their experience and the lived reality which they then express. The artists of the sixth to eighth centuries in Badami and Alampur shared a regional dynastic reality as well as their more particular site and chronological situations. The Aihole style, the Karnatak Nagara, and the eighth-century Dravida styles are abstractions of limited use without consideration of the concrete reality of the political and regional culture within which they were actually created.

The crucial level of tradition in the Deccan seems to be a socio-political one founded upon the cultural limits of language and political sovereignty. That is the dynastic region, the area within which trade and travel are most convenient and within which the surplus economic wealth and ritual patronage are connected and coordinated. I cannot say that such regional dynastic autonomy will always be as coherent as it is in the art of the Chalukyas of Badami, but no other category serves the understanding of these monuments so well.

Among the early Chalukya monuments no one has been able to usefully distinguish the monuments along lines of religious style. Iconography and ritual are distinguishable here, but not style. The same artists apparently worked on Jain, Buddhist, and Vaishnava temples and on the temples of the Saktas, Shaivas and the Sun-worshipping Sauras. The essence of the early Chalukya style was its regional span and the coherence of its traditions over the course of the dynasty's two centuries. There is thus an early Chalukya style of Jain architecture, though there is no Jain style of early Chalukya architecture.

The frame for understanding the Durga temple's significance is found in its genre. It is an elite Brahmanical stone temple of the Puranic age, a palace and vehicle of the supreme lord Aditya, the Sun. It is the sacrifice of the *yajamana* Komarasinga, which served to expiate not only his own sins, but those of his father and his father's father. It is the soteriological *yantra* or instrument devised by Komarasinga's spiritual guide and brought into material form by his orthodox architect to fit his essential being with the requirements of Aditya worship. It is the place where great men of the Chalukya period and their families could worship Komarasinga's image of lord Aditya, and where, in the time of the emperor Vikramaditya II, the Chalukya ruling family sanctioned this worship with the contribution of funds from their share of local customs revenue. In the feudal world of peasant farmers and aristocratic warriors it was a devotional gift to the God Aditya, from his devotee Komarasinga. This much is clear from the temple's inscription and the Brahmanical texts.

From our knowledge of its place in the Chalukya tradition we can say that the Durga temple is the most luxurious structure of its day and one of the most elaborate and refined monuments of the hundred and fifty that the Chalukya dynasty has left us. It is also the largest and most lavishly constructed of the nearly four dozen early Chalukya temples constructed in the holy temple city of Aihole. It is the only one of these to have required or received its own independent stone gateway or a set of more than three *parivara* images. It was the most lavishly developed of all early Chalukya temples before the super-scale temples of Vikramaditya II's reign.

Komarasinga, who paid for the Durga temple, is not given a regal title. He seems more likely to have been a *mahajana*, one of the great men of the town or the region. He may well have been a leading member of the Aihole Five Hundred, the site's powerful and well-recorded merchant guild. That he could build such a splendid temple seems to indicate that wealth outside the royal family was sizeable and allowed to manifest itself in dramatic public display. On the other hand the presence of a donation of dynastic revenue to the temple's upkeep demonstrates royal sanction and support. Only a few of the Chalukya structures are known to be royal dedications. A number of others received royal donations. So we can recognize the collaboration of court aristocracy and commercial or other political interests so familiar in later times. The inscription of the Meguti is eloquent testimony of this.

Indeed there seems to be a conscious expression of political and social interests along with the religious imagery found on these great stone temples. When we look at the inscriptions upon them we see dynastic nationalism as well as religiosity. Inscriptions telling of the deities within the structures and offerings to them celebrate the glory of the reigning dynasty's military achievements as much as its piety.

If we look to the temple's visual imagery we find the same mix of interests. The presence of Ganga and Yamuna flanking the Durga temple's doorway refers to the Chalukya claim to have won them in battle with opposing rulers of north India.[139] Their symbolic purifying of the path to the temple's sanctum also represents a symbolic claim of the dynasty to sovereignty over the Brahmanical heartland of Aryavarta, whose control they denote. The Rastrakuta, who claimed the same status as conquerors of north India, also continued use of this symbolism. No other southern dynasty either made the claim or decorated its temples with images of the twin river goddesses. The Chalukya's unusual use of both the northern and southern styles and their mixture of the two also seem to be a conscious attempt to claim possession of both traditions as well as familiarity with them. It is too prominent and clearly controlled to be an accident. The presence of the *Ramayana* in the basement of the inner porch retells the national religious epic, but it also vaunts the glories of warrior kingship.

Beyond the dynastic distinction that I have pressed here we can see a distinct possibility that the monuments of the early Chalukya period were also conceived with a conscious eye to regnal distinctions. The chronology I have shown here shows a continual stylistic development during the two centuries of Chalukya rule, but it also reveals emphatic jumps at each change of reign. The monuments of Vijayaditya's time show a gradual development, which I have indicated in my discussion of basements and temple sizes. The shift between the later temples of Vijayaditya and those of Vikramaditya II is more dramatic. The new scale is already established in Vijayaditya's great temple at Pattadakal, but a new pillar form and the addition of figurative and narrative sculpture on the interior all draw our attention to something consciously intended to be distinctively new.

The religious development of the early Chalukya period was diverse and included all the major sects of the day. There are Jain and Buddhist temples along with Shaiva and Vaishnava in the dynasty's first century, when the rulers all claimed to be *paramabhagavata*, or primarily worshippers of Vishnu. During the next century there was a marked preference for Shaiva temples, following the first Vikramaditya's special Shaiva initiation in 658 or 659. But there certainly was room for other cults, as indicated by the Sakta nature of the Sarangi-math and Bhagavati temples and the Saura dedication of Badami's Malegitti and Aihole's Surya and Durga temples. Aditya also holds an important place in the central (western) niche on the sanctum of the Shaiva Papanatha temple and the miniature shrine atop the Shaiva Lad Khan.

Since Saura temples are relatively rare, the Durga temple's imagery is interesting in itself. The imagery of the Durga temple seems to fit quite nicely with Shaiva associations in contrast to the Malegitti at Badami, where Vaishnava associations predominate. The significance of this is difficult to distinguish at the present stage of our understanding. One of the weakest aspects of our grasp of the period's elite culture is the specific nature of local religious cults. Vaishnava, Shaiva, Sakta and Saura sects were undoubtedly present, but these are only very general terms for practices expressed through a more particular sectarian reality. Suggestions such as Susan Buchanan's that Pasupata Shaivism was important in the Chalukya realm await fuller development. Her explanation of the image in Fig. 51 as a form of Bhiksatana showing his combat with the Pine Forest *Rsis*, when noted along with Bhiksatana's two other occurrences on the temple as a major icon (on the left in Fig. 6 and in the decorative course below the mithunas in Fig. 60), would suggest a particular importance of Pasupata Shaivism for the Durga temple. Pasupata Shaivism emphasizes the identity of Siva and Vishnu.

The hundred and fifty early Chalukya temples are spread unevenly across 450 kilometres, from Banavasi in the west to Satyavolu in the east, covering two major linguistic cultures. Only a dozen sites and barely two dozen structures are found outside the major concentrations around Alampur in Andhra and the Badami-Aihole region in Karnataka. It thus seems clear that these temples were created more for the narrow interests of the ruling elite that patronized them than for the possibility of public worship for the realm's population. It is no more likely that common peasants would be allowed into their precincts than Chaya, the maid of Aditya's wife, who is corralled by the doorguardian of the Durga temple's entrance.

It would be most interesting to know how the site of Aihole came to have its amazing concentration of temples within such a small area, never evidently one with a particularly large population. What made this a temple town? Was it a particular holiness or association with the famous trading guild?[140]

The continuity of institutions at Aihole is also to be considered. The Durga temple reflects the general rule there, having a temple and a stepwell added to its compound in the later Kalyani Chalukya period (Fig. 85). Just why some temples like the Konti-gudi group (including the Sarangi-math) received additional structures in Rastrakuta times and others like the Durga temple waited for the Kalyani Chalukya resurgence is not clear. No stone temples were created at Aihole after the fall of the Kalyani Chalukyas at the end of the twelfth century.

NOTES TO PART TWO

1. Benjamin Rowland, *The Art and Architecture of India*, Baltimore, 1953, p. 125.
2. The early Chalukya, early western Chalukyas, or Chalukyas of Badami (or Vatapi) are all names regularly used for this dynasty that ruled progressively larger swathes of the Deccan from around 542 to 757. Later dynasties claiming descent from them such as the Eastern Chalukyas ruling in north-eastern Andhra and the later or Kalyani Chalukyas indicate their derivation by lengthening the initial 'a' to 'ā'.
3. This history is traced from the inscriptions of the dynasty. The most recent major views are summarized in D. C. Sircar, 'The Chalukyas', in R. C. Majumdar, ed., *History and Culture of the Indian People*, vol. III, *The Classical Age*, Bombay, 1954, and K. A. Nilakanta Sastri, 'The Chalukyas of Badami', in G. Yazdani, ed., *Early History of the Deccan*, London, 1960, and more recently in P. B. Desai, ed., *A History of Karnataka*, Dharwar, 1970, and K. V. Ramesh, *The Chalukyas of Vātāpi*, New Delhi, 1984. The individual inscriptions are edited in *Indian Antiquary* and *Epigraphia Indica* and a few other places, cited in the aforementioned works.
4. This work was in the form of a Masters thesis at the University of California at Los Angeles: Gary Tarr, *The Cave Temples of the Early Western Chalukyas*, 1966. A refined version of it was later published as 'Chronology and Development of the Chāḷukya Cave Temple', *Ars Orientalis*, VIII (1970), pp. 155–84. ('Tarr' is a shortened version of the family name, to which I returned in 1973.)
5. Burgess (1874), and 'Rock-Cut Temples at Bādāmi in the Dekhaṇ', *Indian Antiquary*, VI (1877), pp. 354–66. R. D. Banerji, *Basreliefs of Badami*, Calcutta, 1928, (Archaeological Survey of India, Memoirs, no. 25).
6. Gulam Yazdani, *Archaeological Department Hyderabad, Annual Report for 1926–27*, Calcutta, 1928, pp. 7–12, and Pls X–XIII. Though Yazdani noticed and published the temples, and even compared them to the Papanatha at Pattadakal, he believed them to be of the tenth or eleventh century. It was not until after their inscriptions were published that Percy Brown described them as early Chalukya. (Percy Brown [1942], ch. 14.)
7. S. R. Balasubrahmanyam, 'The Date of the Lad Khan (Sūrya-Nārāyaṇa) Temple at Aihole', *Lalit Kalā*, X (1961), pp. 41–4.
8. R. S. Panchamukhi, 'The Badami Inscription of Chalikya Vallabhesvara: AD 578', *Epigraphia Indica*, XXVII (1947), pp. 4–9. I see no reason to alter the conception outlined at that time. K. V. Soundara Rajan's *Cave Temples of the Deccan*, Archaeological Survey of Temples, vol. III, Archaeological Survey of India, New Delhi, 1981, is the latest word on these temples. It seems to take only glancing notice of scholarship in the field.
9. Herman Goetz, *India; Five Thousand Years of Indian Art*, p. 124, and Klaus Fischer, *Schöpfungen Indischer Kunst*, Koln, 1959, Figs 103–5.
10. M. Rama Rao (1960), pp. 71–80, and *Early Cāḷukyan Temples of Āndhra Deśa*, Hyderabad, 1965.
11. James Fergusson, 'On the Identification of the Portrait of Chosroes II among the Paintings in the Caves at Ajanta', *Journal of the Royal Asiatic Society*, April 1879.
12. For my conclusions at that time see Tarr, 1970, pp. 173–4 and 181–4. There is little difference in Gary Michael Tartakov, 'The Beginning of Dravidian Temple Architecture in Stone', *Artibus Asiae*, XLII (1980), p. 76. For a more detailed reconsideration noting a few more parallels but making the break more clear see 'Ajanta and the Early Calukyas', in Ratan Parimo *et al.* eds., *The Art of Ajanta*, New Delhi, 1991, pp. 453–66.

13. For a contemporaneous summary of his views see Walter Spink, *Ajanta to Ellora*, Bombay, 1967.
14. E. g., Stella Kramrisch, *Indian Sculpture*, London, 1933, p. 36, and Benjamin Rowland, *The Art and Architecture of India*, Baltimore, 2nd edn, 1959, p. 177.
15. E. g., J. C. Harle, *The Art and Architecture of the Indian Subcontinent*, Harmondsworth, 1986, p. 124.
16. The concept has subsequently been rejected altogether by some scholars. See Odette Viennot, 'Le Problème des temples à toit plat dans l'Inde du nord', *Arts Asiatiques*, XVIII (1969), pp. 23–84, and Gary Michael Tartakov, 'Reconsidering the Flat-roofed Temple Hypothesis', in Joanna G. Williams, ed., *Kalādarśana, American Studies in Indian Art History*, New Delhi, 1981, pp. 147–57.
17. This temple is well known as the Malegitti Sivalaya, but since it has now been shown to be an Aditya temple, I am dropping the misleading element of the name while retaining its still useful identification with the garland sellers in its inscription.
18. Since that time we seem to have reversed places. The case for the early eighth-century date of the Mahakuteswara and Malegitti temples is presented in Gary Michael Tartakov, 'Interpreting the Inscriptions of Mahakuta Art Historically', G. S. Gai and F. Asher, eds., *Indian Epigraphy: Its Relation to Art History*, New Delhi, 1981, pp. 140–52.
19. B. R. Prasad, *Chālukyan Architecture of Mahbubnagar District*, Deccan College Graduate Research Institute, Pune, 1967, since published in refined and updated form as his *Chalukyan Temples of Andhradesa*, Atlantic Highlands, 1983.
20. My dates are all in the Common Era (CE). The Chalukya inscriptions are dated in the *Saka* (*s.*), which was initiated in 78 CE.
21. This was true as far as I could tell in 1969, when my first work was completed, and it remains so to a large extent. I did not yet know about the Jambulinga of 699. And I was only later to learn of several significant, and still controversial inscriptions in Andhra.
22. These stairs actually seem to be a recent construction.
23. The Archaeological Survey of India's repairs in the 1970s cleaned up this face in a manner that seems to be carefully representative of the original form. Michell's drawing 23 (Fig. 25), which shows the lower mouldings rounding the corner, above the stairs, is mistaken, as is his deletion of them on the east.
24. This moonstone is currently flush with sandstone paving laid down by the Archaeological Survey in the 1970s, and it looks as if there are only seven risers.
25. This is the most elaborate variation of this form, combining elements of the Virupaksa and Mallikarjuna's rampant-lion porch-basements with the Durga temple-type of twin lateral staircases. Michell (1975), Plate IIf shows the basement's turn, which indicates that it was originally intended as twin lateral. In this it fits the rest of this outer *mandapa*, signed by Baladeva, who worked on the eastern and southern entrances to the Virupaksa as well.
26. See Michell (1975), drawing 20. The Bhagavati temple has long been known as the Gauda(r)-gudi. It gained a momentary notoriety after a counterfeit excavation in the early seventies. See S. R. Rao, 'A Note on the Chronology of Early Chālukyan Temples', *Lalit Kalā*, 15 (1972), pp. 9–18.
27. The Sarangi-math is the south-eastern temple in the Konti group; Michell says 'Kunti'. See Michell (1975), drawings 18 and 19. S. Rajasekhara, *Early Chālukya Art at Aihole*, New Delhi, 1985, fails to mention it. Before the 1970s it was largely buried within the structure of the adjacent house.

28. An unfinished *candrasala* of similar proportions was found in the rubble north of the Durga temple's stairs also (Fig. 11, here).
29. *Purna ghata kaksasana* are particularly characteristic of this region. The form seems first to occur in the straight-backed *kaksasana* of the last great Chalukya monument, the Virupaksa at Pattadakal, where it can be seen on the eastern gateway (Fig. 92) and on the north-eastern temple in the Konti group. Unlike these early examples, those on the Bhagavati or Huccimalli-gudi are added around pillars that are already standing, and not part of the initial design.
30. See Tartakov (1980), pp. 80–4.
31. Michell (1975) was the first writer to consider the gateway seriously or to illustrate it. Aschwin Lippe, 'Additions and Replacements in Early Chālukya Temples', *Archives of Asian Art*, vol. XXIII, 1969–70, pp. 14–17, mentioned it previously, and it has been mentioned since by Rajasekhara (1985), p. 95, and K. V. Soundara Rajan in the Michael W. Meister and M. A. Dhaky, eds., *Encyclopaedia of Indian Temple Architecture; South India, Upper Drāviḍadēśa, Early Phase, A.D. 550–1075*, Philadelphia, 1986, p. 51.
32. There are fragmentary remains of two passages to the river at Alampur. The passage which is still intact, east of the Bala Brahma, is set in a wall that is now a palimpsest that is difficult to decipher. A passageway to the north has been lost in this century, though the important inscription associated with it preserved. The lost entrance to the Kudaveli Sangameswar *prakara* was quite modest. The entrance passage in the platform of Badami's Cave III is more modest yet. For the last see Tartakov (1980), Fig. 28.
33. This formula can be seen earlier in rock-cut Deccan example at Jogesvari, and later in most *gopura*.
34. I take a *gopura* to be an independent or at least a distinct structure with multiple storeys capped by a keel or tunnel-shaped *sala* or *valabhi* vault, and intended to have an associated wall. I am using the more generic term, *pratoli*, to indicate an equivalently distinct entrance pavilion without upper storeys and vault.
35. Aschwin Lippe (1970) was the first to call attention to this *candrasala* as original and significant. Michell (1975) calls it 'almost certainly misplaced'. While recognizing it as early Chalukya work, while at the site I supposed it to be a bit of *bricolage* restoration, despite the presence of its surviving twin on the ground nearby. It was not until later study convinced me that the temple was dedicated to Aditya that I realized it was probably original.
36. The designation—another title for the Sun God—is modern, and the image on its altar is from the time of the Kalyani Chalukyas, but there is no reason to doubt both represent the temple's original dedication to this deity or its early Chalukya date. Michell (1975), pp. 31–2 and drawing 22, calls it the Narayana temple; Rajasekhara (1985), pp. 131–2, calls it the Surya temple.
37. John F. Fleet, 'Sanskrit and Old-Canarese Inscriptions, No. LVIII', *Indian Antiquary*, VIII (1879), pp. 285–6, and Ramesh (1977), p. 87.
38. Ramesh (1984), p. 184, is the most recent. Soundara Rajan (1986), p. 52, seems to think that Ramesh dates the gateway inscription to Vikramaditya II (733–45), but the brief stairway references to before 700. However, Ramesh's published work does not suport this statement. In conversation he assures me that he sees no such distinction. He has even written an article arguing that distinctions of less than a century should not be made on the basis of letterform.
39. Srinivas Padigar makes the point well that names engraved on early Chalukya monuments are probably by those who constructed them. Earlier scholars suggested that they may have been the names of pilgrims, but they hold no dedicatory content and are thus meaningless other

than as signatures. Other than those who did the stone-cutting, no one had the tools with which to make such engravings, the quality of which is professional and not mere graffiti. See Srinivas Padigar, 'Epigraphy and Some Aspects of the Early Chalukyan Art', *The Journal of the Karnatak University: Social Sciences*, XXII (1986), pp. 74–80.

40. This was not yet accomplished in the northern Deccan in the creation of the Kailasa at Ellora, a decade after the Virupaksa. It was eventually recognized a generation later in Ellora's Chota Kailasa. It already existed in Tamilnadu at the Kailasanatha of Kanchi by 727, and the Shore temple of Mahabalipuram, *c.* 700.

41. I learned of Sulebhavi from S. Rajasekhara. It is discussed in *The Encyclopaedia of Indian Temple Architecture; Upper Drāviḍadēśa*, pp. 90–1, by Carol Radcliffe Bolon.

42. Still intact when I studied the temple in the 1960s, it was subsequently removed by the Archaeological Survey.

43. The walls of the Virupaksa and the Mallikarjuna are reproduced widely. Michell (1975) drawing 39 has diagrams of the Virupaksa's walls. The Kudaveli Sangamesvara walls (Fig. 102, here) can be seen in detail in Carol Radcliffe Bolon, 'The Durga Temple, Aihole, and the Sangamesvara Temple, Kudaveli: A Sculptural Review', *Ars Orientalis*, XV (1985), Figs 1–6. The temple on the hill at Panyem is unpublished to my knowledge.

44. The Ajivika remains surviving at Barabar hills include four apsidal plans. See S. P. Gupta, *The Roots of Indian Art*, Delhi, 1980, pp. 189–93. A variety of Jaina examples begin with the Maurya period remains at Udayagiri, Orissa. See A. Ghosh, ed. *Ancient India, A Review*, (1958–59), pp. 38–40, or Debala Mitra, *Udayagiri and Khandagiri*, New Delhi, 1960, pp. 38–9 and Pls XII and XIX. Brahmanical and proto-Brahmanical examples can be seen in Mathura, Besnagar and Nagarjunakonda. See Herbert Hartel, 'Some Results of the Excavations at Sonkh', pp. 69–99, *German Scholars on India*, vol. II, Bombay, 1970, p. 95 and Figs 38–40; S. P. Gupta, op. cit., pp. 258–9; K. V. Soundara Rajan, *Architecture of the Early Hindu Temples of Andhra Pradesh*, Hyderabad, 1965.

45. Subsequent Jain examples can be seen in the Tiruparuttikkunram temple in Jaina Kanchi. See A. Gosh, ed., *Jaina Art and Architecture*, vol. II, p. 325, Pl. 209. Brahmanical examples can be seen illustrated in the *Encyclopaedia of Indian Temple Architecture; Lower Drāviḍadēśa*, at the Bhaktavatsala complex at Tirukkalukkunram, pp. 105–6 and Fig. 86, at the Apatsahayesvara temple at Tenneri, pp. 295–6 and Fig. 326, the old Siva temple at Magaral p. 325 and Figs 383–4, etc. I have photographed vernacular examples near Ajanta village.

46. Contemporary Pallava apsidal temple remains are found at Mahabalipuram (Sahadeva Ratha) and Kuram (Vidyavinita-Paramesvara-grha). Two more Pallava examples can be found in the early ninth century in the Tirunagesvara temple at Kalambakkam and the Virattanesvara at Tiruttani. See the *Encyclopaedia of Indian Temple Architecture; South India, Lower Drāviḍadēśa*, pp. 40, 44, 99–100 and 101–2; Figs 11–13, 49–50 and 77–8.

47. These solid, miniature temples can be found around many early Chalukya temples and some others in Karnataka and Andhra. There are several lined up on the east of the Mahakuta tank and others within the shelter at Bhadranayika Jalihal. At Alampur there is one inside the Kumara Brahma, more surrounding the Bala Brahma and others in the museum. See Gary Michael Tartakov and Vidya Dehejia, 'Sharing, Intrusion, and Influence: The Mahiṣāsuramardinī Imagery of the Calukyas and the Pallavas', *Artibus Asiae*, vol. XLV, no. 4 (1984), Figs 15–16 and 25, and Tartakov (1980), Fig. 53. They can be seen around the Satyavolu temples, Kadamarakalava and around the courtyard of the Mahanandisvara temple. See Prasad (1983), Figs 63, 64, 75. In Andhra they can be seen surrounding the Kapotesvara at Cejerla, Coomaraswamy,

Fig. 147. Those found at Yelleswaram are now in the museum of the Archaeological Survey at Gun Foundry in Hyderabad.

48. My measurements for the Cekki group's apsidal temple come from Carol Radcliffe Bolon's dissertation, *Early Chalukya Sculpture*, New York University, 1981, p. 154. My measurements for the Cikka Mahakuta temple come from Carol's plan in *The Encyclopaedia of Indian Temple Architecture; Lower Drāviḍadēśa*, figure 34. My Durga temple measurements come from George Michell's drawing (Fig. 25, here).
49. Hartel, p. 95 and Figs 38–40.
50. Soundara Rajan (1965), pp. 14–15.
51. For the Bhagavati see Michell (1975), Drawing 20, or Soundara Rajan (1986), pp. 28–31, Fig. 19 and Pl. 50. The gallery surrounding the Bala Brahma at Alampur is an addition to the original conception, though some of its pillars are early Chalukya in date.
52. See Tarr (1970) and Tartakov (1980).
53. John F. Fleet, *Indian Antiquary*, VI (1877), p. 364. The italics here have been added. C. Sivaramamurti translates this as 'exceeding the height of two men and of wonderful workmanship', *Art of India*, New York, 1977, p. 219.
54. My use of the term '*mandapa*-temple' here is simply descriptive: a temple with a *mandapa*. It should not be connected to James Harle's usage in his article 'Three Types of Walls in Early Western Calukyan Temples', *Oriental Art*, vol. XVII (1971), pp. 45–54. I have left stair measurements out of other temples because they go beyond the basements. The Durga temple is twenty-three metres in length, its 'inner temple' is a smallish fourteen-and-a-half.
55. See Tartakov (1980), pp. 68–9 and Figs 8–9.
56. Michell (1975), Drawing 34. This is a jump of five metres or twenty per cent over the Andhra size.
57. This is not effectively shown on Michell's site plan, Michell (1975), Drawing 13 (Fig. 27, here).
58. A photograph of this temple can be found in Stella Kramrisch, *Art of India*, New York, 1955, Pl. 57. A more detailed development of this chapter will be found in L. K. Srinivasan et al., eds, *Śrī Nāgābhinandanaṁ*, New Delhi, 1995.
59. I am taking my Sanskrit terminology here largely, though not entirely, from Prasad (1983). In fact, we do not know which of the bewildering number of Sanskritic terms available are most appropriate.
60. In the top *bhumi*, the *surasena* are reduced to a split *candrasala* and then a closed one. The two most developed versions of the Karnatak Nagara at Pattadakal, the Papanatha and the Jambulinga, also have decoration inset between the *lata*.
61. These are the *pidhanaphalaka* 'upper plank', which is likely to be untouched by the *lata*, and the *skandha* 'shoulder', which is likely to be encroached by the *madhyalata*.
62. See Michell (1975), drawing 25, or Gupte (1967), Pls 49–50, or Kramrisch (1955), Pl. 58.
63. Cousens' Temple 10.
64. For Mahakuta see Kramrisch (1955), Pl. 57.
65. E.g., the southern temple at Cikka Mahakuta and the so-called Lakulisa temple at Mahakuta, Tarr (1969), pp. 247–8, Figs 201–2, pp. 243–4 and Fig. 198.
66. F. H. Gravely and T. N. Ramachandran, *The Three Main Styles of Temple Architecture Recognized by the Śilpa-Śāstras, Bulletin of the Madras Government Museum*, 1932 (reprinted 1962). This is an ambiguous transformation of Moreas' Kadamba style (described in his *Kadamba Kula*, Bombay, 1931, pp. 304–5 (and Fig. 38, here) achieved by calling it Nagara

in their text pp. 10–12 and 'Kadamba (? Nagara) temple' on the label to Pl. I, Fig. 2 (which features a drawing of a similar tower). Many have followed their suggestion.

67. M. A. Dhaky *et al.*, eds., *Encyclopaedia of Indian Temple Architecture; North India, Foundations of North Indian Style*, particularly p. 174.
68. See M. Rama Rao (1960) and (1965), and B. Rajendra Prasad (1983).
69. The earliest, the Kumara Brahma at Alampur, has three *bhumi*; see Prasad (1983), Pl. 1.
70. This temple is also called 'Temple 17' on Cousens' site plan, 'Narayana' in Michell (1975), 'Surya' by Rajasekhara (1985) and 'Suryanarayana' in Soundara Rajan (1986).
71. There has been some confusion introduced here by the misplacement of several fragments at the upper levels in the 1950s. Beginning with Louis Frederic's photographs of 1959, we can see three top elements on the eastern face that were not there in earlier photographs. They appear at the same time as the tusk-like brackets of the facade's central pillars. Percy Brown's publication of 1942 (Fig. 18, here) shows neither was yet in place in his time.
72. This is true of early Chalukya temples and is fairly common, if not universal, elsewhere.
73. It is also possible that this image could be from a *candrasala* intended for the stair screen, comparable to the one at the Sarangi-math. The location of its find suggests this, though my belief is that it would be the *nasika* image.
74. See Prasad (1883), Pls 1 and 15.
75. Its location can be seen in Michell (1975), drawing 34. I am using style here as a synonym for substyle.
76. Examples from Roda may be seen in Deva (1969), Pls 12–13; Harle (1986), Fig. 110; or the *Encyclopaedia of Indian Temple Architecture; North India, Period of Early Maturity*. I admit that this is an intuitive guess, not a contention I can support.
77. E.g., Sircar, pp. 148–57.
78. H. V. Sreenivasa Murthy and R. Ramakrishnan, *History of Karnataka (From the Earliest Times to the Present Day)*, New Delhi, 1978, p. 79.
79. George Michell, 'Temples of the Early Calukyas', *Mārg*, December 1978, p. 31.
80. See Gary Michael Tartakov, 'Reconstructing a Vaishnava Temple at Badami', in *Ṁadhu—Recent Researches in Indian Archaeology and Art History in Honour of M. N. Deshpande*, ed. M. S. Nagaraja Rao, Delhi, 1981, pp. 179–83.
81. For example, the Huccapayya-math (Cousens' temple 7), the Konti-gudi north-west (Cousens' temple 5), the Sarangi-math, the Hanuman temple, and Cousens' temples 46, 48 and 62, most of which are illustrated by Michell (1975).
82. This is argued for Gupta temples in Viennot (1969) and for Chalukya temples in my article 'Reconsidering the Flat-roofed Temple Hypothesis', in Joanna G. Williams, ed., *Kalādarśana, American Studies in Indian Art History*, New Delhi, 1981, pp. 147–57.
83. In one recent survey of the field, Susan B. Huntington upholds the possibility of Gupta temples without towers, but acknowledges the existence of arguments against them. See Susan B. Huntington, with John C. Huntington, *The Art of Ancient India*, New York, 1985, p. 636. But James Harle (1986), p. 111 and p. 500 dismisses the possibility. In the *Encyclopaedia of Indian Temple Architecture; Foundations*, pp. 22–3, Krishna Deva accepts the old view.
84. I am following the terminology of the *Encyclopaedia of Indian Temple Architecture; Upper Drāviḍadēśa*, ch. 20, as it seems the most authoritative source at this time. The *khura-kumbha* may be considered two mouldings, but since it is almost always seen in this combination and it is normally manufactured as a single piece, I feel it is conceptually a single unit.

85. This is either the only temple in the tradition that omits the *khura-kumbha* or the stones intended to represent that course were left unfinished.
86. See Tartakov (1983).
87. This combination course can be broken down into constituent elements, but it is better understood as a single conceptual unit. The animals overlapping the capping element and the *makara* that usually ends each course connect the two elements.
88. There are many ways to read these mouldings. Soundara Rajan (1986), Fig. 5a, omits the *vajana-patta*, but since it is necessary to reach the inner floor I include it. On the Mallikarjuna and Mahakutesvara temples of Mahakuta, the *vyalamala* and *vajana-patta* rise up the wall above the level of the floor inside. The upper *patta* in both cases contains narrative friezes. This element is particularly wide in the Mahakutesvara, where the *vyalamala* also contains narrative imagery. I am calling this course a *vyalamala* because of the *makara* that emerge from its ends, which are with the caryatid animals that emerge along its course its two typical characteristics. Other identifications might be as accurate, but this one recognizes its comparability with its pair on the Mallikarjuna.
89. I take the Sangamesvara of Pattadakal as the very end of Vijayaditya's reign on the basis of the thoroughly unfinished nature, which belies its exaggerated size and importance. The pillar inscription that gives its original title, the Vijayesvara, leaves no doubt that this is the great temple of Vijayaditya. And yet, in spite of the super-scale size and importance—equalled within the tradition by only his son's two great temples in the same place—it was left unfinished at his death. Additions such as hall *mandapa* pillars were continued for several generations, as indicated by inscriptions. But the temple's hall, sanctum doorway and major sculpture were all left unfinished.
90. Soundara Rajan (1986), p. 49, makes the most reasonable suggestion, that he is an architect. This is more fully discussed above.
91. Carol Radcliffe Bolon, 'The Pārvatī Temple, Sandur, and Early Images of Agastya', *Artibus Asiae*, XLII (1980), pp. 303–26. Bolon thinks Jinalayan may be a pilgrim, but it is difficult to see anyone not significantly connected to the structure's building or patronage being allowed to have such prominent notice engraved in the stone of a temple's facade. Despite Henry Cousens' comment to the contrary, such an inscription could not be 'scribbled' on a stone. It would have required serious labour by a highly skilled artist and sanction by temple authorities.
92. In the 1970s the lion was moved to the garden of the office of the Governor of Karnataka in Bangalore, where it now sits as an unnoticed bureaucratic trophy.
93. Such a concept can be seen at Angkor Wat and elsewhere in South-east Asia.
94. This is a rare inaccuracy in Michell's cross-section (Fig. 25, here), which mistakenly shows all the courses of the basement running around the west of the stairs and none on the east. Only one turns the corner on the inside, none on the outside.
95. Srinivas Padigar mentions the one on the east, 'The Durga Temple at Aihole, An Aditya Temple', *Archaeological Studies*, II, pp. 59–64, quoted in ch. 1. Ramesh pointed out the other to me at the site.
96. Harle (1972).
97. An important Chalukya example of temple building divided between distinct northern and southern sides is found in the Virupaksa at Pattadakal, where it is noted in an inscription. The phenomenon is noted regularly in Hoysala temple inscriptions.

98. For other *mithuna* pillars from the site see James Harle, 'Le Temple de Nāganātha à Nagarāl', *Arts Asiatiques*, XIX (1969), pp. 53–83, or Soundara Rajan (1986), Fig. 182.
99. I have written at length on my reasons for dating the Lad Khan in the first part of the eighth century, Tartakov (1980).
100. Harle (1972).
101. See Susan Locher Buchanan, *Calukya Temples: History and Iconography*, (Doctoral Dissertation) Ohio State University, 1985, pp. 204, 369, and notes 114–19 on pp. 298–9.
102. This is the figure mistakenly attributed to the Virupaksa by Goetz.
103. The arching brackets there today are modern restorations, not appearing in photographs of the temple until the 1950s. See note 71. The presence of the supporting corbel boss on the column, however, indicates that a bracket was intended as the restoration suggests.
104. This is mentioned in two inscriptions of Vijayaditya's reign and two of his grandson's: the Nerur plates of 700 CE, *Indian Antiquary* vol. IX, pp. 125–30; the Rayagad plates of 703 CE, *Epigraphia Indica* vol. X, pp. 14–17; the Kendur plates of 749–50 CE, *Epigraphia Indica*, vol. IX, pp. 200–6, and the Vakkalēri plates of 756–7 CE, *Epigraphia Indica*, vol. V, pp. 200–5.
105. See Tartakov (1980), Fig. 23, for the doorway entablature.
106. See Tartakov (1981) for discussion and illustration of this and Soundara Rajan (1986), Fig. 37 for an illustration.
107. I see this upper cutting as an aid to placing the block into its position, not as the remains of previous image as Lippe (1970) suggests. It is a notch out of the stone, not a form raised above it.
108. Despite the existence of Shaiva associations throughout the temple, there is not a single trace of Ganapati within its decoration.
109. Lippe (1970) and Harle (1972).
110. I cannot tell if a third eye was present either in this case or in the Vrsavahana Siva.
111. Harle (1972).
112. Lippe (1970).
113. Yet a third possible Bhiksatana has been pointed out by Susan Buchanan, in the *kaksasana* frieze on the north (Fig. 60), Buchanan, p. 369.
114. The fifth step in place today forms an exceptionally tall still, which rises above the floor of the porch and is probably a relatively recent interpolation.
115. To call this a *mukhacatuski* or 'four pillar porch', as Soundara Rajan (1986) does, seems to miss the point.
116. See also, Tartakov (1981), p. 69, Pls 2 and 4, or Soundara Rajan (1986), Figs 118–21.
117. The lowest pair have been totally vandalized, along with the second up on the left.
118. Pingala is always on the God's right, and often shown stout. Dandi is always shown slim. This is most commonly visible in the imagery of Bengal, but it is known in the Deccan also, in at least two examples in the Kailasa complex at Ellora. See Soundara Rajan (1983), Pl. XCIX B and Fig. 40.
119. This is a blind clerestory, simulating miniature windows but with only a few actually cut through.
120. The Virupaksa's sub-shrine may be seen in Tartakov and Dehejia (1984), Fig. 20. The Papanatha's are indicated at the mid-point of the northern and southern walls of the eastern *mandapa* on Michell's plan [diagram 2f] and Tartakov and Dehejia, Fig. 22.
121. George Michell depicts the bracket capitals of the interior pillars as simple quarter-rounds,

like the colonnade; the reconstruction has them as *taranga* roll brackets with some elements of unfinished outline drawings of projected sculpture. My own notes and photographs from before the reconstruction do not cover this detail, and I do not know which is true.

122. There is no trace of a Garuda, as reported by Soundara Rajan, in my photographs taken before the restoration. Contemporary reconstructions on the *kapota* level of the outer basement (visible in Fig. 57) are also misleading inventions. They include four pointed diamonds taken from the Kalyani Chalukya style of two centuries later (as found on the later structure in the compound, Fig. 85) and some dreadful figurative inventions.
123. Lippe (1970).
124. The most important of the history studies is K. V. Ramesh's *Chalukyas of Vātāpi*, but since its estimates of the temples there do not deal with their visual design, I shall not discuss its rather unique conclusions here.
125. Bolon (1981), pp. 357–69.
126. Bolon (1985), pp. 47–64. Bolon's reasoning and conclusions agree in large measure with Odile Divakaran's important work of a decade earlier, 'Les temples d'Ālampur et de ses environs au temps des Cāḷukyas de Bādāmi', *Arts Asiatiques*, XXIV (1971), pp. 51–101. Bolon has since contributed a chapter on Nagara temples to the *Encyclopaedia of Temple Architecture*, where the discussion of the Durga temple agrees with the view here on every point, with the exception of date. *Encyclopaedia of Indian Temple Architecture; North India, Foundations*, pp. 298–300.
127. J. F. Fleet, 'Sanskrit and Old-Canarese Inscriptions', *Indian Antiquary* VIII (1879), pp. 284–5.
128. I disagree with Bolon's interpretations of the inscriptions she depends upon, particularly the translation of the Svarga Brahma inscription that she believes to refer to Vinayaditya, but which has turned out to refer to the queen who outlived him. Although I agree that the series begins in Vikramaditya I's reign, I see no reason why it cannot run as late as Vikramaditya II's, particularly as the artists of Pattadakal's Galaganatha exterior and Kasivisvanatha interior seem to be so close to those of Alampur's Visva Brahma.
129. Soundara Rajan (1986), pp. 49–52.
130. Ramesh (1976). Ramesh told me the fragments fit the gateway inscription when we visited the site together. Subsequent to the publication of Soundara Rajan (1986), I asked him about this statement, and he saw no reason that it could not have been as late as the mid-eighth.
131. Padigar (1977).
132. Huntington (1985), pp. 232–5.
133. Harle (1986), pp. 175–6.
134. Rajasekhara (1985).
135. Rajasekhara (1985), pp. 94–7.
136. A detailed iconographic study is found in the dissertation of Susan Buchanan (1985), where the Durga temple is discussed on pp. 367–74. Buchanan says (note 104) she agrees with Bolon's early Vijayaditya date, and otherwise her views are more or less similar to the views I have laid out here and below.
137. The problem is revealed by Soundara Rajan's omission of any notice of the mixing of styles. In referring to the temple's tower, whose two appearances in photographs are unique in this volume on the southern style, *Encyclopaedia of Indian Temple Architecture; South India, Upper Drāviḍadēśa* (1986), Soundara Rajan uses the term *latina* (a sub-variety) rather than call it Nagara or northern. In the encyclopaedia's subsequent volume on the Chalukya's northern

style, Carol Bolon recognizes the Durga temple as a 'mature Calukya synthesis of elements from both Drāviḍa and Nāgara traditions'.

138. Both Carol Bolon's study of the early Chalukya sculpture and Susan Buchanan's study of their iconographic traditions avoid these problems by being comprehensive.

139. See note 104.

140. For an interesting if sketchy suggestion see M. S. Mate and S. Gokale, 'Aihoḷe: an Interpretation', in S. Ritti and B. R. Gopal, eds., *Studies in Indian History and Culture*, Dharwar, 1971, pp. 501–4.

45. 'Asvamukhi group, [Lad Khan], Aihole'. Pl. XXXIV (left), 'Some Remarks on Early Western Cāḷukya Sculpture', 1972.

46. 'Nyads and Tritons of Hellenistic typology'. Fig. 2, 'Imperial Rome and the Genesis of Classic Indian Art', 1959.

47. Huccimalli-gudi, Aihole, from the south-west.

48. Durga temple from the south-east.

49. Durga temple from the south-west.

50. Durga temple *pratoli* from the south. Permission AIIS.

51. Shaiva deity (possibly syncreticism with Aditya), Durga temple, south colonnade (3). Permission AIIS.

52. Durga temple *pratoli* from the north-east.

53. Durga temple *pratoli candrasala*, on the south.

54. Unfinished tower *nasika*, with Aditya, Durga temple.

55. Tower, Durga temple, from the south-east.

56. Tower, Durga temple, from the south-west.

57. South-western entrance, Durga temple.

58. The Lion, formerly at southern entrance steps, Durga temple.

59. *Mithuna* of the southern colonnade, Durga temple (4–8).

60. *Mithuna* of the northern colonnade, Durga temple (14–18).

61. Entrance to the Durga temple veranda, from the north-west.

62. North-west entrance, Durga temple.

63. Brahmachari *mithuna*, Durga temple (9).

64. Chastisement *Dvarapala*, Durga temple (10).

65. *Mithuna* on the west, Durga temple (12).

66. *Dvarapala*, Durga temple (11).

67. Ceiling *vidyadhara*, south-western *pradaksina*, Durga temple (V).

68. *Pradaksinapatha* toward the first niche, Durga temple.

69. *Pradaksinapatha* on the south, toward the *mandapa* wall, Durga temple.

70. Narasimha, Durga temple (IV).

71. Vishnu on Garuda, Durga temple (V). Permission AIIS.

72. *Pradaksinapatha* on the north, Durga temple.

73. Harihara, Durga temple (X). Permission AIIS.

74. Nagaraja ceiling, inner porch, Durga temple (a).

75. Detail of inner porch entablature on the west, with Aditya and guardians, Durga temple.

76. Interior, inner porch, Durga temple.

77. Detail of the *mandapa* doorway entablature with Garuda and other deities, Durga temple.

78. *Mandapa* doorway, Durga temple.

79. Possible Aditya of the entablature's lower storey, Durga temple.

80. Aditya of the entablature's central attic, Durga temple.

81. *Mandapa* interior, Durga temple.

82. Eastern *Dvarapala*, Cave II, Badami.

83. Western *Dvarapala*, Cave II, Badami.

84. Ravananugrahamurti, Cave XXIX (Dhumarlena), Ellora.

85. Kalyani Chalukya structure, Durga temple compound, Aihole from the south-west.

86. Meguti (inscribed 634/5 CE), Aihole, from the north-east.

87. Bhagavati temple, Aihole, from the east.

88. Sarangi-math, Aihole, from the north-east.

94. Destroyed apsidal temple, Cikki complex, Aihole.

93. Apsidal temple, Cikka Mahakuta, sanctum doorway.

92. East *pratoli*, Virupaksa temple (*c.* 733–45), Pattadakal, from the south-east.

91. Sulebhavi *pratoli* and tank, from the south-west.

90. East *pratoli*, Virupaksa temple (*c.* 733–45), Pattadakal, from the west.

89. Western *gopuram*, Tirukalukunram, from the south-west.

95. Pillar *mithuna*, Naganatha temple, Nagaral.

96. Pillar *mithuna*, Lad Khan temple, Aihole.

97. Pillar *mithuna*, Sarangi-math, Aihole. Permission AIIS.

98. Pillar *mithuna*, Virupaksa temple, Pattadakal.

99. Northern *devakostha*, Huccappayya-gudi, Aihole.

100. Window *udgama*, Mahakutesvara temple, Mahakuta.

101. Papanatha temple, Pattadakal, from the north-east.

102. Sangamesvara temple, Kudavelı, from the north-west. Permission ASI.

103. Galaganatha temple, Pattadakal, from the south.

104. Garuda-Brahma temple, Alampur, from the south.

105. Interior pillars, Virupaksa temple (733–45), Pattadakal.

106. Subrahmanya ceiling, porch, Huccimalli-gudi, Aihole.

107. Surya lintel, Surya temple, Aihole.

108. Surya temple doorway, Surya temple, Aihole.

Appendix I

James Fergusson

Iwullee

Though not remarkable for architectural magnificence, the temple represented in [Figs 2, 3, and 4], is to the Indian antiquary one of the most interesting in the whole series; it is the only known example of its class as a structural building, though there are numerous instances at Karlee, Ellora, Ajunta, and elsewhere, of similar edifices. These, however, are all cut in the rock, and, consequently, have no exterior except the facades. It has always, therefore, been a great problem to know how the structural prototypes of these rock-cut temples were formed, and what their interior arrangements may have been. The temple at Iwullee does not answer all these problems, but it goes nearer to it than any other we know.

During the troubles of this country, before it fell into the hands of the British, this temple was used as a fortification. A round keep of rubble masonry replaced the spire, and a parapet was raised surrounding the whole. The interior, too, seems to be encumbered with rubbish, filled in to support the military superstructure. This, with the absence of plans, or any detailed description, prevents our speaking positively on the subject, but there can be little doubt but that the apse represented [Fig. 1], correctly reproduces what the great cave at Karlee would have been had it been a free standing structural building, and the form of the portico is just such as we find at Ellora, Ajunta, and elsewhere.

It is called the 'Sivite' temple, and is no doubt now considered as appropriated to the worship of that deity; but there is nothing in this to prevent our assuming that it was originally appropriated to the worship of Buddha. The great cave at Karlee is appropriated to Siva at the present day, and so are many caves in other parts of the country, though their original dedication to Buddhist worship is quite manifest.

So far as can be made out from the photograph, there is nothing in the sculptures indicative of the worship of Siva, and nothing that might not be found in later Buddhist erections. But, on the other hand, there is nothing improbable in the assumption that the Hindoos may have appropriated a Buddhist structural form in this instance, as they did in their rock-cut arrangements in many instances at Elephanta, Ellora, and elsewhere.

Architecturally it is not so important to which religion it was originally dedicated, as it is to know what its interior arrangements may have been, and the light which an examination of it would throw on the whole subject of cave architecture would be so great that there are few temples in India that would more fully repay a careful survey and detailed illustration.

In the foreground of the photograph [Fig. 2] will be observed two detached slabs lying on the ground, and with two figures in violent action upon them. These are very unlike any sculptures found in Hindoo temples in the neighbourhood, but very much resemble some subjects painted in the fresco in the caves of Ajunta. Indeed, the whole character of this ornamentation recalls these celebrated caves more than that of any structural edifice in the province where the temple stands.

If this is so, and if the temple was originally dedicated to Buddhist worship, it is the oldest temple represented in this work, probably anterior to the tenth century; but the data available are not such as to enable any positive opinion to be pronounced on such a subject. (*Architecture in Dharwar and Mysore*, London, 1866, pp. 67–8.)

Chaityas, or Temples

As before hinted, we are almost wholly dependent on rock-cut examples for our knowledge of these sacred edifices of the Buddhists. There is one structural example at Sanchi, which, as it now stands, is merely a chain of upright stone posts, supporting stone architraves very little less rude than those of Stonehenge, which it very much resembles both in plan and dimensions. It would require excavation, and a more careful examination than it has yet received, to ascertain whether it even was roofed, or was enclosed by another wall. According to present appearances it had neither; but too little is known to justify any inference from this. There is another temple at Iwullee in Dharwar, which, though now dedicated to Siva, seems originally to have been a Buddhist Chaitya. At least, its apse reproduces what we may fancy was once their external form. It, has however, been used as a fortification; its upper part is destroyed, and altogether it will only be when some competent architect examines these examples on the spot, that we shall really know how far they elucidate the matter. [*Note 1*: It is probable that a tolerably correct idea of the general exterior appearance of the buildings from which these caves were copied may be obtained from the *Raths* (as they are called) of Mahavellipore (described further on . . .). These are monuments of a much later date, and belonging to a different religion, but they correspond so nearly in all their parts with the temples and monasteries now under consideration, that we cannot doubt their being, in most respects, close copies of them.]

With these two exceptions, we are left wholly to rock-cut examples. (*History of Architecture in All Countries*, London, 1867, pp. 479–80.)

Plans

Up to the present time only one temple has been discovered in India which gives us even a hint of how the plans of the Buddhist Chaitya Halls became converted into those of the Jaina and Hindu temples. Fortunately, however, its evidence is so distinct that there can be very little doubt about the matter. The temple in question is situated in the village of Aiwulli, in Dharwar, in western India, not far from the place where the original capital of the Chalukyan sovereigns is supposed to have been situated, and near the caves of Badami on the one hand and the temples of Pittadakul on the other. Its date is ascertained by an inscription on its outer gateway, containing the name of Vicramaditya Chalukya, whom we know from inscriptions certainly died in AD 680, and with less certainty that he commenced to reign AD 650. The temple itself may possibly be a little older, but the latter may fairly be taken as a medium date representing its age. It is thus not only the oldest structural temple known to exist in western India, but in fact the only one yet discovered that can with certainly be said to have been erected before the great cataclysm of the beginning of the eighth century.

Mr Burgess is of opinion that it was originally dedicated to Vishnu, but this does not seem quite clear. There certainly are Jaina figures among those that once adorned it; and it seems to be a fact that though the Jains admitted Siva, Vishnu, and all the gods of the Hindu Pantheon into their temples, there is no evidence of the reverse process. The Hindus never admitted the human Tirthankars of the Jains among their gods. Its original dedication is fortunately, however, of very little importance for our present purposes. The religions of the Jains and Vaishnavas, as pointed out above . . ., were, in those days and for long afterwards, so similar that it was impossible to distinguish between them. Besides this, the age when this temple was erected was the age of toleration in India. The Chinese traveller Hiouen Thsang has left us a most vivid description of a great quinquennial festival, at which he was present at Allahabad in AD 643, at which the great King Siladitya presided, and distributed alms and honours, on alternate days, to Buddhists, Brahmans, and heretics of all classes, who were assembled there in tens of thousands, and seem to have felt no jealousy of each other, or rivalry that led, at least, to any disturbance. It was on the eve of a disruption that led to the most violent contests, but up to that time we have no trace of dissension among the sects, nor any reason to believe that they did not all use similar edifices for their religious purposes, with only such slight modifications as their different formulae may have required (Woodcut no. 120).

Be this as it may, any one who will compare the plan of the chaitya at Sanchi (Woodcut no. 40), which is certainly Buddhist, with that of this temple at Aiwulli, which is either Jaina or Vaishnava, can hardly fail to perceive how nearly identical they must have been when complete. In both instances, it will be observed, the apse is solid, and it appears that this always was the case in structural free-standing chaityas . . . it was easy to introduce windows . . . Another change was necessary when, from an apse sheltering a relic-shrine, it became a cell containing an image of a god; a door was then indispensable, and also a thickening of the wall when it was necessary it should bear a tower or sikra to mark the position of the cella on the outside. Omitting the verandah, the other changes introduced between the erection of these two examples are not only such as were required to adapt the points of support in the temple to carry a heavy stone roof, instead of the light wooden superstructure of the Buddhist chaitya [Fig. 1].

It may be a question, and one not easy to settle in the present state of our knowledge, whether the Buddhist chaityas had or had not verandahs, like the Aiwulli example. The rock-cut examples naturally give us no information on this subject, but the presumption certainly is, looking at their extreme appropriateness in that climate, that they had this appendage, sometimes at least, if not always.

If from this temple at Aiwulli we pass to the neighbouring one at Pittadkul, built probably a couple of centuries later, we find that we have passed the boundary line that separates the ancient from the mediaeval architecture of India, in so far at least as plans are concerned (Woodcut no. 122). The circular forms of the Buddhists have entirely disappeared, and the cell has become the base of a square tower, as it remained ever afterwards. The nave of the chaitya has become a well defined mantapa or porch in front of, but distinct from, the cell, and these two features in an infinite variety of forms, and with various subordinate adjuncts, are the essential elements of the plans of the Jaina and Hindu temples of all the subsequent ages. (*History of Indian and Eastern Architecture*, London, 1876, pp. 218–21.)

The great interest of this Ratha [Fig. 33] lies in the fact that it represents, on a small scale, the exterior of one of those Chaitya caves, which form so important a feature in all the western groups, but all of which are interiors only, and not one is so completely excavated as to enable us to judge of what the external appearance may have been, of the constructed Chaityas from which they were copied. There is one temple at Aihole dedicated to Siva which does show the external aisle and apsidal termination, and is probably of about the same age as this Ratha. Unfortunately it has been used as a fortification, and its upper storey and roof removed, so that it is of little more use to us now than an interior would be for judging of what the effect of the exterior may have been above the first storey. From the evidence of this Ratha it seems almost certain that in the larger examples there was a range of small cells in the roof of the aisles, which would naturally be much wider in constructed examples than in caves where there was no possibility of introducing light except through openings in the facade. We may also gather from the Aihole example and other indications that an external verandah surrounded the whole, and if this were so the cells would have been placed over the verandah, and the roof of the aisles used as an ambulatory. (*Cave Temples of India*, London, 1880, p. 136.)

Appendix II

Bhau Daji

Iwullee, Inscription on the Gateway of the Town

This inscription is a short one of the eighth century, and on the wall of a temple; though in the volume it is incorrectly described as being on the gateway of the town.

The two first lines can be deciphered; they contain the name of the Chalukya king Satyāśraya Srī Prithivi Vallabha Mahārājādhirāja.

Iwullee, In a Shivite Temple

This inscription is the oldest of all, being dated in Śaka 506 (Sātampancha śateś ācha), AD 584, and the year of the Kali Yuga 3855, and from the war of the Mahābhārata 3730, thus showing that the war of the Mahābhārata was then regarded as having taken place one hundred and twenty-five years after the commencement of the Kali Yuga. It is clear that enough of confusion existed in Indian chronology even at this early date.

The entire inscription is in Sanskrit verse, and was written in the time of the Chālukya, Pulakeśi II, the contemporary of Hiouen Thsang. In some places the letters in the photograph are indistinct and doubtful, but these have been mostly made out from the context. The inscription, besides giving even a better description of the older Chālukya kings of the Dekkan than has hitherto been published, contains two important names, those of the celebrated poets Kālidāsa and Bhāravi, whose fame in this world is compared with that of Ravikīrti, the author of the verses in this inscription, who was very probably a Digambara Jain. The fact is now placed beyond doubt that Kālidāsa and Bhāravi had achieved fame in India before the end of the sixth century of the Christian era. ('Report on Photographic Copies of Inscriptions in Dharwar and Mysore', *Journal of the Bombay Branch of the Royal Asiatic Society*, vol. IX (1867–70), 1872, pp. 314–15.)

Appendix III

JAMES BURGESS

The little information we had hitherto been able to obtain respecting the curious temple on the north-east outskirts of the village, and locally known as the 'Durga', was most unsatisfactory. It was spoken of as a Jaina temple, and sometimes as a Śaiva one, and was supposed to be the one on which was the important inscription of AD 584 to which I have already alluded. As the only known example of its class as a structural building, it is to the Indian antiquary one of the most interesting temples in the south of India. It was therefore a special object of attention with me. I could find no inscription containing a date upon it, but the style of the interior is so closely allied to that of Cave III at Badāmi that it was evident it must be placed within a century after the cave. The plan, with the round apse [Fig. 8], is unique, and suggests that it might represent a Buddhist Chaitya structural temple. In the absence of plans, however, or any detailed description, all we could previously conjecture was that the apse was a representation of what a Buddhist Chaitya like that at Karlē would have been had it been a free-standing structural building.

Either the roof had fallen in or been destroyed—most likely the latter, and the Marāṭhas of a century or two ago piled up a wall of rubble masonry round the roof and formed a ramp round the spire, utilizing it as a keep and a watch-tower. The interior also is half filled with stones and rubbish. It might be cleaned out, and cattle prevented from entering it as they now do, while the aisles might be used for storing some of the many sculptured and inscribed slabs that lie about waiting destruction . . .

I regretted that the rain forced me to leave Aiwaḷḷi sooner than I had intended and prevented my making so full a survey of this and other temples here as they seemed to require. The temple was neither Jaina nor Śaiva, but a genuine Chālukya temple of Vishṇu. The plan [Fig. 8] will show the size and general arrangements, which need not be more particularly noted here. In the wall of the temple inside the surrounding portico are nine niches in which are mythological figures of Nṛisiñha, Maheśāsurī, Varāha, Vishṇu, Arddhanāri, Śiva, &c. Between the niches are six perforated stone windows—four belonging to the aisles of the temple, and two to the *pradakshina*; and below the level of these is a belt of sculpture consisting of mythological scenes, *gaṇa*, arabesques, &c. Two of the *gaṇa* are represented on Pl. LII, Figs 2 and 3. Of the twenty-eight original columns that surrounded it, twelve in front have sculptures—a pair of figures on the outer sides: otherwise these pillars are plain square blocks. The sketch, Pl. LII, Fig. 4, represents the figures on the front of the left hand pillar at the entrance. The four pillars of the inner porch are more elaborate: besides the larger pairs of figures on the outer sides, they have a band of *gaṇa* near the bottom; farther up the shaft a medallion, usually with three figures; and above this again a deep belt with arabesque drapery below and *gaṇa* above, crowned with a fillet of leaves; and on the neck of the column, resting on this, is another medallion with small figures [Fig. 7]. The brackets over the shaft are not much carved. The ten pillars of the hall of the temple are very similar to those of the porch; and the roof is raised by a deep architrave—a sort of triforium in fact—four feet in height, above the brackets, and further by about one foot, by the cross-beams. The shrine, which occupies the place of the *dahgoba* in Bauddha Cave temples, has a *pradakshina* round it, and is semicircular at the back.

The door of the temple is richly carved, reminding us of the elaborate doorways at Ajaṇṭā, and the carving is continued up to the very roof, 4 feet 8½ inches from the soffit of the lintel, and forms an architrave 2 feet 5 inches wide on the jambs. At the bottom of these are several figures, male and female, from 2 feet 1 inch to 2 feet 9 inches in height. On the lintel is Garuḍa grasping snakes in his hands—the *chinha* or cognizance of a Vaishṇava temple.

The roof in front of the door is carved with a fine Śesha or human-headed snake in the first compartment; and in the second is a circle of fishes with their heads turned towards the central knob (as in Cave II at Badāmi), and round them is a ring of water plants.

From the side columns of the porch to the central beam, there have been brackets possibly like those in Cave III at Badāmi, but they are now gone. The roof of the front of the porch or verandah has fallen and the two larger slabs (represented in photograph, [Fig. 6]) now lying at the south-east corner of the temple probably formed part of this roof. The third seems to have been *recently* extracted from one of the niches in the wall, and was found lying near the gate, over some rods to keep them straight, and I had it set up where it appears in the photograph. The bold free style of these sculptures will strike the artist as quite unusual in Indian art. There are other similar slabs on the roof on each side of the porch, but portions of the stone have peeled off.

At the corner of the temple and partially sunk in the earth is a figure of a gigantic lion or monster with its paw on the back of a small elephant. This was also photographed.

The temple has once been enclosed in a court with gates: the south gate still remains and there are traces of the surrounding enclosure, but it has been divided by low walls built of the *dēbris*, and is used to store hay and straw and to shoot rubbish. On the wall of the south gate are two inscriptions (nos, 30 and 31, [Fig. 9]), the first beginning with the words: *Svasti Vikramāditya Satyāśraya Srī Prithivīvallabha mahārājādhirāja parameśvara bhatāra prithivīrajyageye*. The remainder is Kanarese, but as Vikramaditya died in AD 680. we have here a confirmation of the relation in which, from theoretical considerations, we should place this temple with regard to Cave III at Badāmi.

The inscription was described by Col. Biggs as 'on the gateway of the town', and photographed on a small scale—3 3/10 inches being the length of the lines—so indistinctly that the late Dr Bhāu Dājī could make nothing of it. The second inscription, no. 31, is on the same wall lower down; and on a pillar in the temple is the inscription no. 32; while in the photograph [Fig. 6] is a fourth one of a few letters on the base of the temple. (*Report on the First Season's Operations in Belgaum and Kaladgi Districts*, Archaeological Survey of Western India, vol. I, London, 1874, pp. 40–3.)

Pl. 267 [Fig. 5]—At Aihole, in the Bijāpur district of the Bombay Presidency, is an ancient ruined temple, known as the 'durga' or fort, which most probably belongs to the second half of the seventh century, or, at latest, to the first half of the eighth. It is unique as a structural building, and bears a close analogy in plan to the Bauddha cave-temples, illustrating how the latter developed into the later forms of the Jaina and Hindu temples. . . .

Pl. 268 [Figs 7 and 10]—The sect to which this temple originally belonged has been disputed. Over the doorway [to] the maṇḍapa, which is richly carved, is a figure of Garuḍa holding snakes in both hands; and this is the proper symbol of a Vaishṇava shrine. The sculptures are all executed with remarkable freedom and boldness, and though we have not representations of nearly all of them, there are in the niches of the walls figures of Vishnu, Narasiṇha, and Varāha—agreeing with the symbol on the doorway. But there is on a moulding of the basement on the south side a label bearing—'The holy Jaina temple'. An inscription on the gateway to the south of the temple (seen beyond it to the left) makes a grant 'to Aditya of the temple of Aṭada-Aḷekomara Siṇga' by the king Vikramāditya Satyāsraya 'and the people headed by the mahājans'; but this helps us little, and it is undated—so that though presumed to be of Vikramaditya II, AD 733–46, it may be of Vikramaditya I, AD 655–80, to which period rather the temple itself seems architecturally to belong. Now it is possible that it may have been taken possession of by the Jainas, when they were in special favour, and the words were carved on the basement to indicate the change of proprietors; they would not have been placed there when the temple was first erected. Nor was it originally a Jaina, but distinctly a Vaishṇava shrine. (*Ancient Monuments, Temples and Sculpture of India*, London, 1897, p. 35.)

Till the discovery of the small Buddhist chaitya halls at Tēr and Chezarla and elsewhere, already described [Fig. 34], there was only one temple in India which gave us any hint of how the plans of such halls were related to those of Hindū and Jaina temples. Fortunately, however, its evidence is so distinct that there could be very little doubt about the matter. The temple in question is situated in the village at Aihole in Bijāpūr district, in western India, not far from the place where the original capital of the Chalukyan sovereigns was situated, and near the caves of Bādāmi on the one hand and the temples of Pattadakal on the other. Its date is uncertain to some extent, since an inscription on its outer gateway recording a grant to the temple, during the reign of Vikramāditya-Satyāśraya, is undated; and there were two Chalukya kings of this name—one ruling between AD 655 and 680, and the other between 733 and 746. But the grant was to a temple already established, and even if made in the eighth century the fane might well be of fifty or eighty years earlier date, as its architecture would indicate. It is thus not only one of the oldest structural temples known to exist in western India, but in fact one of the only three yet discovered that can with any certainty be said to have been erected before the beginning of the eighth century.

This temple as the sculptures testify, was dedicated to Vishnu—the special divinity of the Chalukyas; but the words carved in Kanarese on the basement—'the holy Jaina temple'—seem to indicate that at one time it had been claimed or appropriated by the Jains, and this, with some misconception as to the character of the sculptures, has led to the mistake of its being supposed that it was originally Jaina. Its original dedication is fortunately, however, of very little importance for our present purposes. . . .

Be this as it may, any one who will compare the plan of the chaitya at Sānchī (woodcut no. 47), which is certainly Buddhist, with that of this temple at Aihole, which is Vaishnava, can hardly fail to perceive how nearly identical they must have been when complete. In both instances, it will be observed, the apse is solid, and it appears that this always was the case in structural free-standing chaityas . . . Another change was necessary when, from an apse sheltering a relic-shrine, it became a cell containing an image of a god; a door was then indispensable, and also a thickening of the wall when it was necessary it should bear a tower or śikhara to mark the position of the cella on the outside. Omitting the verandah, the other changes introduced between the erection of these two examples are only such as were required to adapt the points of support in the temple to carry a heavy stone roof, instead of the light wooden superstructure of the primitive Buddhist chaitya [Fig. 1].

It may be a question, and one not easy to settle in the present state of our knowledge, whether the Buddhist chaityas had or had not verandahs, like the Aihole example. The rock-cut examples naturally give us no information on this subject, but the presumption certainly is, looking at their extreme appropriateness in that climate, that they had this appendage, sometimes at least, though not perhaps usually. (*History of Indian and Eastern Architecture*, rev. and ed., with additions by James Burgess (Indian) and R. Phene Spiers (Eastern), London, 1910 (2 vols), vol. 1, pp. 319–22.)

Appendix IV

John Faithful Fleet

25. Old Canarese Inscription in the Gateway of the Durga Temple at Aihole . . . [Fig. 9]

The inscription is one of the Western Chalukya Vikramaditya-Satyasraya. It is not dated. But, from the form of the characters, I would refer it to the time of Vikramaditya II, the son of Vijayaditya, not of Vikramaditya I, the son of Pulikesi II.

The grant is to Adityabhatta, a priest of the temple. Atada-Alekomara-Singa, or 'Alekomara-Singa of the games', must be the founder of the temple . . .

Translation

Hail! While Vikramāditya-Satyāśraya, the favourite of the world, the Great King, the supreme king, the supreme lord, the worshipful one, was ruling the world, the gift of Rēvadibadda, the son of Pēsada, to Ādityabhaṭṭa of the temple of Ātada-Ālēkōmara-Siṅga, (*was*) one *māna* on each *pēṟu*, and five *visas* on each *bhaṇḍa-pēṟu*, and fifty (betel-leaves) on each *pēṟu* of betel-leaves, whenever the customs-duty should come in to him. This much . . .

Whosoever destroys this, may he be on an equality with people who kill a thousand tawny-coloured cows and a thousand Brāhmaṇs of Vāraṇāsi.

26. Old Canarese Inscription in the Gateway of the Durga Temple at Aihole

The characters are of the eighth or ninth century. The transcription is: (1) Śrī-Savitaran (2) Piriṟeyya(?) putran. The translation is: Śrī-Savitara, the son of Piriṟeyya.

27. Old Canarese Inscription on a Pillar in the Durga Temple at Aihole

The characters are of the seventh or eighth century. The transcription is: (1) Śrī-Basamayyan (2) Kisuvoḷala bhaṭṭa. The translation is: Śrī-Basamayya, the priest of Kisuvoḷal.

('Inscriptions from Belgaum and Kaladgi', in James Burgess, *Report on the Antiquities in the Bidar and Aurangabad Districts*, A.S.W. I., vol. III, London, 1878, pp. 128–9.)

Sanskrit and Old-canarese Inscriptions No. LVIII

The next of the Aihoḷe inscriptions, in chronological order, is that at the Durga temple . . . Mr Burgess . . . places the date of its construction within a century after that of Bādāmi Cave III, which was excavated, or at least was finished, in the reign of the Chalukya king Mangaḷīśvara, and contains on one of its columns an inscription of his dated Śaka 500 (AD 578–9). He also considers that 'the temple was neither Jain nor Śaiva, but a genuine Chalukya temple of Vishṇu.' I would, however, point out that one of the stones in the base of the temple has on it, as may be seen in the photograph, Pl. LIV, [Fig. 6] of the *First Archaeological Report*, the word *Śrī-Jin-ālayan*, i.e. 'the holy temple of Jina', in characters which may be somewhat earlier, but which seem to me to have been cut by the hand of the very same man who engraved the inscription of Vijayāditya on a pillar in the porch of the temple of Mahākūṭēśvara at Bādāmi.

. . . It is a matter for argument whether it is of the time of Vikramāditya I, the son of Pulikēśī II, or of the time of Vikramaditya II, the son of Vijayāditya. My own opinion—based, partly on the form of the characters . . . is, that it is of the time of Vikramāditya II, who commenced to reign in Śaka 654 (AD 732–3) or 655 . . .

Translation

Hail! While Vikramāditya-Satyāśraya—the favourite of the world, the great king, the supreme king, the supreme lord, the worshipful one—was ruling the world, the gift of Revadibadda, the son of Pesada, to the venerable Āditya of the temple of Āṭada-Ālekomara-Singa, (*was*) one *māna* on each *pēṟu*, and five *visas* on each *bhanda-pēṟu*, and fifty (*betel-leaves*) on each *pēṟu* of betel-leaves, whenever the customs-duty should come in to him. This much was proclaimed by the king, and by (*the people of*) the city, headed by the *Mahājanas* . . . ('Sanskrit and Old-Canarese Inscriptions. No. LVIII', *Indian Antiquary*, vol. 8 (1879), pp. 285–6).

Appendix V

Henry Cousens

. . . we come now to temples in which the shrine is surmounted by a *śikhara* or tower, but which is placed within the body of the building, towards the end of the great hall, and insulated from the back wall, thereby allowing of a passage around it. Among these are the Durgā, Meguti and Huchchimalli-guḍi temples, probably in this order of sequence after Lāḍ Khān's.

The Durgā temple is, without doubt, the finest and most imposing temple at Aihoḷe; and it is one of the most unique in India, in that the plan follows the lines of the apsidal cave *chaitya* of the Buddhists, the place of the shrine occupying that of the *dagoba*. And, like its prototype, two rows of columns separate the body of the hall into a centre nave and two side aisles. Stone, as the building material, at a time when constructive arching was unknown, determined that the roof should be flat and not arched, but sufficient likeness to the *chaitya* was obtained by making the central roof lofty and that of the side aisles low and sloping, the slope being the nearest approach to the half vault of the *chaitya*. The deep entablature, sculptured with friezes of figures, foliage, and arabesque, reminds one forcibly of the same as seen in the cave *chaityas*, above pillars, such as that in Cave XXVI at Ajanṭā.

There is an added outside verandah, all around the central hall. A description of this temple is given in the First Report of the Archaeological Survey of Western India, so I need only supplement that account here. That the temple is Vaishṇava there is no doubt; the sculptures, and Garuda over the door lintel, proclaim that fact sufficiently. The central flat roof has collapsed and the columns and superstructure are shattered. The accompanying illustrations, together with those already published, will give a good idea of the building as it stands to-day [Fig. 11].

As to its age, Dr Burgess says 'the style of the interior is so closely allied to that of Cave III at Bādāmi that it was evident that it must be placed within a century after the cave.' But I would not place it so late as this. Rather, would I say, within a century before the cave. There is no departure here, as in the cave, from the plain square column, with no capital between the shaft and the brackets above. At the same time, the columns are a great deal less massive than in Lāḍ Khān's [Fig. 37]. One would rather expect to find a forward development in style taking place, first and more readily, in a structural building than an excavated one, where the nature of the construction lends itself more readily to a change to more elaborate forms; and certainly the cave, with its varied types of pillars, shows a very great advance upon the Lāḍ Khān type. ('The Ancient Temples of Aihoḷe', pp. 189–204 of *Archaeological Survey of India, Annual Report 1907–08*, Calcutta, 1911, pp. 194–5.)

The Durgā Temple

Of temples with northern *śikharas* there are two particularly fine ones, namely, the Durgā temple at Aihoḷe (no. 3 [on Fig. 13]) and that of Pāpanātha at Paṭṭadakal, the former being undoubtedly the finest and most imposing temple in the village [Figs 11, 12 and 14]. It is most unique in that it is built upon the lines of the apsidal cave *chaitya* of the Buddhists, the position of the shrine being that of the *dāgaba*; and, like its prototype, two rows of columns separate the body of the hall into a central nave and two side aisles. Stone, as a building material, at a time when constructive arching was unknown, determined that the roof should be flat and not arched, but sufficient likeness to the *chaitya* was obtained by making the central roof lofty and that of the side aisles low and sloping, the slope being the nearest approach to the half vault of the *chaitya*. The entablature, four feet deep sculptured with friezes of figures, foliate and arabesque, built over the columns on either side in order to raise the height of the nave, reminds one forcibly of the same as seen in the cave *chaityas* above the pillars, such as that in cave XXVI at Ajanta. Upon Pl. XI [Fig. 12] will be found a small scale plan of cave XIX at Ajanta, and it is interesting to compare the two plans. It will be seen that the rock-wall periphery of the cave corresponds to the outer pillared periphery of the temple; and the walls of the temple are just the columns of the cave all linked up. The *dāgaba* of the cave, upon the face of which is the principal object of worship—the image of Buddha—is represented by the shrine with its image. The structural necessities of the temple required the addition of these extra columns in the hall. There is no doubt that this type of structure descended from a wooden prototype, which was originally provided with a thatched roof. Such a roof has been reproduced, in brick and mortar, over the old Buddhist *Chaitya* at Tēr in the Nizām's dominions. The temple faces the east.

The pillars in this temple are not quite so heavy and massive as they are in Lāḍ Khān's, though they are very simple in their general outline, being square blocks, without bases, surmounted by very plain bracket-capitals. Those in the front of the temple have been decorated with pairs of figures, in full relief, upon their outer sides. Some of the innermost columns in the porch are further enriched with bands and medallions of arabesque [Fig. 7]. It will be noticed that all the male figures wear a high crown, and thus differ from that in the temple of Mallikārjuna at Paṭṭadakal, which has a very elaborate coiffure of curls . . . The latter looks more like a portrait statue than these, which are probably merely decorative figures.

Garuḍa presides above the shrine door, where he grasps in his two hands the serpent tails of *nāgas*, whose upturned human bodies are a little way down the jambs on either side. The doorway is much after the style of those of the *vihāras* at Ajanta.

Though the image groups, representing Narasimha, Mahiśāsura-mardanī, Varāha, Vishṇu, Ardhanārī, and Śiva, in the niches around the walls in the outer verandah, are an impartial mixture of Śaiva and Vaishṇava subjects, it is very likely that the temple was originally dedicated to Vaishṇava worship—possibly to Sūrya-Nārāyaṇa. The central niche at the back, which, in a temple, generally contains the most important image next to that in the shrine, and which gives a clue to the principal object of worship, is empty.

There are two or three short inscriptions on and about the temple, but they are of little interest. On a stone in the basement are the words Śrī-Jin-Alayan' 'Holy temple of Jina' in characters of the same date as Vijayaditya's inscription on a pillar in the porch of the Mahākūṭēśvara temple (AD 696–733). As there seems to be not the shadow of a doubt that the temple was originally Vaishṇava, this may mean that at that early date the temple was either in disuse, when some Jaina stranger, mistaking it for one of his own shrines scribbled this upon it, or that it had been temporarily in the possession of the Jains. In either case it shows that the temple was then of considerable age and had been deserted. On a pillar is another short inscription in letters of the eighth or ninth century, which reads 'Śrī-Basamayya, the *bhaṭṭa* of Kisuvoḷal' (Paṭṭadakal). This may be connected with the time when these temples were restored for Śaiva worship. Yet another on the north wall of the south gateway records a grant to Āditya, a priest of the temple.

The northern type of tower is the most marked feature on this temple—so like the *śikharas* of the oldest temples in Orissa. Unfortunately the upper part has fallen, but we have a more complete example in that of Huchchimalli-Guḍi next to be considered . . .

At different points in the walls are perforated stone windows of curious patterns which serve the purpose of ventilation better than that of admitting light. On Fig. 12 are shown some examples of these among which will be seen one in the familiar Greek fret or key pattern, but worked into the form of the favourite *śvastika*.

The temple stands within the ruins of a fort-like enclosure, which has probably given the present name to the temple—*durga* or 'fort'. It has nothing to do with Durgā, a name of Pārvatī. (*Chālukyan Architecture of the Kanarese Districts*, A.S.W.I., N.I.S., vol. XLII, Calcutta, 1926, pp. 38–40.)

Appendix VI

E. B. Havell

The finest of the very few structural chaitya-grihas yet discovered is one which Fergusson and his followers, to the confusion of their readers, put into his Dravidian compartment, though he points out its resemblance in plan to the ancient Buddhist chaitya-hall at Sānchī. This is a stone building, probably of the sixth or seventh century AD. . . .

It is somewhat remarkable that this temple belonged apparently to the Jain sect: it was an exception to the rule that Jains in their temple-building kept to orthodox Brahmanical types, as their individualistic ritual demanded. Possibly, however, their ancient ritual differed from modern practice, and resembled that of the Buddhists more closely than it does now. But, in any case, in this temple a hall of the Sangha is provided, as if for an order of devotees distinct from the lay community. [*note 1*: The Sangha, like other Buddhist institutions, was only an adaptation of the organization of the Aryan clans to the rule of life propounded by Sākiya Muni: it was an Order within the larger Order of the Aryan community.] . . . the roof of which is supported by a massive Vishnu pillar [Fig. 7]. The roof over the chaitya shrine has fallen, and the loose rubble which has been piled round the ruins makes it difficult to determine whether it was a sikhara of the Vishnu type, or whether it was domed like a Siva shrine. The latter might be expected over a chaitya, and it is significant that it is known locally as a Dūrgā temple, a fact which makes a domed 'Siva' roof, derived from the stūpa, almost a certainty.

This Aihole temple is, or was, distinguished by its extraordinarily fine sculpture, as will be seen from Pls XIV [Fig. 5] and XV (sic). The two superb high relief flying Devas in the last plate, which shows the condition in which they were discovered, have since probably been destroyed; for the photographs taken by Dr Burgess in 1874, and published in his Report of the Archaeological Survey of Western India for that year, show them already in a shockingly mutilated state. Such is the treatment of great works of art which archaeological historians contemptuously dismiss as 'Puranic'. (*The Ancient and Mediaeval Architecture of India: A Study of Indo-Aryan Civilization*, London, 1915, pp. 67–9.)

Appendix VII

ANANDA K. COOMARASWAMY

The Brāhmaṇical Durgā temple at Aihoḷe [Fig. 15] is probably of sixth century date, and rather early Cāḷukya than Gupta, but is connected with the types now described. Entirely of stone, it follows the plan of the apsidal *caitya*-halls, but the roof is flat and constructed of stone slabs, a northern *śikhara* rises above the *garbha-gṛha*, and there is a verandah, roofed with sloping slabs, supported by massive square columns with heavy brackets. The whole stands on a high basement of several horizontal courses, of which one is fluted, another decorated with *caitya*-arches, and another with reliefs. (*History of Indian and Indonesian Art*, New York, 1927, p. 78.)

There are other low, massive, flat-roofed, cave-like temples, not unlike the Lāḍ Khān, but provided with simple Nāgara *śikharas* above the cella; these shrines, originally Vaiṣṇava, have been later converted to Saiva usage, and it is just possible that their *śikharas*, together with that of the Durgā temple, are later additions. (*History of Indian and Indonesian Art*, New York, 1927, p. 79.)

Appendix VIII

Percy Brown

. . . illustrating another experimental stage in the development of the temple structure, is the Durga temple at Aihole [Figs 15–18]. This example is a Brahmanical version of the Buddhist chaitya hall, adapted to suit the service of the former creed. It has already been established that Buddhist buildings of a similar type were not uncommon in many parts of India in the early centuries of the Christian era, while there is an actual example at Ter, not far distant from Dharwar (Chapter IX). The Durga temple, which most closely follows this model, was probably erected during the sixth century, and is an apsidal-ended structure measuring . . . 84 feet. Raised on a particularly high and heavily moulded plinth or stereobate, the topmost tier of its flat roof is 30 feet from the ground; over the apse a short pyramidal tower, or *shikara*, has been subsequently added. Among other notable features in the design of the Durga temple is its peripteral exterior, or pteroma, a passage formed by the colonnade of a verandah which is carried right round the building, and joins up with similar pillars comprising the portico. This portico is approached by two flights of steps, one on each side of the front . . . The interior consists of a single hall 44 feet long, and divided by two rows of four pillars into a nave and two aisles, with an apsidal shaped cella, recalling the naos of the Greeks, at its far end . . . The roof of the nave is raised higher than that of the side aisles, so that in almost every particular, not only in the treatment of its parts, but in the nature of the building as a whole, it is a literal re-statement of the Buddhist chaitya hall. (*Indian Architecture, Buddhist & Hindu Periods*, Bombay, [1942], pp. 61–2.)

It is not improbable that an early phase of the tower consisted of a series of mouldings or layers of masonry of a very simple order, diminishing as they ascend, thus taking the shape of a stepped pyramid, truncated above and crowned by a ribbed stone, as shown in several smaller shrines on the site. (Pl. XLVI, Fig. 4). But one of the earliest, judging by its primitive appearance, to assume the *shikara* form is that over the Durga temple. This, when complete, instead of being curved in outline, as in the later examples, is almost straight-sided, like an elongated pyramid, but inclined inward at the apex to support the fluted finial (*amala sila*), a large ribbed stone now thrown down and lying at its foot. There is something singularly interesting in the formation of this temple, particularly in the superposition of its distinctly Hindu tower on an apsidal structure obviously derived from a Buddhist chaitya hall. (*Indian Architecture, Buddhist & Hindu Periods*, Bombay, [1942], p. 78.)

Appendix IX

Benjamin Rowland

It would be impossible and unprofitable to attempt to prove that the chaitya-hall type is specifically Buddhist and the cella-and-porch type of temple a Hindu invention: the fact remains that both are used with modifications for ritual by both sects throughout the Gupta period.

Many varying examples of these types can be found at Aihole, near Bādāmi. There, in the squalid modern village and in the overgrown wasteland of prickly-pear forest surrounding it, are about seventy old temples, variously used for dwellings, storerooms, and cowsheds. Only a handful have been reclaimed by modern archaeologists. A late Gupta shrine of the chaitya type at Aihole is the Brahmanical Durgā temple [Fig. 11]. It is an example of a modified structural chaitya-hall with the familiar basilican plan of nave, aisles, and apse. A flat roof with stone slabs over the nave replaces the barrel vaults. In place of the ambulatory of the rock-cut chaityas, it has a *pteroma* running round the exterior of the cella. The plain and very massive bracket capitals of this arcade are a type that reappears with variations in all later periods of Indian architecture. These capitals are in a sense a severe or rustic version of those in Cave XIX at Ajaṇṭā. Another and even more interesting new element is the little spire or *śikhara* rising above the apsidal end of the structure. (*Art and Architecture of India*, Middlesex, 1953, pp. 124–5.)

Appendix X

Sherman E. Lee

The second temple is the Durga temple built about a century later in the sixth century AD, paired with the Buddhist cell-temple at Sanchi, to demonstrate the derivation of the Hindu temple . . . While the Hacchimalagudi [cf. Fig. 47] Temple is, in a sense, the end of a tradition, the Durga Temple is a beginning. It has a porch, and a stone megalithic roof—that is, a single stone covering the main area, deriving from archaic architectural construction in stone. It has an ambulatory that has been placed outside the building; that is, the porch is extended around the building so that one can walk outside the shrine, rather than in the building proper. The base has been elevated considerably; and there is a rudimentary tower placed over the main shrine area. These last two are of particular significance because they tend to remove the building from the realm of architecture and to place it in that of sculpture. And as we shall see, Hindu architecture must be considered primarily as sculpture. The tower will develop until it dominates the temple; the base will develop until it seems to dominate the lower part of the structure. The apse end of the Durga Temple shows more clearly the influence of the Buddhist *chaitya* hall, but with an outer ambulatory. The rudimentary tower is carved in great detail, with numerous representations including figures and miniature *chaitya* arches. We have seen such decorations on the Buddhist *chaitya* facades and in the caves; and they will develop into fantastic ribbonlike ornaments in the later Hindu Medieval style. (*A History of Far Eastern Art*, New York, 1964, p. 178.)

Appendix XI

HEINRICH ZIMMER

The heritage of Amarāvatī, as brought to perfection by the artists of the Gupta period, was carried forward in masterly variations by the sculptors who decorated the temples of the early Cāḷukya dynasty, in the sixth and seventh centuries AD, and the artists of the other contemporary dynasties of the Deccan. The structural temple of the goddess Durgā at Aihoḷe (Aivali) [Fig. 15], a few miles from the Cāḷukya capital of Bādāmi, in the central Deccan, was erected by kings who reigned 550–642. It comprises a porch, a main hall, and an innermost sanctuary surmounted by a spire that is now in ruins. The pillared porch on the two sides, running the length of the building, widens to a gallery that encircles the structure and is meant for the ritual of circumambulation. The devotee should walk clockwise around the inner block with his right side to the monument—the usual form to be observed when approaching or leaving any shrine, image, or living saint to whom reverence is due. The pillars within are decorated with ornamental friezes representing chains of pearls and others representing dancing girls; these indicate that the sanctuary was designed as a copy of the celestial abode of the goddess. For such decorations represent the sensual pleasures and amorous delights held in store in the next world for all faithful worshippers who approach with due devotion the benign mother of life. Such devotees become gandharvas, consorts of the apsaras or divine dancing damsels, and enjoy this position for the period of their residence in the heaven; that is to say, as long as the treasure of the fruits of their meritorious behavior lasts. The reliefs show numerous couples of this kind in this beatific celestial abode [cf. Fig. 6], enjoying in youthful bodies a heavenly period of sensual bliss following their earthly lives of virtuous devotion. (*The Art of Indian Asia*, completed and edited by Joseph Campbell, New York, 1955, vol. I, p. 84.)

Appendix XII

Jitendra Nath Banerjea

If we compare this very lively panel from Ellora with two sculptures, one from Aihole and the other from Haripur (Mayurbhanj, Orissa), we are confronted with the fact [of] how the earlier traditional mode of the combat between the Devī and the Asura was given a modified form by the sculptor of the western Calukya country on the one hand and the Orissan artist from Mayurbhanj on the other. The Aihole relief (earlier in point of date, *c.* sixth or seventh century AD) shows the eight-armed goddess piercing the upturned neck of the Buffalo Demon (no man comes out of the decapitated trunk of the animal, which is a later feature), the lion mount on the left being a silent onlooker [cf. Fig. 22] . . . The early Calukyan artist appears to lay stress on the easy and effortless grace with which the divine act of retribution was carried out, while the Orissan sculpture portrays with success the dynamic vigour underlying the act. (*The Development of Hindu Iconography*, second edn, Calcutta, 1956, p. 499.)

The Aihole sculpture of Vṛṣvāhanamūrti of Śiva shows the four-armed god standing in a *dvibhaṅga* pose and reclining on his mount, his back right hand holding a *triśūla* and the front left hand, a snake, the front right hand rests in the *varada* pose on the horn of the vivacious bull, the back left hand being indistinct. The facial expression of the god is not very distinctive but its lack of character seems to be much compensated by the vigorous expression of the bull mount [cf. Fig. 20]. (*The Development of Hindu Iconography*, second edn, Calcutta, 1956. p. 468.)

Appendix XIII

K. V. Soundara Rajan

. . . that the Brahmanical temple builders . . . had not totally ignored the Buddhist formula for shrines is clear by the deliberate attempt seen in the Durga temple at Aihole (end of the sixth century AD) . . . in which the apsidal chaitya form has been closely copied, with an outer pillared verandah and the inner aisles and nave through the hypostyle arrangement . . . their clear inability to get at the curvature of the roof above the apse end in stone medium (and not brick), made them provide a simple flat roof for the shrine, over which the present and later *śikhara* arose. The original *śikhara* consisted of a rubble core with stone casing and of *gajapṛishṭha* form as can be deduced from the photograph taken by Meadows Taylor a hundred years ago. ('Beginnings of the Temple Plan', pp. 74–81, *Bulletin of the Prince of Wales Museum of Western India*, no. 6, 1957–59, Bombay [1960], pp. 77–8.)

Another example of this kind, not entirely in stone medium but in a mixed brick and stone structural form, is now known from the Pushpabhadraswami temple near the Krishnaghat at Nagarjunakonda (Lower Deccan) datable to the early fourth century AD by inscription. This had the apsidal plan, in which the framework was of stone pillars while the intervening spaces were closed by brick work. Presumably it had the rear side curve backed roof as well though we do not know this for certain as only the ground plan was extant. It is clearly the forerunner of the Durga temple and was the earliest Hindu experiment of an apsidal shrine. But it did use, in the main, a more plastic medium of construction, namely brick, which was in vogue for the earlier Buddhist edifices in the valley. ('Beginnings of the Temple Plan', pp. 74–81, *Bullentin of the Prince of Wales Museum of Western India*, no. 6, 1957–59, Bombay [1960], p. 78, note 1.)

Appendix XIV

K. R. SRINIVASAN

The Durga temple is essentially of the southern type, with a later norther type superstructure imposed upon it—an incongruity apparent from the fact that the superstructure is a square structure clumsily fitted over an apsidal cella. The temple stands on a high moulded *upapītha* (sub-base), apsidal on plan and carrying a peripheral row of columns on its edge that surround the moulded *adhishṭhāna* and walls of an apsidal *vimāna* and its front *maṇḍapa*. Thus the colonnade forms a covered circumambulatory with a sloping roof. The open *maṇḍapa* is continued forward on a base of smaller width. The peripheral pillars of the front *maṇḍapa* and those at the forward end of the circumambulatory have large statuary on them. The *adhishṭhāna* inside is again apsidal, moulded with all the components, and carries the apsidal wall enclosing the inner apsidal wall of the cella or *garbha-griha* and a closed *mahā-maṇḍapa* in front of it, with two linear rows of four columns in each row that divide it into a central nave and lateral aisles. The central nave has a higher flat roof raised over a sort of clerestory in front of the cella-entrance, and two lateral aisles have sloping roofs, at a lesser height than the central roof. The aisles of the *mahā-maṇḍapa* are continuous on either side, with a closed inner circumambulatory between the inner and outer walls of the cella, which again have a sloping roof. The *adhishṭhāna* of the apse is projected forward into the porch-like front *maṇḍapa* of a lesser width with four pillars in two rows. The reliefs on the *adhishṭhāna* and outer wall are cantoned by pilasters and enclose niches which are framed by shrine-fronts of all the patterns of northern and southern *vimānas, kūṭa, śālā, pañjara, udgama*, etc., and contain bold sculpture. The four recesses, two each between the three bays on the north and south sides and two more between the three bays round the apse-end, are provided with perforated windows. Over the inner wall of the cella perhaps rose the original apsidal *grīvā* and *śikhara*, as in temples at Ter and Chejarla . . ., either with a wholly-solid core or supported by props inside. The advanced features of the temple, the variety of evolved shrine-fronts displayed in its niches, the style of its sculpture, its diverse corbel-forms and the existence in it of a chute, water-spout and the gargoyle-like *praṇāla*—a late feature—would justify placing the temple in the eighth century. This is also indicated by an inscription of Chāḷukya Vikramāditya II (733–46) on the ruined *gopura* at the south-eastern part of the enclosing-wall. The name 'Durgā' for the temple is misleading, since it was not dedicated to Durga, and is due to the fact that till the earlier part of the last century the temple formed part of a fortification (*durga*), probably of the Marathas. ('Southern Temples', in A. Ghosh ed., *Archaeological Remains, Monuments & Museums*, New Delhi, 1964, pp. 195–6.)

Appendix XV

GEORGE MICHELL

Aihole Durga

External Elevation: . . . The outer faces of the twelve columns at the eastern end of the building are carved with *mithuna* couples, *dvarapalas* and various icons. Tusk-like brackets emerge from the two columns either side of the entrance. Slabs set between these columns provide balcony seating for the outer *pradaksinapatha* . . . The undersides of some [ceiling] slabs are carved with *gandharva* couples. The ruined superstructure is supported on the *garbhagrha* walls. The awkward way in which the superstructure fits onto the semi-circular ended *garbhagrha* and the cutting back of the slabs roofing the *mandapa*, as if to permit space for its base, suggest that the superstructure may be a later addition. If this is so, then it must have been added within the Early Western Calukyan period. It is of the *kapota* and *amalaka* type divided into ascending and diminishing tiers of three elements across. The central band is projecting and on its east face must have been provided with a carved slab which is now missing.

Elevation of the Interior Temple: . . . The niches of the outer walls are created by pairs of pilasters whose designs vary, and include those with double-circle or cushion capitals with curved brackets. These carry elaborate and deeply carved pediments which display a large repertoire of designs. *Kutas*, *salas*, *kudus*, and *makaras* are freely employed. Sculptural panels have been inserted into some of these niches. Windows also employ contrasting designs and are set between pairs of pilasters whose brackets support elaborate pediments. The walls are completed by a *kapota* cornice with uncut *kudus* . . .

Interior: The *garbhagrha* doorway is now mostly ruined. That to the *mandapa* is well preserved and is created by a pair of fluted pilasters set among decorated bands supporting an eave. Above rises a series of mouldings culminating in an elaborate pediment of the *kuta-sala-kuta* type with *kudus*. Garuda appears over the opening and there are river goddesses and attendants carved in the panels beneath at either side. [cf. Fig. 78] . . . As the whole structure has been in danger of collapsing, four columns have been added in recent times . . . The beams and panels above are now mostly destroyed. The roof system has been partly replaced, but consists of raised and horizontal slabs over the central aisle, and sloping slabs over the side aisles and *pradaksinapatha*. The ends of the horizontal slabs are bevelled and are set on a short vertical course provided with a band of pilasters . . . The brackets of the porch columns support beams and panels above, which are divided into projecting and receding niches. These are created by pairs of pilasters upon *vyalas* and *makaras*, and an eave on a frieze of *hamsas*. Miniature icons are placed in the niches which are headed by *salas*. [Fig. 24]. (*Early Western Calukyan Temples*, London, 1975, pp. 32–3.)

Aihole Durga Gateway

To the south of the Durga is a gateway obviously intended to be part of some enclosure [Fig. 26]. Curiously the gateway is not aligned in any way with the temple itself and nothing remains of the enclosure walls. The only evidence for such walls having been built is the markings on the west wall of the gateway suggesting abutting stones. The importance of this small structure is the inscription carved on the north wall recording a gift dating from the reign of Vikramaditya II.

Plan: A central passageway at ground level, connects two doorways on the north and south sides and is flanked by two raised areas. Four free-standing columns and four engaged-columns against the walls are found in each of these raised areas.

External Elevation: The plinth is composed of an *upana*, a vertical course, and a *kapota* furnished with blocked out *kudus*. The walls have pilasters at the corners of the building and either side of the two doorways. Their curved brackets support an eave on a frieze of *hamsas*. Above is a short vertical course supporting the bevelled ends of the roof slabs. The doorways are created by pairs of pilasters supporting an eave, above which rises a series of mouldings culminating in a pediment consisting of three *salas* with intermediate *kudus*. Garuda appears over the opening. Only the southern doorway is complete. The small trefoil *kudu* that now surmounts this doorway, being placed on the roof slabs, is almost certainly misplaced.

Interior: The columns have their shafts divided by raised bands and two part-circles, the brackets being fluted. These support beams are carved with a *kapota*. The roof slabs are raised and are horizontal over the central passageway but sloping over the side areas. Many of these slabs are now missing. (*Early Western Calukyan Temples*, London, 1975, pp. 33–4.)

Appendix XVI

SRINIVAS PADIGAR

. . . The *garbha-griha* of this temple exhibits both *Śaiva* and *Vaishṇava* deities as also *purāṇic* episodes and *mithunas*. The provision of a rectangular socket within a circular *piṭha* in the *garbha-griha* indicates that it enshrined the image of a deity and not a *linga*. The problem as to which deity it was has been there and no serious attempt has been made to set it at rest.

Cousens remarked that the temple was originally a Vaishṇava one, probably dedicated to the god Surya-Nārāyaṇa. Since then it is usually considered as having Vaishṇava affiliation. Recently, however, some scholars have described it as the temple of goddess Durgā, of Surya, or of Brahmā. In the following lines these opinions are reviewed in the light of epigraphic and sculptural evidence concerning the temple.

Epigraphic Evidence

Inscribed on the north wall of the South gateway of the Durga temple is a Kannada epigraph in characters of *c.* eighth century AD. After referring to the reign of the Bādāmi Chālukya king Vikramāditya (II), the epigraph records the remission of certain taxes. Fleet's text and translation of the relevant lines of this epigraph are as follows:

Rēvadibaddar = Āṭada-Āḷekomara-Singana
dēgulada Āditya-bhaṭarage koṭṭudu, etc., i.e.,
'The gift of *Rēvadibadda* . . . to the venerable *Āditya* of the
temple of *Ātada-Ālekomara-Singa*.'

In a recent work of his, Annigeri has interpreted the purport of the inscription more or less the same way as done by Fleet.

Of late, K. V. Ramesh has offered a fresh reading of the above lines and his text and translation read as follows:

Rēvadi baddarāula āle
Komarasingana dēgulada Āditya—
bhaṭarange koṭṭudu etc., i.e.,
'the gift made to the god Āditya of the temple of *Komarasinga*
by *Revadi* who was administering the *baddaraul* tax.'

This new rendering and interpretation of the epigraph has not only taken back the antiquity of the *vaddarāula* tax to the age of Bādāmi Chālukyas, but has brought to light the existence of an *Āditya* temple in the vicinity.

The confusion about the *Āditya-bhaṭara* was obviously on account of the use of the word '*bhaṭara*' in association with the name of the deity. For '*bhaṭara*' is found used often in association with the name of kings [note: In most of the early Chālukya Kannada inscriptions the usage is found; e.g., in the present inscription: '*Vikramāditya Śri-prithivi-vallabha Mahārājādhirāja Paramēśvara bhaṭarar*'] and, sometimes, venerable persons . . . A Kannada inscription in *Sangamēśvara* temple, Pattadakal, after recording a certain grant reads:

Idarkke sa(kshi) Vijēśvara (bha)ṭara etc.

It is obvious that *Vijēśvarabhaṭara* here implies the god *Vijēśvara*, we know that the Sangamēśvara temple was originally known as *Vijayēśvara*, its deity being named after king Vijayāditya of the Early Chalukya dynasty who is known to have got this temple built . . .

Thus it becomes evident that *Ādityabhaṭara*, Vijēśvarabhaṭara and Bhutēśvarabhaṭara of the above inscriptions were the deities of the respective temples and not venerable persons associated with the temples.

A point of interest that needs notice is that in all the three inscriptions cited above, '*bhaṭara*' is used in singular form and not in plural form (*bhaṭarar*), as is normally done in the case of kings or, for that matter, venerable persons.

The '*Ādityabhaṭara*' of the inscription in question was, therefore, no other than the god enshrined in the temple in the vicinity which was enclosed by the *prākāra* on the gateway of which the present inscription is found. And it is known for certain that this gateway once served as an entrance to the Durgā temple. This fact is attested to by another undated inscription, also in Kannada language and characters of *c.* eighth century AD, which is found on the right flanking wall of the flight of stairs leading into the temple from the south side. Although the legible lines of this inscription make no sense, reference is made in it to a *Komarasinga*, apparently the same as the one mentioned in the first epigraph, who was probably the patron of the Durga temple (*Komarasingana Dēgula*). Reference is also made in it to *(Ā)ditya, Navagraha, Diśā* and *Bhumandala*, but the context of their usage is not clear.

It is thus apparent that the *Āditya-bhaṭara* of the inscription belonged to the Durga temple itself.

Sculptural Evidence

At this stage it is worthwhile considering the different views in regard to the religious affiliation of the temple in question. These are mainly based on sculptural evidence.

The inappropriateness of taking the presence of the *Garuda* on the *lalāta-bimba* of the doorway as an indication of the Vaishṇava affiliation of the early Chalukya temples has been pointed out more than once, and hence needs no repetition here. The connection of the goddess *Durgā* with this temple has been aptly ruled out by Cousens and Annigeri; the name is a misnomer derived from '*Durgadagudi*' meaning 'the temple of the fort'.

The recent view that the temple was dedicated to the god *Brahmā*, however, needs a detailed consideration. The grounds for this view are: (i) the presence of a *Brahmā* figure in the central miniature shrine (*kudu*) on the architrave of the doorway of the *sabhāmaṇḍapa*; (ii) the presence of a circular *piṭha* in the *garbha-griha*; and (iii) the image of a four-headed *Brahmā* in round relief, found in the locality and now preserved in the Sculpture Gallery at Aihole. These arguments can be answered as follows: (i) Just above the *Brahmā* figure pointed out above, but within the *chaitya* niche that adorns the same *kudu*'s roof, is the figure of a standing *Surya*. And in the Mallikarjuna temple of the same place a temple dedicated to Śiva, the place of *Brahmā* is occupied by a lady with a flower in her hand, and that of *Surya* by a *linga*; the latter obviously suggesting the Śaiva affiliation of that temple. It is usual with the early Chālukya temples to represent the central deity within the *chaitya* motif (sometimes looking like a trefoil design). (ii) The presence of a circular *piṭha* was necessitated by the apsidal nature of the *garbha-griha*. So far as our knowledge goes, no *vāstu* text bars the use of a circular *piṭha* for *Vishṇu* or *Surya*. (iii) As regards the *Brahmā* image, it is not certain if at all it was found in the vicinity of the Durga temple.

To the above may be added further evidence. Just opposite the Brahmā-Surya figure referred to above, on the architrave of the *maṇḍapa* entrance, again within the central *kudu* is a standing Surya figure (facing west). He is flanked by *dvārapālas* carved within *kudus*. On the north face of the pillar to the right of the main doorway of the temple is a sculpture that reminds us of the story of Chastisement of *Chhāya* by *Surya*, which occurs in some *Purāṇas*. A similar sculpture (also facing north) finds place near the *garbha-griha* of the Malegitti Śivālaya, Bādāmi, which, it is confessed, is a *Surya* temple. The circular, wheel-like, pierced windows on the wall enclosing the inner *pradakshiṇāpatha* and the beautiful *matsya-chakra* on the ceiling of the entrance *maṇḍapa* may not be without significance. So much for sculptural evidence within the temple.

The *toraṇa* (south gateway) is adorned by a sculpture of seated *Surya*. Near the same gateway is another sculpture of seated *Surya* carved within what looks like a *chaitya* design, which must have once adorned the temple's *sukanāsi*, now no more. Also, there is a beautiful but mutilated image most probably of *Surya*, near this gateway, the connection of which with the temple in question cannot be ruled out. . . . ('The Durgā Temple, Aihole: an Āditya Temple', *Archaeological Studies*, vol. II, 1977, pp. 59–64.)

Appendix XVII

SANSKRIT TERMINOLOGY USED IN THIS VOLUME WITH FULL DIACRITICAL APPARATUS

The following is a list of the Sanskrit terms used in this volume with their full diacritical markings, for scholars whose interest requires the fullest linguistic precision.

āchārya
adhiṣṭhāna
āditala
Āditya
Ādityabhatara
Agastya
agrahāra
Ājīvaka
akṣamālā
ālīḍhāsana
āmalaka
ambigēr
ānanda
ananta
Āndhra
antarāḷa
apasmāra
apsarās
Ardhanārī
Ardhanārīśvara
ardhoruka
Aruṇa
Aśura
aśvamūkhi
āvaraṇa
āvaraṇadevata
avatāra
āyudha
bandha
Basamayya
Basavarayyan
bhaṭara
bhaṭarar
Bhikṣāṭana
bhūmandala
bhūmi
bhūmika
Bhūtanātha
Bhūteśvara
biṁba
Brahmā
brahmachārin
brāhmaṇa
caitya
cakra
Calukya
candraśālā
catuṣkī
cauri
chajja
channavira
Chāya
cikka
damaru
dagoba
deva
dēvakōṣtha
dēśa
devī
dhārāvṛtta
dhōti
drāviḍa
drāviḍadēśa
Durgā
dvāra
dvārapāla
dvāraśālā
dvibhaṅga
ekāvali
gajapṛṣṭha
Galaganātha
gaṇa
gandharva
Gaṅgā
garbhagṛha
Garuḍa
gavākṣa
gōpuram
grīvā
guḍi
Gupta
Gurjara
haṁsa
Hanuman
hāra
Hari
hastijatiya
Hiraṇyakaśipu
Hoysaḷa
Huccappayya-guḍi
Huccimalli-guḍi
jāḷi
Jambuliṅga
Jambunātha
Jamunā
jaṭāmukuṭa
Jayāśraya
Kailāsa
kakṣāsanas
kalā
kalaśa
Kallēśvara
Kannada
kapōta

Kapōtēśvara
Karṇāṭak
Kāśiviśvanātha
kevala
khaṇḍa
khura
kinnara
kinnari
kirīta
Komarasiṅga
kōṣṭha
kuḍu
kumbha
kumuda
kuṇḍala
kuta
Lakṣmī
lalāta
liṅga
Lokeśwara
madhyalatā
mahādvāra
mahājanas
mahāpaṭṭikā
Mahāpraśasta
Mahiṣāsuramardinī
makara
Mālegitti
Mallikārjuna
maṇḍapa
Mangaliśvara
mālā
mālāsthāna
maṇi
mārg
maṭha
Mēguṭi
mēkhala
mithuna
mudrā
mukha
mukuṭa
mūrti
Mūṭṭasila
nāga
Nāganātha
nāgara
nāgarāja
nāgarī
nakara
Nandi
Narasiṁha
Nārāyaṇa
Navagraha
nirandhāra
paduka
pāga
pañjara
Pāpanātha
paramamāhēśvara
paraśu
Paraśurāmeśwara
parivārālaya
Pārvatī
paṭṭa
Paṭṭadakal
phāṁsanā
Piriṛeyya
pīṭha
pradakṣiṇapatha
prākāra
praṇāla
pratīhāra
Pṛthivi
Pulakēśin
purnakalasa
rāja
Rāmaliṅgeśvara
Rāṣṭrakūṭa
ratha
Ravikīrtti
rāvuḷa
rekhā
rucaka
Rūpam
sabhāmaṇḍapa
sainyavadha
Śaka
śālā
Samaranganasutradhara
sāndhāra
Saṅgamēśvara
saṅgha
śaṅkha
Sāraṅgī
Savitaran
śikhara
śilā
śilpa
Śiva
smṛti
Śrayāśraya
sthapati
stūpa
stūpika
sukanāsa
śurasēna
Surēndrepāḍa
Sūrya
svasti
tālapatra
taraṅga
telingāṇa
tōraṇa
tribhaṅga
Trilokeśwara
tripaṭṭa
triśūla
Trivikrama
tulāpītha
udgama
upāna
upapīṭha
Uttareśvara
vaḍḍa
vāhana
vājana
Vākāṭaka
vallabha
varada
Varāha
vāstu
Vāstupuruṣa
vēdī
vēdikā
veṇukośa
vesera
vidyādhara
vihāra
Vijayāditya
Vijayēśvara
Vikramāditya
vimāna
Vinayāditya
Virūpākṣa
Vṛṣavāhana
vyāla
yajamāna
yāḷi
Yamunā

Bibliography

Agrawala, P. K. *Gupta Temple Architecture*. Varanasi, 1968.

Anand, M. R., Setter, S., Michell, G. *et al. In Praise of Aihole-Badami-Mahakuta-Pattadakal*. Bombay, 1978. Also published as *Mārg*, vol. XXXII, no. 1 (December 1978).

Annigeri, A. M. *A Guide to Badami*. Dharwar, 1960.

Banerjea, Jitendra Nath. *The Development of Hindu Iconography*. 2nd edn, Calcutta, 1956.

Banerji, R. D. *Basreliefs of Badami*. Calcutta, 1928. A. S. I., Memoirs, no. 25.

Balasubrahmanuam, S. R. 'The Date of the Lad Khan (Sūrya-Nārāyaṇa) Temple at Aihole'. *Lalit Kalā*, vol. X (1961), pp. 41–4.

Barnett, L. D. 'Lakshmēshwar Pillar Inscription of the Yuvarāja Vikramāditya'. *Epigraphia India*, vol. XIV (1917–18), pp. 188–91.

Bhau Daji. 'Report on Photographic Copies of Inscriptions in Dharwar and Mysore'. *Journal of the Bombay Branch of the Royal Asiatic Society*, vol. IX (1867–70), pp. 314–15.

Bhandarkar, R. G. 'Early History of the Dekkan Down to the Mohamedan Conquest'. *Bombay Gazetteer*, vol. I (1896), pp. 132–275.

Bhattacharyya, H. D. 'Minor Religious Sects', in R. C. Majumdar, ed., *The Age of Imperial Kanauj*, History and Culture of the Indian People, vol. IV. Bombay, 1955.

Bolon, Carol Radcliffe. 'The Mahakuta Pillar and Its Temples'. *Artibus Asiae*, vol. XLI, nos 2–3 (1980), pp. 253–68.

——— 'The Pārvatī Temple, Sandur, and Early Images of Agastya'. *Artibus Asiae*, vol. XLII (1980), pp. 303–26.

——— 'Early Chalukya Sculpture'. Doctoral Dissertation, New York University, 1981.

——— 'Supplementum', pp. 59–66 and 90–4, in Meister, M. and Dhaky, M. A., eds., *Encyclopaedia of Indian Temple Architecture: South India: Upper Drāviḍadēśa, Early Phase, AD 550–1075*. New Delhi, 1986.

——— 'Calukyas of Bādāmi: Karṇāṭa', pp. 277–311 in Meister, *et al.* eds, *Encyclopaedia of Indian Temple Architecture: North India: Foundations of North Indian Style, c. 250 BC–AD 1100*. New Delhi, 1988.

——— 'The Durga Temple, Aihole, and the Sangamesvara Temple, Kudaveli: A Sculptural Review', *Ars Orientalis, XV (1985)*.

Brown, Percy. *Indian Architecture (Buddhist and Hindu Periods)*. Bombay (1942). 5th edn, Bombay, 1956.

Buchanan, Susan Locher. *Calukya Temples: History and Iconography*. Doctoral Dissertation, Ohio State University, 1985.

Burgess, James. *Report on the First Season's Operation in the Belgām and Kaladgi Districts*. A.S.W.I., vol. I. London, 1874.

——— 'Rock-Cut Temples at Bādāmi in the Dekhaṇ'. *Indian Antiquary*, vol. VI (1877), pp. 354–66.

——— *The Ancient Monuments, Temples and Sculptures of India*. London, 1897.

Bussagli, Mario. *Oriental Architecture*. New York, 1973.

Bussagli, Mario and Sivaramamurti, *c. 5000 Years of the Art of India*. New York, 1971.

Chandra, Pramod. 'Visual Arts of the Indian Subcontinent', vol. XXVII, pp. 759–91, *Encyclopaedia Britannica*, 15th edn, Chicago, 1974.

——— 'The Study of Indian Temple Architecture', pp. 1–39 in Pramod Chandra, ed., *Studies in Indian Temple Architecture*. New Delhi, 1975.

——— *On the Study of Indian Art*. Cambridge, 1983.

——— *The Sculpture of India; 3000 BC–1300 AD*. Washington, 1985.

Chatham, Doris Clark. '*Pratīhāras* from Paṭṭaḍakal to Ellora: The Early Western Chāḷukya Basis for the Sculpture Style of the Kailāśa Temple', pp. 71–9 in Anand Krishna, ed., *Chhavi II*. Benares, 1981.

Ananda K. Coomaraswamy. *The History of Indian and Indonesian Art*. New York, 1927.

Cousens, Henry. 'Ancient Temples of Aihoḷe'. *A.S.I., Annual Report for 1907–8*, pp. 189–204. Calcutta, 1911.

——— *Architectural Antiquities of Western India*. London, 1926.

——— *The Chālukyan Architecture of the Kanarese Districts*. A.S.I., N.I.S., vol. XLII. Calcutta, 1926.

——— 'The Temples of Alampur'. *Annual Report of the Archaeological Department of the Nizam's Dominions for 1926–27*, pp. 9–13.

——— *Mediaeval Architecture of the Dakhan*. A.S.I., N.I.S., vol. XLVIII. Calcutta, 1931.

Craven, Roy C. *A Concise History of Indian Art*. New York, 1976.

Craig, Maurice. 'James Fergusson', pp. 140–52 in John Summerson, ed., *Concerning Architecture*. London, 1968.

Cunningham, Alexander. *Archaeological Survey of India*, vol. IX (1873–76) and vol. X (1874–77). Calcutta.

Desai, P. B., ed., *South-Indian Inscriptions* vol. XV (Bombay-Karnatak Inscriptions vol. II), Archaeological Survey of India. Delhi, 1964.

——— ed., *A History of Karnataka*. Dharwar, 1970.

Deva, Krishna. 'Northern Temples', pp. 157–89 in A. Ghosh, ed., *Archaeological Remains, Monuments & Museums*. New Delhi, 1964.

——— *Temples of North India*. New Delhi, 1969.

Divakaran, Odile. 'Le Temple de Jambuliṅga (daté de 699 ap. J. C.) à Bādāmi'. *Arts Asiatiques* t. 21 (1970), pp. 15–39.

——— 'Les Temples d'Ālampur et de ses environs au temps des Cāḷukya de Bādāmi'. *Arts Asiatiques*, t. 22 (1971), pp. 51–101.

——— 'The Beginnings of Early Western Chalukya Art', pp. 59–64 in *Chhavi II*. Benares, 1981.

Dhaky, M. A. 'Rāṣṭrakūṭas of Ēlapura and Mānyakhēṭaka', pp. 343–9 in *Encyclopaedia of Indian Temple Architecture: North India: Foundations of North Indian Style, c. 250 BC–AD 1100*. New Delhi, 1988.

Elliot, W. 'Extracts from the Society's Proceedings'. *Journal of the Bombay Branch of the Royal Asiatic Society*, vol. IV (1853), p. 460.

Fabri, Charles. *An Introduction to Indian Architecture*. Aligarh, 1963.

Fergusson, James. *An Historical Enquiry into the True Principles of Beauty in Art*. London, 1849.

——— *The Illustrated Handbook of Architecture*. London, 1855.

——— *History of the Modern Schools of Architecture*. London, 1862.

——— *Rock Cut Temples of India*. London, 1864.

——— *A History of Architecture in All Countries*. London, 1867.

——— *On the Study of Indian Architecture*. London, 1867.

——— *History of Indian and Eastern Architecture*. London, 1876.

——— 'On the Identification of the Portrait of Chosroes II among the Paintings in the Caves at Ajanta'. *Journal of the Royal Asiatic Society*, April 1879.

——— *History of Indian and Eastern Architecture*, rev. and ed., with additions by James Burgess (Indian) and R. Phene Spiers (Eastern). London, 1910.

Fergusson, James and Burgess, James. *The Cave Temples of India*. London, 1880.

Fergusson, James and Meadows Taylor. *Architecture in Dharwar and Mysore*. London, 1866.

Fischer, Klaus. *Schöpfungen Indischer Kunst*. Koln, 1959.

Fleet, John F. 'Inscriptions from Belgaum and Kalādgi Districts', pp. 103–38 in James Burgess, ed., *Report on the Antiquities in the Bidar and Aurangabad Districts*, A.S.W.I., vol. III. London, 1878.

——— 'Sanskrit and Old-Canarese Inscriptions. No. LVIII'. *Indian Antiquary*, vol. VIII (1879), pp. 285–6.

——— 'Sanskrit and Old-Canarese Inscriptions. No. LXXXXIV'. *Indian Antiquary*, vol. X (1881), pp. 102–4.

——— 'Dynasties of the Kanarese Districts of the Bombay Presidency from the Earliest Times Down to the Musalman Conquest of 1318'. *Bombay Gazetteer* vol. I (1896), pp. 278–584.

Ghosh, A., ed., *Jaina Art and Architecture*. New Delhi, 1975.

Goetz, Herman. 'A New Brahmanical Mural of the Sixth Century at Aihole'. *Mārg*, vol. V, no. 1 (1952).

——— 'The Sculptures of the Lad Khān at Aihole'. *Bulletin-Vereenigin van Vriender Aziatische Kunst*, N. S. 36 (March 1952), pp. 142–5.

——— 'Andhra', 'Deccan Art', 'Hinduism', 'India', 'Indian Art', 'Structural Types and Methods'. *Encyclopaedia of World Art*, New York, 1959.

——— 'Imperial Rome and the Genesis of Classic Indian Art'. *East and West*, vol. X, no. 3, 4 (September, December 1959), pp. 153–4, 261–2.

——— *India, Five Thousand Years of Indian Art*. London, 1960.

Gongoly, O. C. *Indian Architecture*. Calcutta, 1920.

Gravely, F. H., and Ramachandran, T. N. 'The Three Main Styles of Temple Architecture Recognized by the Śilpa Śāstras'. *Bulletin of the Madras Government Museum* vol. III, no. 1 (1934), pp. 1–26.

Gupte, R. S. 'An Apsidal Temple at Chikka Mahākuṭa'. *Marathwada University Journal*, vol. IV, no. 2 (Feb. 1964), pp. 58–63.

——— *The Art and Architecture of Aihole*. Bombay, 1967.

Hartel, Herbert. 'Some Results of the Excavations at Sonkh', pp. 69–99 in *German Scholars on India*, vol. II, Bombay, 1970.

Harle, James. 'Le Temple de Nāganātha à Nagarāl'. *Arts Asiatique*, t. XIX (1969), pp. 53–83.

——— 'Three types of Walls in Early Western Cāḷukyan Temples'. *Oriental Art*, vol. XVII (1971), pp. 45–54.

——— 'Some Remarks on Early Western Cāḷukyan Sculpture', pp. 65–9 in P. Pal, ed., *Aspects of Indian Art*. Leiden, 1972.

——— *The Art and Architecture of the Indian Subcontinent*. New York, 1986.

Havell, E. B. *Ideals of Indian Art*. London, 1911.

——— *The Ancient and Mediaeval Architecture of India: A Study of Indo-Aryan Civilization*. London, 1915.

Huntington, Susan B., with contributions by John C. Huntington. *The Art of Ancient India*. New York, 1985.

Karmarkar, A. P. *A Cultural History of Karnataka*. Dharwar, 1947.

Kielhorn, F. 'Vakkalēri Plates of Kīrtivarman II; Śaka-Saṁvat 679'. *Epigraphia Indica*, vol. V (1898–99), pp. 200–5.

——— 'Aihole Inscription of Pulikēśin II; Śaka Saṁvat 556'. *Epigraphia Indica*, vol. VI (1900–1), pp. 1–12.

Kramrisch, Stella. *Indian Sculpture*. London, 1933.

——— *The Hindu Temple*. Calcutta, 1946.

——— *The Art of India*. London, 1955.

Lee, Sherman E. *A History of Far Eastern Art*. New York, 1964. 2nd edn, 1982.

Lippe, Aschwin. 'Unusual Icons at Badami'. *Summaries of Papers of the 26th International Congress of Orientalists*, ed., R. N. Dandekar, New Delhi (1964), p. 151.

——— 'Some Sculptural Motifs on Early Cāḷukya Temples'. *Artibus Asiae*, vol. IXXX (1967), pp. 5–24.

——— 'Additions and Replacements in Early Cālukya Temples'. *Archives of Asian Art*, vol. XXIII (1969–70), pp. 6–23.

——— 'Supplement, Additions and Replacements in Early Chālukya Temples'. *Archives of Asian Art*, vol. XXIV (1970–71), pp. 80–3.

——— 'Early Chālukya Icons'. *Artibus Asiae*, vol. XXXIV, no. 4 (1972), pp. 273–330.

——— *Indian Mediaeval Sculpture*. Amsterdam and New York, 1978.

Louis-Frederic. *The Art of India; Temples and Sculpture*. New York, 1959.

Majumdar, R. C. ed., *The Struggle for Empire*, The History and Culture of the Indian People, vol. V. Bombay, 1966.

Marshall, John. *Mohenjo-Daro and the Indus Civilization*. London, 1931.

Mate, M. S. and S. Gokhale. 'Aihoḷe: an interpretation', pp. 501–4 in Ritti, S. and Gopal, B. R., eds., *Studies in Indian History and Culture*. Dharwar, 1971.

Mathur, N. L. *Sculpture in India: Its History and Art*. New Delhi, 1972.

Meister, M. W., Dhaky, M. A. and Deva Krishna, eds., *Encyclopaedia of Indian Temple Archtiecture: North India: Foundations of North Indian Style, c. 250 BC–AD 1100*. New Delhi, 1988.

Meister, M. W. and Dhaky, M. A., eds., *Encyclopaedia of Indian Temple Archtiecture: North India: Period of Early Maturity, c. AD 700–900*. New Delhi, 1991.

Michell, George. *Early Western Calukyan Temples*. London, 1975.

——— *The Hindu Temple: Introduction to its Meaning and Form*. London, 1978.

——— 'Temples of the Early Chalukyas', *Mārg* (December 1978).

Mitra, Debala. *Udayagiri and Khandagiri*. New Delhi, 1960.

Monod-Bruhl, Odette. *Indian Temples*. Oxford, 1937.

Moreas, George. *Kadamba Kula*. Bombay, 1931.

——— 'Constituent Elements of Kartnataka Culture', pp. 1–10, *Studies in Karnataka History and Culture*, vol. II. Mysore, 1987.

Myradal, Jan, and Gun Kessel. *Angkor: an Essay on Art and Imperialism*. New York, 1970.

Nagaraja Rao, M. S., ed., *The Chalukyas of Badami (Seminar Papers)*. Bangalore, 1978.

Naik, A. V. 'Structural Architecture of the Deccan'. *New Indian Antiquary*, vol. IX, nos 7–12 (July–December 1947), pp. 187–329.

——— 'Inscriptions of the Deccan: An Epigraphic Survey (circa 300 BC–AD 1300)'. *Deccan College Post-Graduate and Research Institute, Bulletin*, vol. IX (1948), pp. 1–161.

——— 'Cult Characteristics of the Hindu Temples of the Deccan'. *Deccan College Post Graduate and Research Institute Bulletin*, vol. XI, no. 1 (1950), pp. 83–119.

Nilakanta Sastri, K. A. *A History of South India*. 2nd edn, Madras, 1958.

——— 'The Chāḷukyas of Bādāmī', pp. 201–46 in Gulam Yazdani, ed., *The Early History of the Deccan*. London, 1961.

Padigar, Srinivas. 'The Durga Temple at Aihole: An Aditya Temple'. *Archaeological Studies*, vol. II (1977), pp. 59–64.

——— 'Some Sculptures of the Mālegitti Śivālaya and Their Identification'. *Journal of Karnatak University, Social Sciences*, vol. XIII (1977), pp. 62–4.

——— 'Epigraphy and Some Aspects of the Early Chalukyan Art'. *The Journal of the Karnatak University: Social Sciences*, vol. XXII (1986), pp. 74–80.

Panchamukhi, R. S. 'The Bādāmi Inscription of Chalikya Vallabhēśvara: Śaka 465'. *Epigraphia Indica*, vol. XXVII (1947), pp. 4–9.

Pathak, K. B. 'Kēndūr Plates of Kīrtivarma II, Śaka Saṁvat 672'. *Epigraphia Indica*, vol. IX (1907–08), pp. 200–6.

——— 'Rayagad Plates of Vijayāditya; Śaka Saṁvat 625'. *Epigraphia Indica*, vol. x (1909–10), pp. 14–17.

Prasad, B. Rajendra. *The Chālukyan Architecture of Mahabubnagar District*. Doctoral Dissertation, Deccan College, 1967.

——— 'Śukanāsā in Drāviḍian Architecture'. *Journal of the Oriental Institute Baroda*. vol. xx, no. 1 (1970), pp. 62–9.

——— 'Temples of the Latina Form at Alampur'. *Journal of the Indian Society of Oriental Art*, N. S. vol. v, no. 2 (1972–3), pp. 53–75.

——— *Chalukyan Temples of Andhradesa*. Atlantic Highlands, 1983.

——— 'Calukyas of Bādāmi: Āndhradēśa', pp. 312–35 in Meister, *et al.*, eds., *Encyclopaedia of Indian Temple Architecture: North India: Foundations of North Indian Style, c. 250 BC–AD 1100*. New Delhi, 1988.

Rajasekhara, S. 'Identification of the Early Chalukyan Temples'. *Srīkanthikā—Dr S. Srikantha Sastri Felicitation Volume*. Mysore, 1973, pp. 16–22.

——— *A Study of the Aihole Temples*. Doctoral Dissertation, Karnatak University, 1975.

——— 'Surya Sculptures at Aihole'. *Archaeological Studies*, vol. II (1977), pp. 35–8.

——— *Early Chālukya Art at Aihoḷe*. New Delhi, 1985.

Ram Raz. *Essay on the Architecture of the Hindus*. London, 1834.

Rama Rao, M. 'Chalukyan Temples of Satyavolu'. *Archaeological Society of South India, Transactions, 1959–60*, pp. 72–8.

——— 'Early Chalukyan Architecture—A Review'. *Journal of Indian History*, vol. XXXXI, no. 3 (Aug. 1963), pp. 431–57.

——— *Early Cāḷukyan Temples of Āndhra Deśa*. A. P. Government Archaeological Series 20. Hyderabad, 1965.

Rambach, Pierre, and de Golish, Vitold. *The Golden Age of Indian Art*. Bombay, 1955.

Ramesh, K. V. *Presidential Address to the Epigraphy Section of the XXXVII Session of the Indian History Congress, Calicut*, Reprinted in 'On Some Inscriptions Edited By Fleet'. *Journal of the Epigraphical Society of South India*, vol. IV (1977).

——— Chalukyas of Vātāpi. Delhi, 1984.

Rao, S. R. 'A Note on the Chronology of Early Chālukyan Temples'. *Lalit Kalā*, vol. XV (1972), pp. 9–18.

——— 'New Light on Chalukya Architecture', pp. 272–5 in M. S. Nagaraja Rao, ed., *The Chalukyas of Badami (Seminar Papers)*. Bangalore, 1978.

Rawson, Philip. *Indian Sculpture*. London, 1968.

——— *Indian Art*. New York, 1972.

——— *The Making of the Past; Indian Asia*. New York, 1977.

Rea, Alexander. *Report of the Southern Circle*, Archaeological Survey of India, April 1889.

Rodin, A., Coomaraswamy, A. K., Golobuew, V. *Sculpture Çivaites*, Arts Asiatiques, t. III. Paris, 1921.

Rowland, Benjamin. *The Art and Architecture of India*. Baltimore, 1953. 3rd rev. edn, 1967, 1st integrated edn, 1970.

Ruskin, John. *Aratra Pentelici*. London, 1872.

Said, Edward W. *Orientalism*. New York, 1978.
Saraswati, S. K. 'Architecture', in Majumdar, R. C., ed., *The Classical Age*, History and Culture of the Indian People, vol. III. Bombay, 1954.
Sarkar, Gurudas. 'Notes on the History of Shikhara Temples'. *Rūpam*, vol. X (1922), pp. 45–6.
Sinor, Denis, ed., *Orientalism and History*. Bloomington, 1970.
Sircar, D. C. 'The Chālukyas'. pp. 227–54 in Majumdar, R. C., ed., *The Classical Age*, History and Culture of the Indian People, vol. III. Bombay, 1954.
Sivaramamurti, C. 'Some Recent Sculptural Acquisitions in the National Museum'. *Lalit Kalā* vol. I (1955), pp. 113–20.
——— *Royal Conquests and Cultural Migrations in South India and the Deccan*. Calcutta, 1955.
——— *Indian Sculpture*. New Delhi, 1961.
——— *The Art of India*. New York, 1977.
Smith, Vicent A. *A History of Fine Arts in India and Ceylon, from the Earliest Times to the Present*. Oxford, 1911.
Soundara Rajan, K. V. 'Beginnings of the Temple Plan'. *Bulletin of the Prince of Wales Museum of Western India*, vol. VI (1957–59), pp. 74–81.
——— *Architecture of the Early Hindu Temples of Andhra Pradesh*, A. P. Government Archaeological Series, no. 21, Hyderabad 1965.
——— *Early Temple Architecture in Karnataka and Its Ramifications*. Dharwar, 1969.
——— *Indian Temple Styles*. New Delhi, 1972.
——— 'Temples of Aihole and Pattadakal', pp. 258–71 in M. S. Nagaraja Rao, ed., *The Chalukyas of Badami (Seminar Papers)*. Bangalore, 1978.
——— 'Calukyas of Bādāmi', pp. 3–59 and 70–90 in Meister, M. and Dhaky, M. A., eds., *Enclyclopaedia of Indian Temple Architecture: South India: Upper Drāviḍadēśa, Early Phase, AD 550–1075*. New Delhi, 1986.
Spink, Walter. *Ajanta to Ellora*. Bombay, 1967.
Srinivasan, K. R. 'Southern Temples', p. 69 in *Indian Archaeology 1960–61—A Review*. New Delhi, 1961.
——— 'Southern Temples', pp. 191–240 in Ghosh, A., ed., *Archaeological Remains, Monuments & Museums*, New Delhi, 1964.
——— *Temples of South India*. New Delhi, 1971.
Sundara, A. 'Some Early Calukyan Temples: Notes on Further Traces and Additions'. *The Quarterly Journal of the Mythic Society*, vol. LXX, nos 1–2 (January–June 1979), pp. 97–110.
Taddei, Maurizio. *Monuments of Civilization: India*. London, 1977.
Tadgell, Christopher. *History of Architecture in India, From the Dawn of Civilization to the End of the Raj*. London, 1990.
Tarr (Tartakov), Gary. 'The Architecture of the Early Western Chāḷukyas'. Doctoral Dissertation, University of California, Los Angeles, 1969.

——— 'Chronology and Development of the Chāḷukya Cave Temples'. *Ars Orientalis*, vol. VIII (1970), pp. 155–84.

Tartakov, Gary Michael. 'The Beginning of Dravidian Temple Architecture in Stone'. *Artibus Asiae*, vol. XLII (1980), pp. 39–99.

——— 'The Significance of the Early Chalukya Art of Andhradesa'. *Archaeological Studies*, vol. V (1980), pp. 49–62.

——— 'Reconsidering the "Flat-Roofed Temple" Hypothesis', pp. 147–57 in Joanna Williams, ed., *Kalādarśana: American Studies in the Art of Indịa*, New Delhi, 1981.

——— 'Reconstructing a Vaishnava Temple at Badami', pp. 179–83 in M. S. Nagaraja Rao, ed., *Madhu—Recent Researches in Indian Archaeology and Art History in Honour of M. N. Deshpande*. Delhi, 1981.

——— 'Interpreting the Inscriptions of Mahakuta Art Historically', in Gai, G. S. and Asher, F., eds., *Indian Epigraphy: Its Relation to Art History*, New Delhi, 1984, pp. 140–52.

——— 'Changing Views of Orientalism', pp. 509–22 in Lokesh Chandra ed., *Dimensions of Indian Art*. New Delhi, 1986.

——— 'Art and Identity'. *Art Journal*, vol. XLIX, no. 4 (Winter 1990), pp. 409–16.

——— 'Ajanta and the Early Calukyas', pp. 453–66 in Ratan Parimoo *et al.*, eds, *The Art of Ajanta, New Perspectives*. New Delhi, 1991.

Tartakov, Gary Michael, and Vidya Dehejia. 'Sharing, Intrusion and Influence: the Mahiṣāsuramardinī Imagery of the Calukyas and the Pallavas'. *Artibus Asiae*, vol. XLIV, no. 4 (1984), pp. 287–345.

Viennot, Odette. 'Le Problème des temples à toit plat dans l'Inde du nord'. *Arts Asiatique*, t. XVIII (1969), pp. 23–48.

Volwahsen, Andreas. *Living Architecture, Indian*. New York, 1969.

Wu, Nelson I. *Chinese and Indian Architecture*. New York, 1963.

Yazdani, G. *History of the Deccan*, vol. , Part VIII: 'Fine Arts', London 1952, p. 42 and Pl. XXXVI a. (Reprinted as chapter X, *Early History of the Deccan*, London, 1960, p. 756 and fig. XXXVIa).

Yazdani, G., ed., *The Early History of the Deccan*. Oxford, 1961.

Zimmer, Heinrich. *The Art of Indian Asia*, ed., Joseph Campbell. Princeton, 1960.

Index